DOC MAYNARD

The Man Who Invented Seattle

By Bill Speidel

D0962428

Seattle, Washington
Nettle Creek Publishing Company 1978

THE WAY WE WERE

A SNOQUALMIE PASS
B NORTH BEND, SPOT WHERE INDIANS MET TINKHAM
C LOWER SNOQUALMIE VALLEY
D TIGER MT.
E SQUAK MT.
F LAKE SAMMAMISH
G SAMMAMISH RIVER VALLEY
H LAKE WASHINGTON
I MERCER ISLAND
J CEDAR RIVER
K BLACK RIVER
L GREEN RIVER
M DUWAMISH RIVER
N MUD FLATS
O ELLIOTT BAY
P WEST POINT
Q FOURMILE ROCK
R QUEEN ANNE HILL
S LAKE UNION
T CAPITOL HILL
U FIRST HILL
V BEACON HILL
W ALKI
X POINT PULLY

■■■■ DR. MAYNARD'S TRADE ROUTE BETWEEN THE UPPER SNOQUALMIE VALLEY AND THE VILLAGE OF SEATTLE VIA CEDAR RIVER, LAKE WASHINGTON, BLACK RIVER AND THE DUWAMISH RIVER.

MAYNARD'S POINT
BIRTHPLACE OF
SEATTLE
AT THE MOUTH OF THE
DUWAMISH RIVER

FIRST EDITION

CIP Library of Congress Cataloging in Publication Data

Speidel, William C.   1912-1988

    Doc Maynard : the man who invented Seattle

    Bibliography: p.
    Includes index.
    1. Maynard, David Swinson, 1808-1873. 2. Seattle—Biography
    3. Seattle—History 4. Physicians—Washington (State)—
       Seattle—Biography.
    I. Title. II. Title: The Man Who Invented Seattle.

F899.S453 M397   979.7'77   78-10146
ISBN 0-914890-02-6

International Standard Book Number 0-914890-02-6

Library of Congress Catalog Card Number 7810146

Nettle Creek Publishing Company
600 First Avenue—Suite 310
Seattle, Washington 98104

Printed in the United States of America
by George Banta Company, Inc., Menasha, Wisconsin

A SPECIAL TRIBUTE TO THE OMBUDSWOMAN

The reader owes a debt of magnificent proportions to SHIRLEY PORRO, who served as ombudswoman in this manuscript. She cut through the red tape and got down to the meat of the coconut. And all of us should be thankful. I'd look like an idiot and the reader would have been hopelessly confused in and among the fascinating side trips that didn't have anything to do with either Doc Maynard or the invention of Seattle.

Also by Bill Speidel

You Can't Eat Mt. Rainier!— *(1955—out of print)*
Be My Guest! In the Pacific Northwest *(1957—out of print)*
You *Still* Can't Eat Mt. Rainier! *(1961—out of print)*
Sons of the Profits—Seattle Story 1851-1901
 (1st Ed. 1967, 9th printing 1978)
The Wet Side of the Mountains *(1st ed., 1974)*
It Was a Hell of a Blast! *(1975)*

David Swinson Maynard

"So I went down to my cabin pretty mad and climbed into the sack and read a lesson in my Correspondence Course on American history, but I didn't find a thing there to cheer me up—it was the same selection of bums we have today, only they wore funny clothes and had never heard of bubble gum."

Richard Bissell, *High Water*

TABLE OF CONTENTS

LIST OF ILLUSTRATIONS

I

Doc

A book called *Sons of the Profits,* which I wrote a decade ago, starts out with: "I'm sure there must have been *somebody* who participated in the construction of Seattle without first determining whether there was a buck in it for himself, but this book isn't about him."

During the intervening years, I found the somebody . . .

And this book *is* about him.

His name was David Swinson Maynard.

He was a licensed medical doctor. At the age of forty-four, he was half again as old and a thousand times more knowledgeable than the backwoods folk who generally have been credited with founding our town. And (this one will visit heart attacks upon a lot of our present citizens) he patterned it after Cleveland, Ohio.

If the men in *Profits* could have made more money by *not* building a city, then that's what they would have done. But the doctor invented a money-making machine. The profiteers just used it. In *Profits,* I said, "Seattle lucked out on a lot of things, the most important of which was her geographic location in the center of the Sound."

Doc Maynard put Seattle where she is on purpose!

Historian Hubert H. Bancroft wrote that "the rage for laying out towns (in the Pacific Northwest) was at its height between 1850 and 1852." Doc Maynard's shrewd intelligence was in competition with at least twenty-five other men who were trying to come up with the most important city in the northwest at that same time.

1

Portland was the one that gave him the best run for his money. It had a population of 2,000 when he got Seattle going. It would take fifty years for Seattle to forge ahead. And we did it by simply cranking the machinery the doctor had invented.

He was monarch of all he surveyed—and what some of the others surveyed as well—for the first seven years of Seattle's existence. And as he bent the twig, the city grew for the next fifty years . . . until the Christers took over and passed the State's 1909 Blue Laws, which made anything that was fun illegal.

Concomitant with the invention of Seattle, the doctor created what has become our state out of the massive Oregon Territory . . . and won King County as kind of a booby prize.

Doctor Maynard was the first person to call Seattle the "Queen City of the Pacific Northwest," and "The Gateway to the Orient." He put Seattle on the map of the United States as the terminus of the transcontinental railroad. He was the first resident to recognize the importance of Snoqualmie Pass, which is the lowest pass in the Cascades.

He named the town. He brought the first residents here . . . the first store . . . pharmacy . . . restaurant . . . hotel . . . gambling joint . . . saloon and whorehouse.

It was his specific ambition to make Seattle the greatest city on earth.

Today, the viable essence of our town is the same as it was 126 years ago when he slapped the baby's bottom and delivered her, squalling and protesting, to the rest of the world.

And, oh, yes, he had one other thing going for him that too often is missing today . . .

A magnificent sense of humor.

A man called Maynard

There are a lot of people with medical degrees whom you wouldn't dare call "Doc." It would injure their dignity . . . a dignity that is at best precarious. But Doctor Maynard was of the earth earthy.

He rolled through life like a solid gold ball, without worrying that somebody else might scratch the surface and find it was just gilt paint.

He loved to tell the story of a couple of his progenitors, a Maynard and a Swinson, who were picked up by a British press gang and lodged aboard a warship at the start of the American Revolutionary War. When they protested, they were informed that their services were required to put down the revolution. When they continued to protest, their clothes were removed and they were tossed in the brig.

That night they broke out of the brig, jumped overboard and swam ashore. To the astonishment of a townswoman, they appeared at her door inquiring as to the shortest route to General George Washington's camp. They presented themselves in their long johns to George, himself. And they fought at his side throughout the war.

Throughout his years, the doctor carried on the tradition of the two young men who had presented themselves to General Washington. He liked their spirit, enjoyed telling that story, and incorporated that kind of thing in his own life. Most of the people he met in the Pacific Northwest got a kick out of him. But the Christers—who were the ones he fought with during his invention of our town—were horrified. And I have to believe that he did a lot of the things he did for the pure pleasure of throwing them into a tailspin.

How can you call anybody like that anything but "Doc?"

Little is said in our current history books about him before he got to the Pacific Northwest. But the truth is that he had made and gone through two fortunes before he arrived here. And then he set about building his third and using it for the construction of his town.

He was older than anybody else who participated in the original construction of our town . . . nearly twice the age of some of the men who played key roles. The creation of a new town represented a chance to start life all over again when most of his contemporaries long since had gone to their rewards.

Doc Maynard was a man with a powerful physique. He hovered around six feet in height. He had the shoulders of a lineman on a professional football team, sloping to a strong neck. He had curly black hair, a broad forehead, wide set china blue eyes and a prominent nose, wide mouth and squared, determined chin . . . powerful arms with hands that could be as gentle as a whisper when the need arose. His was an elongated torso on top of legs that were as sturdy as fenceposts . . . a weight-lifter of championship proportions.

Physically, there was nothing he didn't think he could do—and usually did it . . . to the astonishment of those around him . . . even in a society that was highly "physical" to begin with. Only once did he use his strength to chastise another living creature—and I suspect she had it coming.

The doctor detested violence.

If there was one outstanding characteristic, this was it. If at all possible, he avoided confrontations. He manipulated people as a matter of personal preference and I doubt that ever, in his whole life, did he let his right hand know what his left hand was doing.

The doctor was a highly emotional man who threw himself completely into any project he felt required his attention. Thomas Prosch, his principal biographer, said: "There was no holding back with him. If a thing was desirable he was in favor of it; if wanted, he would go at once; if it had to be done or it was well to do it, he was ready to devote to it his money to the last dollar."

That's the man who invented Seattle.

The man and the medicine

Born on March 22, 1808, near the town of Castleton, Vermont, David Swinson Maynard gobbled up the necessities of preparatory education by the time he was seventeen years old and showed such bright promise that he was accepted as a student at Castleton Medical School. Unlike a lot of other medical schools in those days it had a solid foundation in legitimate medical education and subsequently became the medical school at Middlebury College.

As was his wont on any project during his entire life, he went about learning what there was know about the practice of medicine flat-out, full-speed-ahead and no-holds-barred. And being top man in his class, he got the coveted position as apprentice to one Dr. Theodore Woodward, professor of obstetrics and surgery and the most important teacher in the school.

You have to keep in mind that in those days getting a medical degree was not exactly the same process people go through today. Whatever formal education he got, he got by the time he was twenty years old. With the possible exception of Philadelphia and New York, the medical schools were operated privately. The free enterprise system ran rampant. For as little as fifty bucks and a six-months correspondence school course, a butcher could put the name "doctor" in front of his own . . . and a lot of them did. At best a man—and there were very few women—blew about $500 and three years of his time in some kind of medical institution. This included his room and board. And he could get into medical school right out of high school.

These schools were only supplementary, however, for the backbone of medical education then was preceptorship, the American form of Europe's apprentice system. The student kept the doctor's office clean, compounded the powders and salves, and looked after the horses, in return for the use of his preceptor's library and the privilege of watching him in the task of examining and prescribing.

A book about the Mayo Brothers notes that, "When an alert young mind, observant, curious and full of questions, met with a seasoned practitioner, able and willing to impart the wisdom he had gained from his years of experience, preceptorship was a reasonably satisfactory form of medical education, certainly far superior to classroom lectures alone."

There wasn't a drug store at every corner of America as there is today. The doctor had to gather his own roots and berries, plant his own herb garden in his own back yard.

And when the doctor came west, he brought the seeds for his herbs with him. There's the story of one man who nurtured a small tree all the way across the Great American Desert—doing without water himself so he could keep his specimen alive. And what did he bring to the Pacific Northwest? A fir tree. Doc Maynard had his own variation of the same thing. He was using dandelions as a diuretic and laxative and brought some seeds of this flower with him . . .

Only to discover cascara bark when he got here.

Calomel was big in his black bag. A mercurous chloride, it was used as a purgative and fungicide, along with another mercuric compound called "blue mass." At any rate, these were the ones which cropped up with the greatest frequency in the diary he kept on the Oregon Trail. Sulphur and molasses were a part of his thing . . . soda and soap.

Soap was big with the doctor.

He used it himself with great regularity—and he required those around him to use it, too . . . a custom that got him into no end of trouble among the hardy westerners who took a bath once a year— and then only if they felt they really needed it. Doctor Maynard was an oddball who took a bath once a week whether he needed it or not— and washed his hands and face several times a day.

Whatever else he got out of his medical education is somewhat hazy, but he sure got habits of cleanliness that lasted him a lifetime. He also acquired the costume of a doctor. It was on occasions so rare that historians made special mention of it that he failed to appear in public immaculately clad in white linen, black suit and vest.

Malaria was called the "ague" in those days—and there was plenty of it around the Pacific Northwest. Fortunately, the doctor had a specific for it in quinine. He also had ipecac, which induces vomiting. And both of these would play their own major roles in the creation and development of Seattle—along with what the doctors, the patent medicine people and just about everybody else called "tonic."

The active ingredient of tonic was opium. The resulting state of genial euphoria made them think they were better, whether or not they in fact were. It was used with the careless abandon of the aspirin tablet of today, and it was cheaper than booze.

For instance, when Sears, Roebuck & Co. got going half a century or so after the doctor got his medical education, you could buy opium-based tonic through the catalogue at $2.50 a pint. By 1900, America was a nation of opium addicts.

At any rate, opium as a tonic, and dissolved in alcohol and called laudanum, was a major part of the doctor's little black bag . . . perhaps too major a part. On the other hand, it was too major a part of the black bag of any doctor in the world. Doc Maynard was an obsessive enemy of pain. And opium often was the only weapon he had.

The final result of Doctor Maynard's medical training was Seattle's first hospital, which he founded in 1863 and in which he practiced medicine as he thought it ought to be practiced. Once more, Prosch provides us with proper insights: "As a physician Seattle had no better during his time. He was one of the olden school, not the modern, which relies too much upon surgery, upon the use of the knife and the saw. Nor was he a great medicine doser. He depended largely upon the most simple means—upon pleasant surroundings, a cheerful atmosphere, confidence on the part of the patient, the alleviation of pain, fresh air, sanitary conditions, and an occasional bit of pardonable deception. Many a person who imagined himself or herself dangerously ill was cured by him with a prescription of water, disguised, perhaps, by the addition of salt or other harmless ingredient."

That's a thumbnail sketch of the first successful physician in the city of Seattle . . . and it's not a bad description of what a physician ought to be doing today.

But we also fell heir to something else that happened to the doctor about the time he was twenty years old . . . shortly before he graduated, and before he could serve his internship with Dr. Woodward.

He fell in love.

The phantom lady

He did it with the same intensity that marked everything else in his life, and that episode provides us with a further insight into his personality.

There are a lot of men, and women, too, for that matter, who practice the philosophy that if they can't be near the one that they love they will love the one they are near. Many of his friends, for instance, flitted from one love affair to another. But the doctor was not of this genre.

He was a one-woman-at-a-time man.

History records two of the women, but the third—who really was the first—probably will always remain as the phantom lady. At any rate, while he still was a medical student, he succumbed to a pair of beautiful brown eyes . . .

Or were they blue?

It doesn't matter.

What does matter is that he fell very hard and the young lady in question put him to the first tough decision of his young life. She wouldn't wait for him to get his license to practice medicine. If he would give up his medical career and go to work she would marry him. If not, too bad.

She was a beautiful young woman and sought after by a number of other young men. The doctor had to choose between her and his medical career. It cut him up something awful, but he chose the medical career. It was a choice between love and medicine and he chose the latter . . .

A bitter pill which he never forgot . . .

The choice was between his head and his heart.

He chose his head . . . and lost the girl.

Years later, when he was confronted with a similar situation, he took the opposite course. You make the best decision you can at any given moment. And that's the way he played both of these decisions. He was right and he was wrong in both, but without them he would not have brought the city of Seattle as we now know it into existence. Somebody else might have created "a" city. But it wouldn't have been "our" Seattle.

That, however, is the long range look.

The phantom lady initiated a not unprecedented course in human events known as "marrying on the rebound."

The perfidy of Lydia A. Rickey

Doc Maynard made the biggest mistake of his life on August 28, 1828 . . .

Her name was Lydia A. Rickey . . .

Doc did not leave a lot of progeny around the Pacific Northwest to extol his virtues—either real or fancied. He had his own built-in ego, so he didn't have to go around rubbing other peoples' noses in an imaginary concept of his importance. Although he was an emotional man who usually let his emotions dictate his actions, this time he used his head. In those days, family ties were big in the doctor's life. The Maynards and the Swinsons were long time friends. Prosch says, "The two families lived in the same neighborhood, fought in the same wars, educated and reared their children together, intermarried, and otherwise associated in the many ways incident to the life and times of the eighteenth century, first in the British province and later in the young American possession and state in which their lot had been cast . . ."

In the same bunch was the Rickey family.

Lydia Rickey was a part of his peer group. He was twenty. The first great love of his life had told him to go jump in the lake. And there was Lydia . . . member of a fine family . . . approved by his peers. She came from fine stock. How could he go wrong letting her be the mother of his children? He wasn't in love with Lydia, but look what love had done to him.

It's too bad we trust something as difficult as marriage to the young.

Anyway, they were "properly" married, and it ended up providing a permanent cure of "propriety" with the doctor.

He never would be "proper" again after Lydia.

Very properly the young couple produced a daughter, Frances, in 1830, and a son, Henry, in 1834.

The closest we can come to the next important date is April, 1841. The doctor was out making a call on a patient. And if you'd like to make a comparison between today and those days, he got four-bits for house calls—two-bits for office treatments. No wonder doctors turned their talents to other enterprises . . . you could buy a doctor or five pounds of pork chops for fifty cents.

Anyway, here's how the story goes in an affidavit which the doctor signed under oath a decade later: "That in the month of April of the year last aforesaid (1841) on returning home from visiting a patient at about the hour of ten o'clock in the night—found his wife lying with a certain John Hemrick in an obscene manner. That the undersigned had previously doubted her chastity but had never before seen anything positively confirming his suspicions . . ."

There's really no point in going into detail about the perfidy of Lydia except to note that the various documents introduced into the doctor's affidavit would indicate that Lydia had been sleeping with every available man in Cleveland, Ohio, at the time. Not only was she sleeping around, she was proud of her record. One of the great quotes in the records came from a witness who saw Lydia "kissing Ormsby and that, too, in the bushes."

In view of the fact that she and the doctor no longer were in love with one another—and as far as the doctor was concerned a deep and passionate attachment never had been part of the picture—it's hard to fault Lydia for infidelity.

Stupidity, yes.

Promiscuity, yes.

But infidelity . . .

The doctor had that one coming.

It's the doctor's reaction to this traumatic confrontation which is important in this book. He still was hidebound by convention—an ailment from which he recovered with maturity. In those days there were two clearcut grounds for divorce: adultery and desertion. If the doctor had marched out of the house and into court with the adultery charge, he would have saved himself a lot of financial trouble later on. He was sore enough at Lydia to do it. But, as he testified later, he couldn't do it to her family. The disgrace would have destroyed their standing in the community and he couldn't bring himself to do that to them.

And then there were the children. He had to preserve the marriage for the sake of the children . . . what a fallacy!

Also, under his code of ethics, he had to leave Lydia with what he called "a sufficient competence."

Let's see, the children were eleven and seven at the time. The doctor stuck around for the next nine years . . . until Frances was twenty . . . and Henry was sixteen. What a friendly atmosphere there was in that family; the doctor grimly trying to put together that damned "competence," and Lydia out sleeping with anybody she could get to lay hands on her.

Great family unit.

By 1850, the doctor acquired the "competence" he was aiming for. This included a home that he could give to Lydia and a pile of money big enough that, properly invested, would enable her to live comfortably for the rest of her life. But her idea of comfort tended more toward things like kissing Ormsby in the bushes. She never remarried. She just hung around where she later could make the most possible trouble for the doctor.

On the other hand, knowing something about her helps us understand him. In later years, when he had mellowed some on the subject, he opined that while she had been sleeping with every man in Cleveland, it wasn't a very big town at the time.

Blueprint for Seattle

For nearly a hundred years now, a place called Cherry Grove, Illinois, has been rammed down our children's throats as the place from which our pioneer forefathers originated . . . and presumably they built a town out here just like the one they had left back there.

It's going to come as something of a surprise to everyone concerned— especially to the people who write the history books for the Seattle Public School system—that Cleveland, Ohio, is the town after which Seattle is patterned, not Cherry Grove.

For most people, Cleveland is the last place on earth they would like to live.

Last place?

Well, not quite the last. Los Angeles is the *last*. Then come Pittsburgh, Chicago and New York. But Cleveland is right up there in the top ten. A lot of folks living here today are fugitives from Cleveland. There's a certain stuffy side to Seattle that reminds us of Cleveland, but we can put our minds to rest on that subject. The stuffy side of Seattle came from Cherry Grove. Cherry Grove went to sleep one night about a century ago, and never woke up. If you want to see what Seattle would have been like if it had been patterned after Cherry Grove, you'll have to take a trip to Port Gamble on the Olympic Peninsula where the Pope & Talbot people have restored the sleepy little lumber town that used to be there.

Cleveland, at least, as the third largest city in the country, is alive and well.

And Maynard was a fugitive from Cleveland.

He and a whole collection of Swinsons, Maynards and Rickeys had joined a general migration to the Western Reserve, in which Cleveland is located, some time in the early 1830's. For the next eighteen years or so, he would dedicate to Cleveland the same overboard enthusiasm he gave to any project he got into . . . and would make and dispose of two fortunes in the process.

To calm the nerves of people who might be concerned about this kind of thing, Cleveland did not develop into a steel town until after the doctor left there is 1850. During his time there, it was a major distribution center, a lot like Seattle is today. And he picked up a lot of good ideas there which you will find that he used in the invention of Seattle.

For instance, the town fathers made significant attempts to bring in a good "mix" of people. If a man was a good doctor, or a good dentist, or a good blacksmith, carpenter or plumber, he could get an excellent deal on a piece of real estate . . . for twenty-five or fifty bucks, he could buy a town lot.

Had to build on it, however, or it would be repossessed. Doc Maynard would use that one with telling effect in the invention of Seattle.

A device which we find commonplace or even passe today was unique in 1836 when it was introduced in Cleveland. Crowds collected around to look at it in a department store window . . . and there were headlines in the newspaper reading:

"Bathtub arrives in Cleveland!"

You could get in this thing and get wet all over and wash your whole body. To the impressionable young doctor, with whom cleanliness ran well ahead of Godliness—causing him no end of trouble then and in the future—this was the answer to a prayer. Some of those devices even had hot and cold water piped right in!

Another idea which the doctor applied to Puget Sound was the layout of the town and the inclusion in the original plat of a forty-four-acre town square in the center of the plat.

He got another lesson from the bloody battles that were fought between Cleveland and Ohio City, on the other side of the river. The towns ultimately were merged and a whole lot of hard feeling could have been avoided if they had worked together from the beginning. It made an impression on the doctor, and when the chips were down in Seattle, he saw to it that this kind of thing was avoided on Elliott Bay.

The combination of coal and iron ore to create steel was just coming into Cleveland when the doctor left, and in those days, it was a marriage devoutly sought after by any town father. The age of steel was upon the nation. Steel tracks soon would connect the two coasts of this country. Steel steam locomotives would run along those tracks. Coal would provide the fuel for the locomotives and for the steel steamships that soon would connect this continent with other continents of the world.

Doc would waste a lot of time trying to find the combination of iron and steel for his town. But it was only natural. Shortly after his arrival in Cleveland, the first foundry to use steam instead of horsepower for "blowing" was developed. The first locomotive west of the

Alleghenies was built. The forerunners of the New York Central and the Pennsylvania railroads were initiated here.

Cleveland had forged ahead as a trading center because of the canal systems between the east coast and the Great Lakes. But the railroads were replacing them and the doctor made his first fortune investing in railroading. The city of Cleveland encouraged this kind of thing by extending the town's credit for incredible sums of money for those times, like a quarter of a million dollars. Cleveland history relates it like this: "Among the incorporators were men of leadership and vision. A charter was granted in the heat of the speculative period (1836) providing for banking powers and the issuance of paper money, as well as the right to build the railroad . . . Stupendous engineering plans called for the driving of a double row of piles on which rested stringers . . . the expense of grading would thus be saved by utilizing this elaborate stilt system . . ."

Shades of Cleveland in Seattle.

The first railroad arrived here on such a stilt system.

One day, the doctor had a net worth of $30,000 in railroading—the equivalent of $300,000 in today's money. The next day (in the panic of 1837) he was $30,000 in the hole when the railroad went belly-up and because he had co-signed a note with somebody else.

This gives us an insight into Maynard's standing in Cleveland.

How many men in Seattle today can get $300,000 on only their personal signature?

The bankers didn't lose by this, either. The other guy blew town . . . Doc Maynard stayed around to make another fortune, pay off the note . . . pay off Lydia and leave town.

In this connection, Doc Maynard, who would try nearly anything once, got into the Medical School business with one Dr. Horace Ackley. It was Cleveland's first and became the forerunner of the medical school at Western Reserve University. At one time the two young men had 150 students paying something like $200 a year tuition. A proprietary school, it was a going business that dropped dead in the panic of 1837 . . . losing a bundle for Maynard, but Doc regained it and more before he left thirteen years later.

When the doctor arrived in Cleveland, it had a population of 500. By the time he left, it had grown to 17,000 . . . and it had two medical schools . . . a university . . . a homeopathic institute . . . an academy of natural sciences . . . a Roman Catholic Cathedral . . . the famous Case Library. It was a medical, cultural, literary and musical center. It had gaslight, planked roads, banks, churches, industry, commercial enterprises, gambling joints, whorehouses, saloons and railroads.

Cleveland's development resulted from the fact that it was the major crossroads of the mid-west at the time. It was built at the mouth of a meandering river called the Cuyahoga, which emptied into a large body of water called Lake Erie. Canals and then railroads built her into a major town, but in the original instance its prominence resulted from a simple economic fact . . .

The town's hinterland became the breadbasket for the little villages springing up all around Lake Erie. The town, itself, became the center of trade for the lake.

What the doctor looked for when he finally got to the Pacific Northwest was a good site at the mouth of a river that furnished transportation for the products of a rich hinterland to a large body of water where there were small towns which needed those products.

The town also should be the logical location of the terminus of a transcontinental railroad which the doctor believed would be materializing "any day now."

The doctor participated as an active businessman in Cleveland for eighteen years . . . from 1832 to 1850 . . . and by the time he left that location he was thoroughly acquainted with all of the aspects of putting together a major city.

II

It was a tough fuckin' trip

The Oregon Trail and the people who crossed it in wagon trains during the quarter of a century beginning in 1841, have combined to become kind of a religious cult in the Pacific Northwest. I went to a meeting of the Daughters of the Pioneers in Seattle, for instance, and the people there were wearing badges showing the mode of transportation used by their progenitors in getting here. If your ancestor came in a covered wagon, you sat at the head table. If he or she came by train, you could hardly get in the front door.

A lot of movies show the Indians whacking away at the emigrants, but the record massacre, done by a party of Mormons dressed like Indians at Mountain Meadows on September 11, 1857, puts the Indians to shame. Although the raid was not sponsored by the church, the raiders killed 120 people, sparing only the lives of seventeen children under the age of seven. I wouldn't get into the Mormon thing but for the fact that during his trip through Mormon territory, Doc Maynard stayed awake every night, guarding his people after performing incredible feats of strength all day on the trail itself.

Thanks to the Mormons, we know what an iron man Doc was.

But the real fatalities that go to make up the statistics of about a thousand people a year who died on that trail were perpetrated by the people participating in the trip. They tried one another and hung the guilty parties from a couple of wagon tongues stuck up in the air.

They hadn't the slightest idea of antisepsis—and cared even less—and died by the thousands during the cholera epidemics.

Ignorance and sheer stupidity did most of them in. They drove off cliffs. They drowned in rivers. They starved to death. A huge percentage drove their animals to death—which is where Doc Maynard broke his pick with the people on his own wagon train. They quarreled among themselves. They had a terrible time with their leaders. Usually, the guys who started out as leaders got fired before the trip was well under way. This was truer of the people who came to the Pacific Northwest than the ones who went to California. The men who organized the trips to California during the gold rush were well-heeled, tough men who financed wagon trains themselves and didn't brook insolence on the part of those who went along for the ride.

For the most part, the people who came to Oregon were the ones who rode steerage instead of first class on the river boats to St. Joseph and Independence, Missouri. They were the dirt farmers who weren't making it where they were, or they wouldn't have come west in the first place. They were the ones who said their prayers every night and twice on Sundays.

Many really didn't have the least concept of what they were up to and today they couldn't get a driver's license. The most shocking example was that of the guy who was driving along the trail with a loaded and cocked rifle in his lap. It accidentally was discharged and he blew the head off the baby in her mother's arms in the next wagon.

In our day, we seem to equate the trail to one of the transcontinental freeways, but it wasn't like that at all. Writing about it, our most professional pioneer, Ezra Meeker, of Puyallup, tells about crossing the Missouri where wagons were starting four abreast with oxen of one wagon breathing on the tailgate of the one ahead. "I realized it was like this for 500 miles ahead of me."

The emigration started with the arrival of grass in the spring and hundreds of thousands of animals depended on that grass to get the people across the country. Without grass, nobody moved. So, instead of being a four or six-lane highway, the trail was about a hundred miles wide.

Granted they had a tough time, but it wasn't all bad. Those who survived didn't have to take any sleeping pills to get a night's rest. A lot of sickly people got well—or died—in the process. And you didn't have to coax the kids to eat their breakfast cereal. Doc Maynard had his fair share of troubles. And fortunately for someone who wanted to find out what kind of a guy he was, he kept a diary. He was not what you could call a prolific writer, but his casual dismissals of events of heroic proportions are in themselves an indication of what kind of man he was. (He didn't even include his closest brush with death, which came at the end of the trip.)

On the other hand, he had a premarital, transcontinental honeymoon with the woman he loved. That wouldn't raise many eyebrows today, but it sure did then . . . and it sure had a lot to do with the history of our town.

Actuarially speaking, the doctor had a life expectancy of thirty-five years when he was born. So, he should have been pushing up daisies for seven years before he even started west. He was forty-two years old at the time . . . starting a new life and inventing Seattle before he died at the age of sixty-five.

"Took the cars to Sandusky . . ."

On Tuesday, April 9, 1850, Doc Maynard entered the following in the diary he kept during his trip across the United States and for a month intermittently after he reached the Pacific Northwest: "Left home for California. Passed through Norwalk to Monroeville. Took the cars to Sandusky . . . passage 75 cents."

The above, as well as the rest of the diary he kept on his transcontinental trek, needs to be fleshed out for full understanding.

He wasn't really *going* to California.

What he was doing was *leaving* Cleveland.

Where he was going didn't really matter. He might, for instance, have left Cleveland for Columbus two years earlier if his candidate for governor of Ohio, John B. Weller, had not lost by the slimmest margin of votes in Ohio history—311 votes out of 297,201 votes cast.

The doctor had played a major role backstage in that campaign and would have been named to Weller's "cabinet" if he had won.

Weller was the one who finally talked Maynard into leaving Ohio for California, and it always has been assumed that the doctor was headed west for the gold rush. But Weller had a healthy selfishness that reached above and beyond a mundane desire to see the doctor get rich. He wanted to be the first United States Senator from California, where he had gone after his unsuccessful attempt at the Ohio governorship. He offered the doctor a pot of gold in exchange for Maynard's services as a master politician in his senatorial campaign.

For two years, construction of the new Cleveland, Columbus & Cincinnati railroad had absorbed the community. Three weeks before, the Cleveland City Council had officially opened the first fifteen mile stretch. Cleveland history says: "Behind the proud little locomotive, its high, expanded stack belching billows of smoke, they bounded adventurously over that distance in the remarkable time of twenty-seven minutes. Civic pride ran high, and as a humorist observed, the locomotive (The Cleveland) was the only 'motive' that could induce a man to leave Cleveland."

Doc, of course, had yet another motive. Her name was Lydia.

Nonetheless, it was a trip which excited him. The brass-trimmed, wood-burning locomotive moved on a pair of six-foot drivers and four front wheels. It had no cow-catcher or headlight, but it made the most of its shrill whistle. Behind the engine was a boxlike car piled high with wood, followed by the watertender and three forty-foot passenger cars with quaint curtains, railed platforms and handrails . . .

And speed?

Man . . .

It did an incredible twenty miles an hour.

One day people would take the "cars" all the way to California!

Life begins at forty-two

Doctor Maynard's "reincarnation" was into its second month and seventh day on May 16, 1850, in St. Joseph, Missouri, when he made an actuality of his theory about the cheapest way of getting his body across the United States. He had a mule, a buffalo robe, a gun, his precious medicines, his surgical instruments and several volumes of advice on the pitfalls and possibilities of transcontinental travel.

Some 50,000 people would emigrate from St. Joseph and Independence, Missouri, to the west coast of America the year that Doctor Maynard took the trail . . . with about 49,000 of them headed for the gold diggings in California, and the others to Oregon Territory where a single man or woman could get 320 acres of rich agricultural land, although there was beginning to be talk of prosperity to be derived from cutting down a vast crop of timber and shipping it to California.

A spirit of optimism was in the air in St. Joseph.

The town was crowded. A multitude of shops had sprung up to cater to the needs of the emigrants. There was an incessant hammering and banging from a dozen blacksmith shops where the wagons were being prepared or repaired, the horses and oxen shod. The streets thronged with men, horses and mules. Supplies for the emigrant trains overflowed from the shops to the streets. Saloons were booming. Houses of ill repute echoed to the songs of pleasure far into the night, while on the prairie surrounding the town there was a continuation of the confusion as the emigrants for Oregon, who were largely sober and God-fearing, were holding meetings . . . passing resolutions . . . establishing regulations—and having an awful time trying to choose a wagon master.

As a general thing, the people heading for the gold rush in California held themselves aloof from the Oregon immigrants. Many of them were persons of wealth and standing. They were the ones who stayed at the best hotels, provided the gunsmiths and saddlers with patronage for the best equipment. They had arrived here in the first class section of the riverboats and looked down on the travelers bound for Oregon Territory who, in general, had counted themselves lucky to arrive in steerage. In the California group were the speculators, adventurers, gamblers.

With his qualifications as a medical man, it was easy for Doc Maynard to make a connection with the best equipped and managed

California-bound wagon train in the town . . . which he did immediately upon his arrival. And, on May 16, the party with which he had associated himself crossed the Missouri River and encamped.

The travelers from St. Joseph would join with those from Independence at the confluence of the Big and Little Blue rivers in Kansas. They would follow the Little Blue to Fort Kearney, Nebraska, where they would transfer their affections to the North Platte River to Independence, Wyoming, and picking up the Sweetwater River as far as South Pass through the Rocky Mountains. On the west side of the Rockies, the vast majority of the immigrants would head for California . . . which was the doctor's plan.

The man and the cholera

The first inkling of the disease which would change the course of Doc Maynard's life and lead to the invention of Seattle appears with this cursory notation in his diary on May 19, 1850, slightly less than two years before he would stake his claim in what we now know as the Pioneer Square Historic District. The entry reads: "Passed one grave." The next day he notes that he "passed some new graves." Then comes this: "May 21—Tuesday. Passed the grave of A. Powers, of Peoria County, Illinois, died on the 20th inst., about sixty-five miles west of St. Joseph. Traveled eighteen miles. Was called to visit three cases of cholera. One died, a man leaving a wife and child, from Illinois, poor. He lived seven hours after being taken. No wood or water secured."

There are a lot of ways to go . . .

But cholera is not the most pleasant.

It begins suddenly, with terrific purging. The victim has no control over his bowels or his vomiting. The combination of the two creates cramps and prostration. In many instances, apparently healthy people drop in their tracks as though felled by an invisible club. Within hours, the patient loses most of his body fluids . . . like eight to ten quarts in a period of twenty-four hours. His eyes become sunken and the skin clings to the bones, giving the victim the appearance of a living skeleton. Of particular horror is the fact that the patient remains lucid . . . realizes he's about to die.

Today the treatment consists of massive doses of liquids—as one doctor notes, "gallons, not pints"—intravenously. Cholera originally appeared in India and the Orient where the British doctors, for their own reasons, believed that all liquids must be withheld from the victims . . . even to the extent that sentries were placed at the entrances to the hospitals lest some kind-hearted nurse might smuggle in a little water to the patients who were screaming for it.

Nobody clicked that it was a communicable disease. Its incidence was blamed on electricity in the air . . . on swamps . . . on watermelons . . . tomatoes . . . cucumbers. In America the Christians were convinced that it was a scourge in the hand of God, striking down heathens.

It would never appear in our God-fearing society.

Then, in 1832, it crossed the Atlantic, following the channels of trade, and penetrated the United States . . . bringing panic with it. (The doctor was four years out of medical school at the time.) It hit Cleveland the hardest two years later when there were 100 deaths in a town with a population of about 2,000 . . . and that was minor alongside of nearby Cincinnati which lost twenty per cent of its population . . . or New Orleans where 5,000 deaths were reported.

The doctor was never one to participate in the activities of any church, but he was totally turned off by the Protestants' approach to the solution of the problem. They figured that if the President of the United States would declare a day of fasting and prayer, we could lick the disease right now. They believed this was a wrathful deity ridding the premises of sinners.

Doc Maynard believed the disease struck people who had to live in squalid conditions and didn't have enough proper food to eat. It was this epidemic that turned him away from the trappings of the Protestant faith and caused him to join the Masons, a group that would be enhanced by his enthusiasm for the rest of his life.

The American medical profession went through what now is termed the "dark ages of medicine" in this country during the cholera years here—from 1832 to 1834, and in 1849 and 1850. A doctor was left to his own devices to try anything he wanted. One that you may not want to read about was the practice of fastening an electrode to the base of the patient's neck and another up his rectum and turning on the juice from a galvanic battery.

The doctors complained that the patients objected strenuously, but the treatment was continued for five or six hours.

The result was death.

The most ingenious treatment was that of a doctor who provided the patient with a tobacco smoke enema, accompanied by a beeswax plug . . . at least symbolic of the fact that the medical profession was blowing smoke up the patients' asses.

Cholera was particularly frightening on the Oregon Trail. Charles Rosenberg wrote: "Cholera waited in the brackish streams and water-holes, left by one party, to be passed on to the next group following across the plains. The route westward was marked with wooden crosses and stone cairns, the crosses often bearing only a name and 'cholera.' Nowhere could the disease have been more terrifying than on those trails, where men died without physicians, without ministers and without friends."

The wooden grave markers on the trail have aptly been described as a broken picket fence. People died of a lot of things on the Oregon Trail, but none died with more terror than the victims of cholera. Estimates of the number of deaths from this cause run as high as 20,000.

Commenting on the treatment of cholera in the United States in 1850, one of the leading authorities on the disease in the World Health Organization in Geneva, Switzerland, said, "Your chances of sur-viving an attack were about as good as though you had been shot in the stomach at point-blank range . . . maybe fifty per cent. On the other hand, if you fell into the hands of the average doctor your chance of dying rose to about ninety per cent."

To Doc Maynard, fresh from treating the 1849 epidemic in Cleveland, the incidence of cholera was as commonplace as the common cold. His principal weapon was calomel. On two occasions, he contracted the disease himself. And he was in such excellent physical condition that he threw off both attacks with self-administered calomel . . . which at least had a tendency to sterilize the bowels.

The doctor's treatment consisted of keeping the patients warm and comfortable . . . boiling all the water that anybody drank and providing the patients with as much tea as he could persuade them to swallow. And finally, he had opium. It didn't do much beyond relaxing the affected organs of the body as far as treating the patient was concerned.

But it eased his passage to the beyond.

If we got as much as a single case of cholera in Seattle today, it would make headlines in all media throughout the world. There hasn't been a case of cholera in the United States in half a century.

In the three weeks following his call to the first patient, Doc Maynard was summoned to the sides of thirty-five cholera victims. He saved about two thirds of them . . .

Which was spectacular success for the state of the art at that time.

Panic on the plains

On June 3 the doctor wrote: "Fell in with innumerable hosts of immigrants. Rained through the night." The next day he wrote: "Traveled up the Platte River twenty miles. The road was low, level, muddy. The river is about a mile wide. At 2 o'clock it began to rain and blow tremendously, continuing all night. Camped without a spark of fire or warm supper, with our clothes as wet as water. A man died within sight of us. He was a Mason. I was called to see him, but too late . . ."

Writing of the same conditions at about the same place and the same time of year, historian Francis Parkman Jr. fills out the picture with: "The thunder here is not like the tame thunder of the Atlantic coast. Bursting with a terrific crash just above our heads, it roared over the boundless waste of prairie, seeming to roll around the whole circle of the firmament with a peculiar and awful reverberation. The lightning flashed all night, played with its livid glare upon the neighboring trees, revealing the vast expanse of the plain, and then leaving us shut in as by a palpable wall of darkness . . .

"We lay upon India-rubber cloths, placed between our blankets and the soil. For a while they excluded the water to admiration; but when at length it accumulated and began to run over the edges, they served equally well to retain it, so toward the end of the night we were unconsciously reposing in small pools of rain."

It rained steadily for three days and nights.

Doc witnessed three more cholera deaths.

On June seventh the doctor awakened, still wet, to another lowering sky in a desolate land dominated by massive sheets of water . . . grass trampled by the hoofs of thousands of animals and of wagon wheels.

A messenger came from a stricken wagon train, his face pale and agitated. A whole bunch of people were dying. Would the doctor come?

The other members of the doctor's party would have no part of any more cholera. "You stay here and you stay alone," the wagon master said. "We're leaving."

The doctor detached himself from his party, following the panic-stricken messenger through the sea of mud.

He had embarked on a journey that would end with the founding of the city of Seattle.

A tale of two sisters

Hans Christian Andersen's story about the Ugly Duckling to the contrary and notwithstanding, the kid with the curly hair is the girl who gets the handsome prince . . . and the ugly sister gets the shaft. That's the way it always had been between Catherine Broshears and her younger sister, Susanna.

On December 6, 1832, when Catherine was married to a dashing riverboat captain named Israel Broshears, the family put together a "grand" wedding for her. There were four bridesmaids and four groomsmen and a great number of guests. A grand dinner party was provided for the entire wedding party following the ceremony.

Seven years later when Susanna reached the age of sixteen years— which was considered a marriageable age in those days—the family fortunes were dissipated. There was no dashing captain and a whole bunch of suitors seeking her hand. There was only a dirt poor dirt farmer by the name of Samuel Rider. The existence or non-existence of a beautiful face meant nothing to Sam Rider. He was almost entirely sightless.

By that time, Israel Broshears had parted with his glamorous job as a riverboat captain and, along with other members of the family, he was trying to eke out a living on a farm in Pike County, Illinois.

In the meantime Susanna's adored older brother, Michael T. Simmons, had gone west to find the pot of gold at the end of the rainbow, in Oregon . . . and it looked like he had found it in a far-off place called Olympia on Puget Sound in the Oregon Territory. From the letters received at home, Mike had struck it rich. And, all of them should come out there and share his wealth.

They decided to go west.

The relative financial status of the two sisters appears in the kinds of equipment their husbands had been able to purchase for the trip west. Having disposed of his farm, Broshears bought nothing but the best, an enormous Conestoga wagon drawn by five yoke of oxen and two cows, along with a full complement of animals as a relief team. Susanna and Sam Rider had to content themselves with a lighter wagon and a pair of oxen, with some additional back-up animals. All of Catherine's equipment was of the newest and best. Susanna and Sam had to be content with the castoffs of the rest of the family. Catherine was thirty-two, Susanna twenty-five years old.

Hopefully, they were headed for a new and happy life.

But one thing hadn't changed. Catherine was the rich and beautiful sister. Susanna was the poor relation.

Damsel in distress

The Broshears-Morton-Rider wagon train left Illinois in December, 1850, and headed for Missouri where the wagon trains departed. They left March 22, intending to go slow and take plenty of time . . . During the latter part of the first week in June, Israel Broshears was taken with cholera and after him six members of their party.

with fatal results. (Twice as many as that in the train contracted the disease but survived.)

"A stream of rapidly moving immigrants passed by. 'Hurry on!' they shouted. 'Leave the dead! Save yourselves! You'll die if you stop to bury them! Help you? No!' Past the plague spot they went, in abject terror, whipping their animals to hasten their movements to the utmost." (That was Catherine's memory.)

Then a miracle happened.

The messenger who had been sent for help emerged from the mists.

Behind him was a powerfully built man wearing a wide-brimmed hat which dripped rain to a long black cape. He was riding a mule.

"This man's a doctor," the messenger said.

Catherine's narrative continued with: "He was . . . taken first to Mrs. Morton, who was then near death. 'Never mind me,' she said, 'but look after my widowed daughter, my daughter with the blind husband and the others. I am going. Help them, doctor. Don't desert my children.' "

Catherine was too ill to pay much attention to the man who had come to the aid of their stricken party . . . But Susanna had been but lightly touched by cholera. The doctor treated her with a courtesy and respect to which she was unaccustomed. He allowed her to help him with the other patients and praised her for her help.

The praise was music to her.

The doctor looked up at her with kindness and understanding when her mother begged him to take care of "my daughter with the blind husband."

The doctor became a knight in shining armor.

A number of historians have taken cognizance of Doc Maynard's efforts during that crisis with the Broshears-Morton-Rider wagon train on the plains, but none as literally as Robert Cantwell in *The Hidden Northwest*. Cantwell and his wife revisited the scene with the aid of Judge William Dietrich, president of the North Platte Historical Society, retracing the doctor's steps . . . finally producing a map which shows how it was done.

"At first glance his story seems incredible. He wrote that he had remained with the sick and dying from noon of one day, all through the night, until dawn. Then he rode forward 20 miles to catch up with the wagon train with which he had been traveling. Then he rode back 20 miles . . . or 40 miles in all, after a sleepless night. And now after joining Mrs. Broshears he rode forward with her at least another 20 miles . . . He then rode forward another 3 miles to his original wagon train to make arrangements to shift his duds to the widow's wagon the next day. Two days without sleep and more than 60 miles of hard riding were involved . . ."

Cantwell then points out that Judge Dietrich was the great authority of emigrant crossings of the Platte River. The judge showed him the various places where the river could have been crossed. He pointed out the difficulties of travel over the Oregon Trail that the emigrants accepted as a matter of course . . . "He could have done it," Judge Dietrich said . . . "It would have been hard, but he could have done it."

On June 7, with his usual brevity, Doc recorded the crisis with: "Find plenty of doctoring to do."

But by the next day, a literary transformation had overcome him. He expounded with, "Left the camp of distress on the open prairie at half past 4 in the morning. The widow was ill in both body and mind. I gave them slight encouragement by promising to return and assist them along. I overtook our company at noon twenty miles away. Went back and met the others in trouble enough. I traveled with them until night. Again overtook our company three miles ahead. Made my arrangements to shift my duds to the widow's wagon when they come up in the morning . . ."

After nine long years of Lydia, who hated his guts, the doctor had discovered a beautiful damsel in distress . . .

How long can a wagon master survive in a democratic society?

Overnight, the doctor found himself wagon master of a train that probably consisted of ten wagons.

He got the job about the way an office boy might become president of a corporation overnight . . . by virtue of the fact that the president and all of the six vice presidents had died . . . leaving the office boy as the only remaining human being in the organization who understood the filing system.

Seven people in what has become known as the Broshears-Morton-Rider party died in the twenty days succeeding June 6 when Israel Broshears keeled over in his tracks. Because she was the richest survivor of the bunch, the chore of wagon mistress devolved on Catherine Broshears. But from a standpoint of muscle alone, she was far too fragile to drive a team of seven yoke of oxen. It's not exactly like getting behind the wheel of an automobile, you know. Driving seven yoke of oxen was no mean trick . . .

Driving a yoke of *two* oxen is no mean trick.

Prosch wrote: "The widow found in the beginning that the doctor (David S. Maynard) was not a first class teamster. In fact, it was his first experience with an ox team, and to put a novice in charge of seven yoke of cattle under such circumstances was imposing a burden and strain upon him of momentous character . . ."

In short, Doc became what is known as a "bull-whacker." At the time Prosch wrote his monograph, everybody in the United States knew what a bull-whacker was, but that knowledge is considerably more limited today. One General James F. Rusling, U.S. Army, retired, provided us with a fair to middling description of some professional bull-whackers in action in his book, *Across America,* published in 1874. The general wrote his book with the idea that the railroad soon would span the country and an appreciation of the role of the bull-whacker in the development of the West would be lost forever. The scene of the following was that portion of the Oregon Trail across the Blue Mountains in northeastern Oregon between the Snake River and Umatilla, an area which the doctor would reach three months later.

In his chapter on "Journeys by Wagon Through the Blue Mountains," General Rusling wrote that he had thought army muleskinners were the toughest men on earth until he encountered the bull-whacker, and continued with:

"A harder or rougher set than the ox men or bull-whackers (as they call themselves) of the Plains and Mountains, it would be difficult perhaps to find, or even imagine . . . with their many-yoked teams, struggling through the mud and rocks . . . they were in their element . . . red-shirted, big-booted, brigand-looking ruffians, with the in-separable bowie-knife and revolver tucked around their waists, they swung and cracked their great whips like fiends, and beat their poor oxen along, as if they had no faith in the law of kindness here, or belief in a place of punishment hereafter. And when they came to a really bad place—in crossing a stream or when they struck a stump or foundered in a mud-hole—it is hard to say whether their prodigious, multiplied, and many-headed oaths were more grotesque or horrible. To say 'they swore till all was blue,' would be but a feeble comparison, the whole Mountains corruscated with sulphur . . .

"At extra bad places, the teams were doubled or trebled up, and then the wagons were bound to come, if the wood and iron only held together. Twenty or thirty yoke of oxen struggling to the chains; with the 'bull-whackers' all pounding and yelling like mad, their huge whip-lashes thick as one's wrist cracking like pistols, was a sight to see—'muscular,' indeed in all its parts. The noise and confusion, the oaths and thwacks and splashing of mud, made it indeed the very hell of animals; but, for all that, the wagon was sure to reach *terra firma* at last . . ."

Not all of the trip would be that bad, of course.

And some of it would be worse.

So there Doc stood on June 9 facing the seven yoke of oxen—fourteen animals—hooked to Catherine's covered wagon. In his hands was a bull-whip with a handle as thick as his wrist and a plaited rawhide lash twenty-five feet long at the end of it. The object was to crack that whip over and above, under and on these animals for the next 2,000 miles.

Under the amused eyes of the other members of the party, the doctor decided that for the time, at least, he would not be under the necessity of wearing his frocked coat and flowered vest.

Doc, who had been practicing the art with his previous companions, cracked the whip and the wagon lurched slowly under way. Prosch notes that Catherine had a "large strong wagon and first class equipment," which would have included about $1,500 worth of harness animals, along with three sets of harnesses . . . horses and cattle worth some $500. The oxen were capable of hauling 400 pounds apiece, permitting her to carry nearly a ton and a half. Included in the equipment were dutch ovens for stews and for baking bread, a set of kettles that fit one inside of another . . . tin plates, knives, forks, spoons and cups . . . water kegs . . . 600 pounds of flour . . . 625 pounds of bacon . . . twenty pounds of dried apples . . . seventy-five pounds of sugar . . . two bushels of dried beans and bushel of salt . . . fifty pounds of coffee and an equivalent amount of tea . . . thirty-six packets of dried yeast, two gallons of vinegar . . . saws . . . shovels . . . axes . . . and all of the hand tools which Israel Broshears had accumulated in his life as a farmer for the previous decade or so . . . along with rifles, shotguns and hand guns . . . tobacco.

Added to these were a number of family heirlooms which Catherine had been unable to part with—but which she would have to part with before the end of the journey.

The elimination of anything beyond the 2,800 pounds which the team could haul began immediately, and what with six deaths in the family, that meant a lot of discarding—including whole wagon loads.

It was pathetically typical of the conditions on the trail.

It is impossible for me to resist quoting the courtly Prosch with regard to the next period in the reincarnation of Doctor Maynard, one in which there was a lapse in Doc's journal: "Here there is a break in the doctor's journal, there being no entries from June 12 to 24th inclusive . . . it is to be supposed that the troubles were so many and the labors so great incident to the peculiar situation in which he found himself that he was unable to keep the diary written up . . . Mrs. Broshears losing not only her husband and mother but three other relatives, and being left in a most forlorn and helpless condition. The sympathy and assistance she required from the doctor, who became her second husband, accounts reasonably for this much to be regretted omission in the narrative."

Truth impels me to point out another aspect of the human condition with regard to the omissions in the doctor's diary. The chances are that as a precautionary measure, anyone displaying any symptoms of cholera got the full treatment from the doctor on the grounds that it was a lot better to be safe than sorry. So the calomel was passed out with careless abandon. The purgative treatment was followed by the accepted dosages of an opium based tonic to sooth the irritated linings of the collective intestines in the party . . .

Leaving everybody in a happy state of euphoria.

At the end of two weeks—with only Austin Morton hovering between life and death—the folks sobered up some and realized there had been no new cases of cholera in the group . . . enabling them to look at the doctor more as man than magician . . .

And when he cut off the supply of opium, with considerably less than outright enthusiasm.

There's nothing like knowing your business for gaining the respect of the people who are supposed to be your followers, and the doctor was in a tough spot for wagon master when he didn't have a "real" grasp on the fine art of driving oxen . . . a feat in which men half his age on the wagon train could perform better. He adopted the obnoxious policy of requiring that potholes be dug in the banks of the river for filtered drinking water. Unlike the river water which was jovially described as too thin to farm and too thick to drink, it came clear. But it had the awful taste of alkali. The river water came out like cocoa and frequently had tadpoles swimming in the bottom of the cup, but it tasted good. He insisted that it be filtered and boiled, a tedious and annoying process.

Moreover, he was stuffed with "book larnin'." The kind of expertise that the doctor picked up in his preparations for the transcontinental journey was that offered by Peter Burnett who had organized one of the first emigrant trains to cross the Oregon Trail eight years earlier. Appearing in national magazines to which most of the party did not have access, this kind of advice cautioned would-be travelers to take care of their animals early on so the animals could take care of them when the going got rough later on. Without the oxen, mules and horses, they wouldn't get across the Rockies. Burnett wrote. "They should be regularly watered, morning, noon and night. Never maltreat them, but govern them as you would a woman, with kindness, affection and caresses, and you will be rewarded by their docility . . . The best way to save the teams is to drive a reasonable distance every day and stop about an hour before sundown. This gives time for arranging the camp, and for the teams to rest and eat before it is dark. Eight hours' drive in long days—resting one hour at noon—I think is enough. Never drive irregularly if you can avoid it. A prudent care should be taken of horses, teams, and provisions from the start . . ."

The doctor added his own fillip to these instructions.

And that's where he broke his pick.

His insistence on cleanliness was quite a time-consumer, but one they obliged him with as long as there was sickness in the party. But now he was proposing that once a week, when they came to a good watering spot, they not only do their collective laundry, but take baths.

Laundry? Baths!

Too much!

For people driving desperately to leave the source of the dread cholera, this was one delay too many. The first inkling of his dethronement came on the morning of June 25th, just two weeks after he had been voted into power. He wrote in his journal: "Started late, in consequence of our cattle being lost. When I came up from hunting the cattle the company had gone and left us. We drove on to the Bad Hills, about eighteen miles." (Where they caught up with the others and encamped.)

The next day, they buried Austin Morton, in what was his last act as wagon master. They only made two miles that day, and the doctor found himself getting the silent treatment. Nobody would talk to him.

The man and the animals

The campground that night was on the banks of the river where they encountered a disconsolate young man by the name of George Benton. George Benton was in tough shape, as Prosch explains:

"George Benton, a nephew of Senator Thomas H. Benton, had started with another party which met with disaster in the river South Platte. Several wagons and animals were lost at a supposed ford, where the water was both deep and strong. Benton saved his life and his horse, but lost all else, including shoes, coat and hat, and being left entirely alone on one side of the river. He, perhaps, saved the Broshears-Morton people a similar misfortune by pointing out the danger, and he immediately took service with them at $18 per month and clothes, the latter being an advance payment that was absolutely necessary . . ."

Doc's sole comment on the incident was made the next day. It read: "George Benton commenced driving the team."

The big confrontation with the others came on June 27—eighteen days after the doctor had taken over and one day after George Benton had signed on. The party reached Cottonwood Creek. There was excellent feed, fuel and water. The doctor-cum-wagon master announced they would stay here for the next couple of days, do a laundry, bathe themselves and rest the teams.

There were angry mutterings from the others on the train.

Laundry . . .

Rest the teams . . .

Take baths!

No way!

"You can stay if you want," the doctor was told. "The rest of us are leaving."

Samuel Rider, virtually sightless, had no choice. He would be required to go with the others or not continue on the trip.

And that's when Susanna stood up in the doctor's defense. With shining eyes, she announced that she would drive their team if necessary. "We will stay with Doctor Maynard," she announced. It was partly because the doctor had waded for wood for the Riders and had shown them the same kinds of little courtesies that he accorded anyone else who ever needed his help. The little kindnesses were common to the doctor . . . But not to Susanna. She took them as a personal tribute to herself.

The doctor wrote: "Part with Fanings & Co."

The record doesn't show how many wagons there were when the rest of the members of the party voted "Fanings" in as the new wagon master. I'm guessing eight or ten . . . at least the majority of the group . . . leaving the doctor as master of two wagons, Catherine's and her sister Susanna's. George Benton had appeared at a particularly propitious time. Susanna's blind husband was in no position to drive the Rider's oxen, while the doctor, who had mastered the art by this time, could take on the smaller wagon with one yoke of animals.

On June 28, the members of Doc's diminished group did a laundry and bathed. The doctor packed a picnic lunch and he and Catherine and Susanna took their horses on a hunting trip. It was a beautiful day. The flowers were blooming. And the new regime began with pleasure on the part of everybody concerned. That night, the doctor wrote: "I think this is the pleasantest hunting ground I ever saw." That night there was fresh game for dinner for the people involved. That night, as they sat around their bright campfire, the world was pleasant indeed.

The next day, they crossed from the South Platte to the North Platte, where we get another sample of the doctor's free and easy approach to the spending of money. What most travelers described as "those thieving Indians" had established a ferry at the most favorable spot to cross the river. You either paid to cross there or took a drive some-place else where the river could be forded. The doctor cheerfully paid.

Israel Broshears and Samuel Rider had followed the general practice of the time and had brought along as many extra animals as they could afford to buy—as sort of "spares" for hauling the wagons . . . and as an investment. For the most part, they brought along extra cattle. The cows could be milked, providing a welcome additon to the often dubious water on the trail, as well as in the cooking. And, as one writer of the time pointed out, the animals which could be trans-ported to Oregon would be worth "thribble as much as when you started." Another wrote that "If a man had $500 and would invest it in young heifers in the States and drive them here (to Oregon), they would be worth $5,000; and by engaging in stock raising, he could make an independent fortune. Milch cows on the road are exceedingly useful, as they give an abundance of milk all the way . . ."

It wasn't all that easy, of course. The loose animals fell behind those harnessed to the wagons. They also ate all of the grass that otherwise would have been found on either side of the trail. "Trail" is really kind of a loose term. Depending upon the particular conditions at any given time, it could be as much as 100 miles wide. It's been estimated there must have been 100,000 animals crossing the trail every summer. Thus the drovers connected with the wagon trains often strayed far and wide.

And the situation gives us further insight into the kind of a man Doc Maynard was. He took on as his own responsibility the business of scouting ahead for wood, water and feed—with especial emphasis on the latter. If he didn't take care of the animals, they couldn't take care of him. On a good day, the wagons would make twenty miles. The doctor, ranging far and wide, covered twice that amount of ground. Then at night, when the rest of the party collapsed, he took the evening meal to the drovers, wherever they were. There were many notations like the following in his journal: "Had a serious tramp in carrying supper to the boys, after dark, some six or seven miles and back."

How many men of forty-two could ride a horse for forty miles a day, collect the wood and water necessary to make camp, and then tramp twelve to fourteen miles on foot in the dark without the aid of a flashlight? No wonder there were the frequent entries in his diary reading, "went to bed at midnight, (or two o'clock in the morning) . . . tired enough."

"Tired enough," with or without an exclamation point that was the signal that Maynard had reached total exhaustion. Total exasperation was expressed with such expressions as, "oh God, the mosquitoes," and "if they don't beat the devil." But most of the time his strongest editorial comment was the one used when he encountered the Broshears wagon train: "In trouble enough."

Shakespeare, he was not.

The doctor worked for the animals "hard enough."

Some samples of his entries go like this: "The team came in full and lively," or the "team was rested and recruited."

There were other entries, though, like, "feed poor . . . camped without feed or water . . . found plenty of salertus water, by which our teams suffered much . . ." On the third of July, they found no feed. On the fourth, he reported that they "celebrated a little." Other times it was, "found feed very scarce . . . dragged team through sand eight miles to devil's Gate . . . Oxen sick, vomiting like dogs. Old Nig looks bad, got better towards night . . . team comfortably fed . . . team tolerably fed but no water . . ."

Here's as good a sample as any. "July 15—Left camp and passed the forks of the roads, the left road leading to Salt Lake. Traveled eight miles to the Little Sandy. Watered the team, drove three miles more, turned out and camped. Drove the team up four miles further for feed. Set things right about camp, carried supper to the boys four miles, washed, changed clothes and slept in tent . . ."

No guard duty?

A red letter day!

On other days he wrote, "found good feed for team four and a half miles from camp, and stayed to rest our teams in the waters of the Little Sandy . . . went in search of feed; tramped eleven miles and found feed scarce. Returned to camp and sent the boys out with the teams to graze all night . . . Lion and Bright are sick . . . we threw Lion down and found four or five gravel stones in his foot. Came eighteen miles and camped with most excellent water and feed . . ."

The doctor cared for the animals . . .

And the animals took care of him.

The cattle had given him everything they had. "Lion, Sam and Bright are sick," he wrote that night. For several days after that there was excellent feed and water, but the animals were in trouble . . . and he delayed the trip to nurse them, writing, "Doctored Lion's foot and fed poor Bright."

Things began to go bad for Lion and the doctor took him out of the harness. On July 31, he found the mosquitoes too bad for either the people or the animals and they had to move on. August 1, the doctor was sick himself and under the influence of calomel pills, but he drove the animals "eight miles through the sage to a spring, and put old Lion out to rest." The next day he reported, "Started late on Lion's account. Drove two-and-a-half miles and he gave up the ghost . . ."

When they reached the end of the trail, an effort was made to guide them over Naches Pass in the Cascade Mountains, but the doctor opined the animals had given their all . . . could never make it over the pass. They had earned a rest. He could have gotten a handsome price for them, but he sold them for a mere $110 in order to get them a good home.

Doc figured they'd earned it.

That's the way he did things.

Particularly today, when we don't have that much contact with them, people may think it odd that a man could have deep affection for oxen and have that feeling reciprocated. But the doctor did. Those patient, dumb beasts had been his close companions for weary months on the trail. They had done his bidding and had never failed him. They had bivouacked together, slept together, lunched together. They knew him and were eager to obey him. Without them the journey would not have been possible.

It was with sadness that he parted with them.

The doctor's system had worked and in the long haul had passed the people like Fanings & Co. who were stalled by the side of the road, their weary animals at a point of exhaustion.

Ezra Meeker also had a cogent word or two on the subject:

"With so many, the watchword was to push ahead and make as big a day's drive as possible." Of a thousand wagons that crossed the original river with Meeker's group, soon all were ahead of them. He quoted his wagon master as saying, " 'Now, fellers, jist let 'em rush on, and keep cool, we'll overcatch them afore long.' And we did, and passed many a broken-down team, the result of that first few days of rush . . ."

It was a philosophy followed by Doc Maynard.

The man and the Indians

Doc had a great natural curiosity about anything that came down the main street of his life, and he satisfied it with the zest of a gourmet. His diary is peppered with examples of a mouth-breathing amazement at such things as his first sight of a fellow who would be normal in any professional basketball game today. Entered in his journal on April 21, "Saw James Porter, the Kentucky giant, 7⅔ feet." Another in a long series of entries on the natural beauties of the country through which he was traveling west goes: "This pass through the Whitewater is one of the curiosities of nature. Perpendicular height of rocks four hundred feet. Width of stream or valley fifty-five feet." On August 1, there's another sample. Sick all day and on calomel, and driven wild by the mosquitoes, he nonetheless took time off at Fort Hall to take in another human phenomenon. I haven't the slightest idea who it was, but he devoted a precious line or two in his diary to note, "Took in George the Second at the Fort."

He probably picked up the basics of Indian dialect before he ever left Cleveland, and with his facile mind was able to acquire competence in communication with them in their own language as he went along. It is certain that by the time he arrived in the Pacific Northwest, he could converse freely with them—even on abstract subjects. It was a competence that few other whites bothered with and it amazed and delighted the aboriginal residents of this country. To him, they were children, sometimes very dangerous children—children with their backs to the wall against the onslaught of the white civilization.

And he never feared them . . .

It was a condition which seemed to put a magical protection around him.

In this, he was an exception to the rule.

Most of the immigrants to Oregon were scared to death, not only of the Indians, but of the other strangers they met on the trail. Nearly all of the immigrants to Oregon Territory were simple folk who had lived a simple life in a small community before they headed west. And, most of the time, the people headed for California were the sophisticates . . . the traders, gamblers, con men and wealthy adventurers.

Doc was neither.

And he led a charmed life.

Parkman, who lived among the Indians, provides us with at least a partial answer. He wrote: "The timorous mood of the emigrants was doubly unfortunate, as it exposed them to real danger. Assume, in the presence of Indians a bold bearing, self-confident yet vigilant, and you will find them tolerably safe neighbors. But your safety depends on the respect and fear you are able to inspire. If you betray timidity or indecision, you convert them from that moment into insidious and dangerous enemies."

The Indians, and the Mormons, and anybody else who happened to be strategically-located, erected toll bridges and toll ferries at places where your choice was one of going five or ten miles up or downstream or of waiting several days for swollen rivers to subside. Following natural laws of economics, the farther west the immigrants got, the higher the tolls. The doctor's first encounter with an Indian toll ferry came on May 19, in Missouri, while he still was with the original party heading for California. The toll was twenty-five cents a wagon. By the time he got to the Snake River in Idaho, it had been upped to $7.50. This time they swam the cattle across.

On one of the more notable occasions, the doctor was called in by the chief of an Indian village to treat the chief's daughter. As was his usual custom, he visited the Indians in their villages, breaking bread with them, trading with them, and companionably smoking the inevitable peace pipe with them.

On July 28, he noted in his journal that he left camp at 7 o'clock in the morning, traveling leisurely through good roads where there was plenty of fuel, feed and water. The day before, he reported that he and Catherine had passed beautiful springs and that there were

"Indians aplenty." That day he noted that the hot springs were a curiosity. They were sulphur and soda springs and they paused for a time to admire them. Then they went on for about a mile where they paused to satisfy the curiosity of the natives in an Indian village. Catherine's tendency to fear the aboriginals was dissipated when she saw their attitude toward the doctor. On both sides, it was one of easy familiarity. She and the doctor were royally entertained with feasts in half-a-dozen tents, as was the ritual. He sold the Indians five pounds of tobacco for $2.50. And when they finally went on, they were directed to another Indian camp at an interesting location seven miles away . . . which was where they camped for the night.

The doctor covers all of this in his journal with: "Fed forenoon at an Indian camp . . . Sold five pounds of tobacco for $2.50. Went on seven miles and camped near an Indian camp." He also adds a cursory, "Was called to see a sick papoose . . ."

A crying baby is a crying baby, regardless of race, creed or color. And whatever medicine Doctor Maynard had, it was better than that of the Indians, and probably contained just a touch of opium. He had a salve compounded of mercury that, for instance, could provide real relief for the child.

And a grateful mother is a grateful mother in any language.

Catherine was impressed.

In the blindness of their attraction to one another, neither Catherine nor the doctor noticed that somebody else in their group also was impressed. Catherine's sister, Susanna.

Both women were even more impressed on the occasion of an approach by a band of hostiles on July 8. With his usual brevity, the doctor recorded the event: "Started out, and after traveling six miles discovered a party of Indians coming upon us. We heard they had just robbed one train. Prepared for an attack. When within half a mile they sent two of their number to see how strong we were. After viewing us carefully they left us for good. Traveled twenty-two miles . . ."

I could shoot Maynard, myself, for his casual dismissal of this confrontation. How did he do it? What did he say? Was he scared? Did he "con" 'em out of it? Would he have killed them if he had the chance?

Man, this was a page one story in the books written by the immigrants who wrote books.

There are dozens of examples of people on wagon trains who lost their lives in a confrontation like this one. But I suppose it comes in the same category as the fatal traffic accident that is missed by inches. You just drive on. The best Catherine came up with later on was that the doctor was "absolutely fearless when it came to Indians."

For one thing, he could discourse with them in their own language. The strength of his personality showed through to them. He was armed. He probably saw to it that everybody else in the train had guns pointed at the Indians. But there were only four people.

It was some feat.

Doc Maynard was a complex man with insights which none of us ever will fully understand. And he instinctively understood another thing about the Indians which we, with all of our so-called advantages, have not as yet fully grasped. It is something which influenced his attitude toward Indians for the rest of his life.

He sensed the reverence with which the western Indians regarded the salmon, which had been the principal source of protein in their culture for perhaps 5,000 years . . . and the feeling came to him first on August 12, 1850, when he bought one of these beautiful animals from some Indians at Salmon Falls on the Snake River. His entire association with the incident was one of beauty. He wrote, "This place is delightful. The stream is alive with fish of first quality, and wild geese are as tame as the natives." A few days later, he would write, "We killed a noble salmon, taking breakfast out of him, and a fine dish he was. I just wish my family had such a fish to work on."

Salmon was of critical importance to the doctor from then on. He knew that somewhere, somehow, it should be made available to people everywhere. It was a major consideration in the selection of the site for the city of Seattle. The technique of canning it had not as yet been developed, but the doctor sensed its importance . . .

And, as was so often the case, he was ahead of his time.

The Indians also were responsible for a major break-through in his relationship with Catherine. He traded a brass kettle, two blankets, a shirt, a mare and a colt . . .

For a "beautiful beaded Indian dress for Catherine."

It was a big day in the lives of this man and this woman.

An awful day in the life of Susanna Rider.

The man and the woman

There aren't many of us whose lives are visited by the high drama that was so much a part of the bond of unity between David and Catherine that it was commonplace to them. In later years, when he was ill, she had to take care of him. But for the better part of their lives together, he was fiercely protective of her. They developed a love which defied what normally were the irresistible mores of the day.

And the shape and direction of Washington history evolved from it.

Quite a story.

Her epitaph for the doctor was: "There was no better man on earth."

By all standards she was a beautiful woman and a relatively young one when he died. She lived on for thirty-three years, and never found a man who could replace him in her heart.

The doctor's first encounter with her came at a time when everyone in her party and all of the other immigrants around them passed the stricken wagon and demanded that the bodies of the dead be left exposed to the elements. Catherine was distraught and half-sick, and it was one of those times when the temptation to flight was close to irresistible. She couldn't dig the graves of six people all by herself. But, "Mrs. Broshears would not go until her husband, her mother and the others were buried by the roadside, their bodies as safe as they could be made from the teeth of the wolves and the scalping knives of the Indians."

It took all night . . .

But the doctor seized a shovel and helped the woman bury her dead.

There was much for Catherine to admire about the man who would become her husband. His awkwardness in handling seven yoke of oxen was immediately apparent, but he stuck at it and within two weeks could bull-whack the oxen with the best of them. His compassion for man and beast was apparent throughout the three months that they were on the trail. His good cheer was unflagging, and he brought humor into her life—something that previously had been completely lacking. There was no chore too large or too small for him to tackle. He provided her with small, thoughtful niceties that hitherto had been lacking in the man to whom she had been married.

One of the far-reaching impacts he made upon her came during the first week in July. On July fifth, the doctor literally put his shoulder to the wheel of the covered wagon as the oxen floundered through eight miles of desert sand. That night, he drove the animals out three miles to feed. The heat was intense. The next day, he brought the team back, hitched up the wagon and drove back to the spot where he had spent the night with the animals. What an iron man! He had worked for twenty hours straight, without any rest.

The water in the keg tasted of alkali . . .

And was almost too hot to drink.

Catherine dreamed of a drink of cold water.

What neither she nor the doctor realized was that somebody else also was dreaming of a drink of cold water—Susanna.

That day the doctor announced that he would be gone from camp on some mysterious errand. He carried a huge bucket with him. When he covered the subject the next morning in his journal, he noted that he had gone on a trip to a mountain and had returned with a load of fresh snow. "Got into camp about three o'clock." he wrote. "Tired enough."

But Catherine had her drink of cold water . . . so did Susanna.

She looked thoughtfully at this man . . . so did Susanna.

He had saved most of the members of her party from cholera. He had taken command of the party and of her future. He had refused to budge when the others panicked and fled the cholera. "Let them go," he said, "make haste slowly." He had taken her with him to treat the sick Indian papoose. He had out-bluffed a band of hostile Indians. He had exercised calm, cool judgment in every situation to which he had been exposed. He was a tower of strength accompanied by a gentleness that she never had seen in a man.

One of the chores the doctor assumed for himself was that of guard duty at night . . . against the Indians . . . against the Mormons . . . against stampeding buffalo. The various Indian tribes were warring more on one another on the trail than against the emigrants. But what they needed most was horses . . . and their nightly raids were made more for these animals than for any other reason.

During the day, the doctor scouted ahead for fuel, feed and water. Ezra Meeker described the situation: "The grass along the beaten track was always eaten off close by loose stock . . . so we had frequently to take the cattle long distances from camp. Then came the most trying part of the whole trip—the all night watch, which resulted in our making the cattle our bedfellows, back to back for warmth; for signal as well, to get up if the ox did. It was not long, though, till we were used to it, and slept quite a bit except when a storm struck; well, then, to say the least, it was not a pleasure outing.

"But weren't we glad when the morning came, with, perchance, the smoke of the campfire in sight, and maybe, as we approached, we could catch the aroma of the coffee; and then such tender greetings and such thoughtful care that would have touched a heart of stone, and to us seemed like paradise. We were supremely happy."

Meeker was a young man at the time . . . talking about his young wife. But the emotional climate was identical for the lonesome, bereaved widow and for the man who had been living in an atmosphere of hate for nine long years.

The spirit might be willing for morality.

But the flesh is something else again.

And that didn't just apply to Catherine.

It also applied to Susanna. And the part of the marriage ceremony that reads "till death do us part" is honored as much in the breach as not. The law says you have to be married to this woman or this man

. . . but it doesn't necessarily hold that you have to remain in love with him. And a complicating factor had entered into the idyllic picture.

Susanna had fallen in love with the handsome doctor.

On July 11, Susanna found her sister in the doctor's arms.

In the resulting shock waves that hit Susanna, her love for the doctor turned to hate.

Trouble in paradise

Trouble appeared in paradise the very next day. It was fifteen days since the doctor's cursory notation. "Parted with Fanings & Co." This time he wrote: "Left Sweetwater and traveled over the ragged mountains twenty miles. I was well worn out, as well as the team, from watching all night. A miserable company for help."

They were at the Continental Divide.

Things did not improve the following day.

After noting that the team had been poorly fed the night before, he added: "Traveled eight miles to the last of the Sweetwater and turned out with a view to stopping, but the company growled, and we set sail. Went in search of food and water until all power exhausted. Team got ahead about five miles. Camped with little feed and no water."

On the fourteenth, they covered a bare eight miles again and the other members of the party waited disconsolately while the doctor went in search of feed and water. He wrote, "Found some feed but no water. Got no thanks from the company for my labor."

The going was tough at this point. The whole party—two wagons and the various animals connected with them—averaged about twelve miles a day when it hoped to average around twenty. But the doctor, foraging ahead for feed and water and then walking four to six miles each night after they had stopped for the day to take "supper to the boys" was covering thirty-two to thirty-six miles a day, either in the saddle or on foot.

Then he stood guard at night about half the time.

The animals and the people all traveled about half as far as he did and got twice as much rest.

On July sixteenth, after traveling four and a half miles, they found good feed and water and, as wagon master, he called a halt for the rest of the day . . . and would have stayed there the next day but "the company growled so much I consented to start next morning." The next day, they covered twelve miles and he covered an additional eleven miles looking for feed and water.

The eighteenth was a terrible day.

After filling every container with water, they left camp at eleven o'clock in the morning. They were crossing a desert where "dust from one to twelve inches deep on the ground and above the top of the wagon cover a perfect cloud." They traveled all day and all night . . . crossing twelve miles of plain and then "went over a tremendous mountain."

Tension perceptibly increased.

The doctor tried to "rest and recruit" the animals.

The Riders insisted on pressing ahead, regardless of what it did to the animals.

On July twenty-first, the doctor wrote: "Company was not willing to feed the team or for me-to doctor Lion. We therefore started without even watering the team. Came on about four miles and camp."

The next day the split came.

The Riders fell back and the doctor went back to find out what was wrong and learned that their animals were too weak to travel. Harsh words were exchanged. The doctor and Catherine went on for fifteen miles that day. The trail was easy and they could have gone farther, but they were stopped by a violent rainstorm . . . enabling the Riders to catch up with them. The Riders "camped in sight" but not with the doctor and Catherine. Doc Maynard stalked over and got his tent from them.

The last time they saw the Riders on the Oregon Trail was on July

27 when the doctor reported that he saw them "some three miles astern."

On August third, they reached the next important fork in the road of the doctor's life. It was at the confluence of the Snake and the Raft rivers . . .

The last chance to head for California.

Could he leave Catherine alone on the trail?

No way!

George Benton announced that he would leave them there and head for California. "In a pig's eye!" the doctor retorted.

Well, not precisely like that.

The doctor covered it in his diary with: "In quite a hubbub. George is about to leave us for California." The doctor's words on the subject were mild, but the young man got the point.

George didn't leave.

He continued on with them.

For the next sixty days—and *nights*—the doctor and Catherine were alone and unchaperoned on the Oregon Trail . . .

And for the next sixty days—and *nights*—the scorned Susanna followed in their tracks . . . falling farther behind as the days passed . . . burning her cork with increasing intensity every day . . .

Vividly imagining what the doctor and her sister were doing.

On September twenty-fifth, the doctor wrote: "Made our way . . . to M. T. Simmons, our place of destination, where we were received with a degree of brotherly kindness which seemed to rest our weary limbs, and promise of asylum for us in our worn-out pilgrimage."

Oh! Susanna

I can tell you for cotton pickin', boll weevil, gin mill certain that Stephen Collins Foster didn't have *our* Susanna in mind when he wrote the song about the girl with the same name for people to sing around the campfire at night on the Oregon Trail . . . and in the local saloons when they got to Oregon or California.

I also can vouch for the fact that her name has never appeared in many Seattle history books. For that matter, she has barely made it in *any* history book to date.

But, oh, boy, what a wallop she packed in Northwest history.

In order to understand her impact, it is necessary to go back a ways into the Simmons family history which, as far as Catherine was concerned began with her maternal grandfather, Michael Troutman. Michael was married twice . . . had ten children by each wife. He was worth plenty of bucks. At a family gathering for Christmas two years before Catherine was born, there were ten of his children there . . . ninety grandchildren and three great grandchildren. "All of the 122 sat down to dinner in the dining room, the length of which was eighty feet, the house being a three-story brick as large as a European castle . . ."

The landed possessions of the Troutman family included some 30,000 acres.

And, alongside the Simmons family, they were *poverty stricken!*

The Simmons family had three plantations, one for cotton, one for hemp and one for corn . . . and 300 slaves to operate the whole shebang.

When a Troutman and a Simmons were married, it resembled a merger between General Motors and the little company put together by Henry Ford.

But the war of 1812 and a few other similar disasters did in the family wealth. By the time one of the major characters of Washington history, Michael Troutman Simmons had reached young manhood, they were broke.

But they never forgot the "glory days."

Historian Hubert Bancroft describes Simmons as a fine specimen of a man "possessing the fine physique of the early men of Kentucky,

unlettered though not unenlightened, he possessed the qualities which in feudal times made men chiefs and founders of families. His courage was only exceeded by his independence . . ." Mike was seventeen years old and approaching his maximum growth of six feet four inches when his father died and he left the family farm to make his own way.

On January 1, 1835, he married Elizabeth Kindred. Mike was twenty years old. Elizabeth was sixteen.

Mike and Elizabeth moved to Missouri where, "Mike struggled with a text on mathematics. By rule of 'cut fir,' he constructed an excellent grist mill . . . not far from what became the site of St. Joseph. He was known the country over as 'honest Mike' Simmons. His mill was the meeting place for all the countryside where all problems large and small, were discussed . . ."

In the winter of 1843-44, Mike sold his mill and became a colonel in a huge wagon train of 300 wagons headed for Oregon. He had intended to settle in the Rogue River country, but when the train reached Fort Vancouver, he learned that the Hudson's Bay Company, under the autocratic management of Dr. John McLoughlin, was *requiring* all American settlers to take up claims south of the Columbia. The idea of the British at that time was that the Columbia

River would be the boundary between the United States and Canada. And when Mike learned the British wouldn't let him go north, then that is exactly what he had to do. Mike was a man who was easily led—but he couldn't be driven.

In July of 1845, Mike explored Puget Sound as far north as Whidbey Island, but finally staked a claim at the head of Budd Inlet where the Deschutes River dropped eighty feet in a series of falls and was an admirable spot for another grist mill. The mill went into operation in 1846, and was the first on Puget Sound. The following year, he erected a hydraulically operated sawmill—another first on the Sound—in what became the town of Tumwater.

In the fall of 1849, Mike sold his mills to Clanrick Crosby (Bing's grandfather) for $35,000. He was offered free property by Edmund Sylvester, the town proprietor, on the main street if he would come two miles north to the town of Olympia and establish there the first general store owned by an American on Puget Sound. If you will remember to multiply by ten to get the $35,000 in perspective, you will get some notion of the impact Mike's financial condition had on the rest of his impoverished family, which by that time was struggling for an existence in Illinois.

Early in 1850, Mike took a small portion of his fortune and purchased controlling interest in the brig *Orbit,* the first merchant vessel to visit the Sound . . . sent it to San Francisco with a load of pilings and an order for the ingredients of his new store. He erected a two-story building at the corner of First Avenue and Main Street. It became the first American store and postoffice on Puget Sound . . . and Mike, the first merchant and postmaster.

Overnight, Mike was the richest and most influential American on the Sound.

And that's what he was when Catherine and the doctor showed up in Olympia.

They told Mike the story of their suffering and struggle . . . of the deep and turbulent rivers . . . the precipitous mountains and the burning deserts . . . the worry about the animals and the vehicles . . . the sickness and the disease . . . the encounter with the Indians and the fear of the Mormons . . . and some kind of a cockimamy story about the separation from Susanna and Sam Rider.

Catherine got into the touchy ground about the death of her husband and the sixty days and sixty nights she and the doctor had spent unchaperoned on the trail.

In those days, *one* night alone wth a man was ruinous to a woman's reputation.

She admitted that it was a little soon after the death of Israel. On the other hand, this was the age of enlightenment. She and Israel had not been getting on that well in the previous few years. After all she was only sixteen when she and Israel had been married. She still was a young woman, etc., etc.

And they were going to be married.

Mike was something of a man of the world, himself, and could understand the story so far. He had his private suspicions of the doctor even at that point. It has been a long time, for instance, since anybody in the Simmons, Troutman, Morton or Broshears family had been in silks and satins. And here was this guy who *said* he was a doctor . . .

A lot of men *said* they were doctors.

Maynard, who had gotten himself barbered and shaved for the negotiations with Mike, stood there with his string tie and flowered vest, his polished black boots and expensive suit . . . his clean fingernails, white shirt and expensive cufflinks.

Catherine was wearing the Indian Maiden costume the doctor had bought her at great expense near Walla Walla.

Mike was more or less going along with the gag when they dropped the bombshell on him.

"There's this one small difficulty."

"Ah?"

"The doctor already has a wife."

"Holy smoke!"

Well, she knew that when he left, he had left for good. She did not expect him back. She had agreed to get a divorce on grounds of desertion as soon as the legal time had elapsed. However, in view of this new, er, "development," the doctor would arrange to get an immediate divorce. Prosch worded it like this: "He would treat Mrs. Broshears honorably, would marry with her, and in the most correct manner would end the trouble."

Left to his own devices, Mike might have gone along with them. Then, ten days later, Susanna showed up with murder in her head, blood in her eye and a loaded gun in her hands.

The Simmons family histories have been a little diffident about this episode in the family history. As one of the family historians pointed out, nothing ever was said about the "scandal of Catherine and Doctor Maynard."

Catherine pointed out that her brother was a head taller than the doctor, and with considerable pride told her biographer that Susanna tried to kill the doctor but that the "latter was not intimidated, nor more by white men and women than by Indians or disease."

Memory of the phantom lady mocked Maynard . . .

And this time he would not give up so easily.

III

For Love . . .
or Money?

Doc Maynard, who appears to be a mild-mannered man in most instances, could be a rough cob when occasion dictated. For instance, he didn't hit the roof and blow somebody's head off when he found his first wife in bed with another man. What he did was set a course for himself that took nine tough years to achieve results. With no big fanfare, he just plugged away at it; probably driving his first wife right out of her tree in the process . . . but never stopping until he attained his goal.

The doctor was not a huge man, but when necessity demanded that he become a mule-whacker with a twenty-five-foot whip, he flailed away until he got the hang of it and then come hell or high water, he drove that team of oxen across the country. The Indians who approached him on the trail with malice aforethought, didn't find him breathing fire and brimstone, but they got the message just the same. He didn't holler and stir up a storm when an insanely jealous Susanna presented him with the business end of a gun. But she got the message from a pair of steady eyes and didn't pull the trigger.

In the next few months, the doctor would face down and tame a shrewd, cruel and uniquely amoral Indian chief. He determined that Catherine would become his wife and went about accomplishing that result in spite of all the roadblocks her family put in his path.

At the end of this period of his life he liberated what would become downtown Seattle from the custody of a naive young man from Cherry Grove, Illinois, as easily as though he were removing a surface splinter from a man's hand. And then, within a matter of hours, he named and started the City of Seattle.

The honeymoon ended on October 7, 1850, when Susanna tried to kill him . . . and the wedding bells had not as yet rung.

By that time, the doctor realized that California was out as far as he was concerned. All they had down there was gold. What there was in the Pacific Northwest was without a doubt the greatest challenge of his life. For thirty years now, there had been a movement to link the Atlantic and Pacific coasts with some kind of a road.

We think that with all the airplanes flying around we've got a better handle on things than the folks did back in those days . . . but they were as aware of the Great Circle Route across the Pacific then as we are today.

Cognizant of all of this, the legislators of the two-year-old Oregon Territory were regularly sending off resolutions to Congress demanding that we get protection for our waters against the British . . . demanding that Alaska be made a territory . . . demanding that coastal defenses, lighthouses and harbors be mapped and charted . . . demanding that a telegraph line be extended to the new territory.

And demanding a transcontinental railroad.

The rage for laying out towns was at its height.

Some town in the Oregon Territory was going to become the "Queen City of the Pacific Northwest" and the "Gateway to the riches of the Orient" via the Great Circle Route. And at least twenty-five promoters of twenty-five towns during that two-year period had entered the sweepstakes.

If a fella could make his town the terminus of the railroad, he could sit back and make a fortune.

Doc Maynard was the ultimate gambler.

At fifty cents a call, there wasn't enough money in doctoring . . . So, what he did was decide to enter the incorporational sweepstakes.

He'd had a lot more experience in city-building than the average promoter in the Pacific Northwest at the time . . . and this kind of thing would keep him close to Catherine . . .

So, why not give it a fling?

Chance is the golden opportunity of the trained mind

Detective stories tell about how the police department, with all their anti-crime equipment and know-how, have caught the criminal. What usually happens is they dust for fingerprints, interview the neighbors, question the relatives and all like that.

Then some stool pigeon calls up and tells them who done it—and where he or she is at that moment.

And that's how the doctor located the site on which Seattle was built. He could have pored over the reports of Commander Charles Wilkes, who had explored the whole Pacific Coast nine years earlier. And he could have talked to all the experts about the best possible location for a city, etc., but what he did was pick up the *Oregon Spectator* for October 17, 1850 . . .

And there it was . . .

Cleveland West laid out before his very eyes.

Another man with a bright mind and a lively curiosity had arrived in Olympia nine months earlier in search of a place to settle.

The man was Isaac N. Ebey.

Mike Simmons, the only merchant in the place—which was called Smithfield at the time—tried to interest Ebey in settling down in his candidate for "Queen City" and "Gateway to the Orient." And Ebey did plunk up for a couple of town lots. But it didn't look like a very hot spot to him. Beyond suggesting that they change the name from Smithfield to Olympia, he didn't play much of a role in the place.

Ebey wasn't even sure he wanted to promote a town.

What he did want to do was explore Puget Sound. He agreed that he would inform Mike about his progress. And in the summer of 1850 he wrote a letter to Mike extolling the virtues of a place on what then was called Duwamish Bay and now is known as Elliott Bay.

Mike, who figured himself as some kind of an empire builder, forwarded Ebey's letter to the *Oregon Spectator* in the hope that it would encourage more settlers to head north of the Columbia.

The paper ran the letter two days after the doctor showed up in town in search of a divorce.

Maybe it was Mike's name on the letter which caught the doctor's eye. But Maynard was a man of infinite curiosity, and he probably would have read the piece under any circumstances.

Whatever it was, the seed that grew into the city of Seattle was planted in Maynard's head in Oregon City on or about October 17, 1850.

A tale of two Indians

In order to apprehend the history of Seattle, you have to get into the Indian political situation at the time the Americans began to trickle into the area north of the Columbia River . . . and to acquire an appreciation of the toughest Indian chief in the Puget Sound Basin.

All of our history books, for instance, cite Chief Seattle as one of Nature's noblemen . . . a chief of great oratorical abilities and of stature among the other Indians on the Sound . . . when the truth is that he was kind of a big, bumbling idiot who couldn't punch his way out of a cedar bark bag. It was a condition that went double for the other braves in his tribe—or he would never have made it as chief. He was a guy who knew how to play his politics well and could pit various factions against each other. He didn't invent the system, but he knew how to work it. The most important thing he did in his life was butter up Doc Maynard. That's why the town was named for him. But when you think of Chief Seattle, think of Charlie McCarthy on Edgar Bergen's knee. The words came out of Seattle's mouth and you couldn't even see Doc Maynard's lips moving.

The tough Indian on the Sound was Chief Patkanim.

An early history pointed out that Patkanim was "a man of bright, intelligent face, which was broad and full, eyes large and lustrous, set straight in his head, a straight Greek nose, delicate mouth with thin lips and graceful curve at the corners and the 'Cupid's bow.' He was ambitious and knew how to gain ascendancy over others . . . he was shrewd, ruthless, cunning."

Today he could be, say, a vice president of Boeing . . . maybe even president.

Patkanim was chief of the Snoqualmie and/or Snohomish tribe, the biggest and most powerful tribe on the Sound.

The tribes were named for the rivers on which they operated. So Patkanim controlled the rivers to the main passes through the Cascade Mountains (known today as Stevens and Snoqualmie). His headquarters probably was at the spot where the Snoqualmie and Skykomish rivers join to form the Snohomish—or in the neighborhood of Everett.

Chief Seattle held sway over a loose amalgamation of tribes at the mouth of the Duwamish River, which was created by the Black (no longer in existence), the Green and the White. In order to understand the situation, you must know of another chief called "Old Graybeard," who headed up a bunch of Indians near the mouth of the Nisqually River, which lies between Tacoma and Olympia.

In 1848 Chief Patkanim called together a meeting of all of the Puget Sound Indians—of which there were about 8,000—on Whidbey Island, where he pointed out that the "white" situation was getting out of hand and what the Indians should do was kill them all off before they took over the whole Puget Sound region.

Old Graybeard got up and said something like, "Yeah, and if we kill them all off, who will there be to protect my tribe against your periodic raids?" It took all the guts he had to say that.

Chief Seattle proved even more foolish.

He got up and said that his tribe occupied the land between Patkanim and Old Graybeard and he would protect the Nisquallies.

When the general hilarity among the Indians present had subsided,

Graybeard announced he'd rather have "one Boston (American) with one gun protecting us than all of the Duwamish Indians put together."

And Chief Seattle's tit really was in a ringer.

His favorite stamping ground at the mouth of the Duwamish no longer was available to him because it would be too easy for Patkanim to swoop down on him, killing warriors and taking women and children as slaves . . . which was why Chief Seattle and his tribe happened to be wintering in Olympia a couple of years later when Doc Maynard came along.

Patkanim hit the white history books again in 1849 when most of the white population on Puget Sound had departed for the California gold rush.

What he did at this time was stage a raid on the Hudson's Bay Company trading post at Fort Nisqually.

How he did it is the tricky part.

Patkanim went inside the fort, pretending he wanted to register a complaint about Graybeard and Company with factor William Tolmie. While he was there, he "accidentally" discharged his gun. His warriors attacked. Somebody providently closed the gates, but in the meantime two white men were killed.

Patkanim, who had arranged the whole show, could and did disclaim all responsibility for the attack and could get away with it because he was inside the fort at the time it occurred.

By that time the United States had taken over the territory and decided to make a *cause celebre* of the case . . . showing the Indians they couldn't get away with this kind of thing and demonstrating the American Judicial System in action. What Governor Joseph Lane did was move an entire court, including judge, jury and lawyers, up from Salem and stage a big show. The problem they encountered was finding some defendants until Chief Patkanim announced that for a hefty fee, he would produce the culprits.

Chief Patkanim delivered his own brother to be hung.

Thirty pieces of silver?

Hell, no!

Of the $2,000 it cost to stage this show, Patkanim got five hundred bucks.

The sixty-two-cent battleship

Well, it wasn't exactly a battleship.

It was an Indian war canoe. But these were substantial vessels constructed by hollowing out cedar logs, the like of which you can't even imagine today. There was a cedar tree in Doc Maynard's claim with a root system covering an entire city block. And the Indians were so adept at handling cedar that you wouldn't believe that, either.

Of course the Indians didn't work as hard as we do at the same things we do. All they had to do was work a couple of weeks in the fall during the salmon runs.

That gave 'em time to make cedar planks and use the bark of the cedar to make their clothing. And, cutting down a cedar tree with a diameter of twelve or fifteen feet with a stone ax took a little doing.

Hollowing it out into a craft twenty or thirty feet long was another time consumer.

The resulting craft was a thing of beauty with long, tapering lines that raised to a height of maybe six feet at the bow like the prow of a Viking ship. It would hold a dozen or more warriors—or an entire family with all its goods. With a sail in the bow, Indians used them to hunt whales way to hell and gone out in the Pacific. Behind the sail was a tent big enough to keep everybody covered as they sailed along in the rain, pretty as you please.

Patkanim had the best war canoe on Puget Sound.

What he did was take newly arrived white men on trips around the Sound—sort of like Western Tours or Gray Line does today.

Only, Western Tours and Gray Line bring 'em back.

One of the confrontations between the whites and Patkanim came when he took the new engineer for a sawmill on a trip around the

Sound. The engineer didn't come back. But a couple of Patkanim's braves came back wearing his clothes and carrying his watch and wallet. This was a source of considerable agitation among the other newly arrived whites in Seattle.

Patkanim allayed their fears.

He had both of his men hung . . .

Not for being thieves, but for getting caught.

And so it was on November 18, 1850, that Doc Maynard returned to Olympia, checked Catherine's Guilt Complex Temperature, found it still rising . . . and noted in his diary that he was taking a trip "down Sound."

With Patkanim, and a dozen or so of his braves.

The doctor would be gone for the next forty-five days.

But the item of interest here he entered in his diary a week after he started. He notes that he paid for one Indian canoe "one blanket, two shirts, three looking glasses and other iktas . . .

"To the amount of *sixty-two cents!*"

That made the doctor the proud new owner of Patkanim's prized Indian War Canoe . . .

Sixty-two cents.

You couldn't buy one today for $10,000.

Some deal!

How did a gentle pacifist like Doc Maynard do it? Simple. On the night of November 17, he refrained from eating dinner . . . For a simple reason.

He had dumped a dollop of ipecac in the stew.

It wrenched his heart to see those wretched red wretches reeling and retching in the rain—but it was either him or them and he knew it. And while they were engaged in this serious physical exercise he calmly informed them that, unlike other white people in the Pacific Northwest, he was not out to kill them.

On the other hand, if they so much as touched a hair on his head, this is how they would feel for the rest of their lives. He also thought it was a good time to make a deal on his future transportation needs in the new country where all transportation was by water.

If the doctor was going to make house calls, a canoe would have to be his carriage.

From the doctor's standpoint, the "patients" treated with ipecac underwent a complete "cure." From then on—and for the rest of his life—Patkanim couldn't find poles long enough to touch the doctor with. The rest of the trip around the Sound was "on the house." And from then until he died of natural causes in 1859, Patkanim wouldn't make a momentous decision like going to the bathroom without consulting Doc. I must confess the idea was not original with Doc Maynard. He'd picked it up from Dr. Marcus Whitman who had "doctored" a couple of melons with ipecac to keep the Indians out of his watermelon patch in Walla Walla.

A site for sore eyes

Doc Maynard's diary shows that they left camp early on November 19 and made it twenty miles to what we now know as the Tacoma Narrows. On the twentieth, running before a southwest wind, they made it into Commencement Bay where he bought salmon, potatoes and a new tent cover for the canoe from some Indians. This is the site of Tacoma today.

He got a lesson in Puget Sound tides that night.

I wouldn't want to say this is what soured him on Tacoma—a tradition maintained by Seattleites to this day—but he notes that he and the others "camped on the beach, but were driven off before daylight by the tide . . ."

They didn't have tide tables in those days and the tides around the Sound were unpredictable enough that even the Indians got caught short by them once in a while. There must have been some scrambling in the dark, rain and wind of that November night.

But all he notes in his diary is "Got my gun wet. Left the skillet cover."

The next day they picked up what he described as a "stiff breeze and ran around to an Indian camp where we were obliged to stay until the next morning . . ."

This was an empty Indian camp at the mouth of the Duwamish River.

Left empty by virtue of the fact that Chief Seattle and his braves were skulking around the streets of Olympia under the aegis of the white men who protected them against the dreaded Patkanim.

It was the doctor's first look at the site where he later would build the city of Seattle.

Doc Maynard, naturally, didn't describe it.

But he knew all about it from the clipping he had picked up in Oregon City the month before. Ebey noted that the Duwamish River dropped into a "bay which forms a beautiful little harbor about four miles in width and some six miles in length." He also pointed out that the river descended from a fertile valley and had an average width of about "forty yards with a deep channel and placid current." He added that "other plains of more extensive character are represented as being near at hand, and of sufficient fertility to satisfy the most fastidious taste."

It should be noted here that Ebey was more interested in farm land than in a city site. However, he described Lake Washington, which he called Lake Geneva, and adds that, "Between the lake and Admiralty Inlet (Puget Sound) the distance to Geneva Lake (which today is the narrow waist of the Queen City along Yesler Way) in many places cannot exceed a few miles as the Indians make portage across it with their canoes . . ."

The doctor had found the site of Cleveland West.

It didn't click with him at the time because he knew from Patkanim that the Duwamish River did not come down out of the mountains from the lowest pass. The pass from which this river descended (Naches) was not traversible in the winter. Patkanim, Chief of the Snoqualmie and Snohomish tribes, was proud of the fact that his tribe occupied the mouth of the two rivers which provided access to the lowest pass (Snoqualmie) and was eager to get the doctor to his own camping ground.

The doctor's principal objective was finding a good bed of coal. Everybody "knew" there would be plenty of iron ore some place in the Cascade Mountains. But the development of that resource would take time.

The urgent necessity to the doctor was coal.

The role of coal

Those of you who have read *Sons of the Profits* will have discovered, as I did, how important coal was as a resource in King County and how the forthright "sons" got squabbling among themselves and blew away the most important asset the county had—even more important than the timber or fish resources.

What additional research on the part of others and myself has brought to light during the intervening years is the importance with which Doc Maynard regarded this commodity while he still was in charge of the whole operation on Elliott Bay.

Patkanim, of course, was pretty eager to let the man with the magic in the black bag know how important Snoqualmie Pass was.It was the principal "grease trail" in the trade between the Puget Sound and Eastern Washington Indians. It was over this "trail" that the oil from the Eulachon—otherwise known as candlefish—was carried. It was this oil that was used to light the lamps of the wigwams in Eastern Washington. The Indians on the other side of the mountains could get their own salmon when that animal reached the heads of the streams. But the Eulachon oil was a different proposition. Patkanim's key position at the mouth of the important Snohomish made him the richest and most powerful chief on the Sound.

But the doctor was interested in coal.

At the time he came west, the entire nation was talking about railroads . . . more specifically, the transcontinental railroads . . . and even more specifically than that, which of the three potential transcontinentals would be the most important: the one that would terminate in San Diego . . . the one in San Francisco or the one that would terminate either at the mouth of the Columbia or somewhere near the Strait of Juan de Fuca.

As soon as the doctor had settled in his mind that his future lay in the Pacific Northwest, he became a proponent of the Puget Sound route for the major transcontinental railroad. It was his conviction that some town on Puget Sound would become the greatest maritime center on the Pacific Coast. There was talk, for instance, of how fast a person could be transported across the country.

He had just completed a trip of five months.

Railroad experts estimated that it could be done in five days!

One expert put it like this: "The eastern portions of Asia, including China and Japan, and countries adjacent, which are known to contain a population of many millions, in an advanced stage of civilization, in a condition to furnish a very profitable commerce; a commerce which has greatly enriched all that have hitherto participated in it, are situated from three to seven thousand miles from our Pacific Coast."

The big population centers were the cities of Canton, Nanking and Peking in China and Tokyo in Japan . . . each containing populations of from one to two million inhabitants . . . and each having ports accessible to U.S. vessels.

From New York to the Yangtze River, the shortest and most direct line was over the Great Circle which runs considerably north of the boundary between the United States and Canada. But the Strait of Juan de Fuca provided access to U.S. harbors closest to the true curve of the earth. The city of Chicago was the largest western city close to the Great Circle and the natural route for the railroad ran through Chicago via Lake Superior. The route then would go up the great bend of the Missouri River and over one of several passes in the Rockies located by Lewis and Clark and then down the other side along the Columbia.

The route then would abort the valley of the Columbia, somewhere in what we know today as Eastern Washington and cross the Cascade

Range for a more direct shot at the Strait of Juan de Fuca than could be had from the mouth of the Columbia.

The distance from Chicago to the Strait of Juan de Fuca by doing this was 1,960 miles . . .

By far the shortest route from Chicago to the Pacific Coast.

Everybody in the nation at that point knew about Mount Rainier from elevations taken by Wilkes nine years earlier. Surveyors had Mount Rainier at an elevation of 12,330 feet at the time (the official elevation is now 14,408) and figured that mountains on either side in the Cascade Range became progressively lower.

One expert made the estimate that somewhere north of Rainier a pass of 4,000 feet or less would be discovered within the next few years. And this, because it would be the closest to the Strait, would become the most important pass on the transcontinental railroad route.

A further argument for the northern route lay in three things: There were vast mineral resources, especially coal which would be the basic source of energy for the steam engines . . . timber along the entire route that was readily available to be made into ties . . . and that as fast as the line was built, the land around it would be settled by immigrants.

Bituminous coal had been discovered between Mandan and Great Falls along the Missouri.

A New York magazine of general circulation summarized the kind of thing that Doc Maynard was looking for in his first exploration of Puget Sound:

"West of the Cascade Mountains, bituminous coal is now known to exist in large quantities in the vicinity of the waters of the Straits of de Fuca . . . It lies near the surface, is gotten out with crowbars, is near to good anchorage and is of excellent quality, running in extensive folds, and even in clumpy mounds . . . most easily worked all along this part of the country."

At the time the doctor was doing his explorations, no coal had been found south of the Stillaguamish River.

The doctor didn't find the "easy access" supply of coal on that trip.

But nowhere did he find a better harbor than the one he had seen in Elliott Bay his third night out. The Indians told him that Isaac Ebey had preceded him in his explorations.

He decided to visit Ebey and talk things over.

Patkanim had no problem finding the place.

It was the exact spot where he'd called the big conclave of Indians.

The same place where Chief Seattle lost his figurative shirt.

"Colonel Ebey, I presume?"

Isaac Neff Ebey always has had a big ride in Washington history, primarily on account of the fact that the Haida Indians cut off his head and took it north with them, keeping it for two years until it was recovered by Hudson's Bay Company detectives and returned to his widow.

But, outside of the archives, nothing ever had been printed about the critically important meeting between him and Doctor Maynard in the winter of 1850.

Ebey, another Ohioan, was eight years Doc Maynard's junior and had been educated as a lawyer, but never been admitted to the bar. In 1843, he married and two sons were the result of that union. In 1846, when the younger son was but six months old, Ebey came west seeking a permanent home for his family . . .

And didn't see his wife for the next four years.

He filed his donation claim on a beautiful piece of rolling prairie land on Whidbey Island on October 15, 1850, and was living alone in his cabin there in December when Patkanim brought Doc Maynard to the spot . . . and the two men became fast friends. Both of them well educated and with a broad view of the potential of the Pacific Northwest, they had a great deal in common. They were a discouraged pair at the time. Ebey was lonesome for his wife. And the doctor didn't know whether it was up, down or sideways with Catherine.

The doctor had been led to believe in everything he had read that there were enormous coal deposits somewhere around the Canadian border . . . but none of his explorations had turned up anything worthwhile. It has to be presumed that Ebey, who was enthusiastic about the site of what became King County, persuaded the doctor that this was the spot where coal would be found and where the major city of the Pacific Northwest would grow.

The doctor, in turn. learned that Ebey had political ambitions, and filed away this knowledge for future use.

Ebey later would file an affidavit with the Oregon Territorial Legislature that : "This is to certify that I have been acquainted with the bearer, D. S. Maynard, since some time in the autumn of 1850 and am happy in saying that I consider him a man of honest moral principles and believe that he is considered as such among his acquaintances in general."

Doc Maynard returned to Olympia toward the end of December, realizing that what he was, was broke.

Doc Maynard's incredible woodpile

The way Prosch put it was: "Urgent necessity stared him boldly and harshly in the face. Undaunted, he took off his fine coat, donned the garments of a laborer, and proceeded to cut cordwood for the San Francisco market." Being the kind of man he was, however, it couldn't be just any old woodpile.

It had to be the biggest pile of wood on earth.

There also had to be an angle or two that didn't meet the naked eye.

If anything ever was prime example of the inventor of Seattle in action, the pile of wood that he cut in Olympia between January and August, 1851, is it . . . because, of course, he had another ax to grind than the one he was using to cut down those trees and then split them up into four-foot sections of cordwood for the San Francisco market. All he has ever gotten in our official history books on this one is a couple of lines in a footnote or two saying that he, personally, cut 400 cords of wood in a period of eight months.

However, for 125 years, historians have agreed that he did cut them and he did cut them all by himself. He interrupted his woodcutting from time to time to take an interest in the future state of Washington and to thwart the mighty Mike Simmons, which he could be persuaded to do as easy as you could spit in the street . . .

Easier.

And to pursue the hand of the beautiful maiden that Mike kept locked up in the castle on the other side of the moat.

Well, it really wasn't much of a moat.

It was Mike's combined house, store and post office at First and Main Street in Olympia . . . although during the rainy winter months, both First and Main were muddy enough to satisfy the qualifications of a moat, which the dictionary describes as a "deep and wide trench around a fortified place, usually filled with water."

Take a look at "General" Maynard's strategy.

In those days a man could keep all the wood he could cut. And the place he chose to do his cutting was on the outskirts of Olympia along Budd Inlet where every passing ship could see the results of his work.

Every night he could tramp into town and sit someplace jawing with the boys and keep an eye out for Catherine. Mike couldn't keep a guard on Catherine all of the time. And the second mighty Mike turned his back, the two lovers were in one another's arms making the most of their limited opportunities.

There also was a subtle psychological battle going on between the doctor and the merchant prince of Olympia. The folks around and about admired a man with guts. The doctor was a nobody. Mike was the man who had broken the lock the British had kept on the land north of the Columbia River. For thirty years it had been the policy of Great Britain to divert emigrants to that part of the Oregon Territory south of the Columbia River.

Great Britain figured she would have to reach a compromise with America over this ground . . . she hoped the border would follow the westward flow of the Columbia.

Mike was the first to defy Dr. John McLoughlin, chief factor of the

Hudson's Bay Company, and move north of the Columbia to settle on Puget Sound with the first American hydraulically operated saw and grist mills.

He was the most important man on the Sound.

Men didn't cross him lightly. He ran things with a strong hand. They might resent him, but they didn't cross him. And here was this mild-mannered and genial doctor, quietly and thoroughly driving Mike nuts.

It must be remembered that this was an extremely physical society. There was no electricity. There was no steam power . . . with the exception of the *Beaver*, ships that entered Puget Sound were sailing ships. Olympia was the only town on the Sound. Mike Simmons was the only merchant in the town. He had a monopoly which might make him unpopular on some fronts, but which, it was generally believed, would soon make him a millionaire.

In order to understand this, you have to understand one of the peculiarities of existence in the Pacific Northwest at that time and place.

For two or three decades the Hudson's Bay Company had, to all practical purposes, owned and operated the vast Oregon Territory.

And the company had done it through its merchandising policy. It charged reasonable prices, but it did not permit anybody else to enter the merchandising business in opposition. The company wasn't about to let somebody else enter the fur trade by importing goods to swap with the Indians for fur. As someone put it, "If you wanted to buy a new pair of trousers, you had to show the clerk the rent in the ones you were wearing before he would sell you the new ones."

When the United States got the Oregon Territory at what is generally the same boundary as today, merchants began opposing the Bay Company south of the Columbia, and because of the competition, prices were reasonable.

But Mike was the only *American* merchant on Puget Sound.

Where brooms sold for twenty-five cents in Portland and Oregon City, Mike was selling them for a dollar. Mike got a dollar a yard for calico and a dollar a pound for sugar—items that sold for two-bits south of the river. For a stove that sold for $7.50 in New York . . . $15 in San Francisco and $22.50 in Portland or Oregon City, Mike got a whopping $80.

They might not like it . . .

But if they wanted a stove, they paid it.

And here was this little old man (Doc was forty-three) with his crosscut saw and his ax and his wedges felling trees that were as high as a twenty-story building and ten or fifteen feet in diameter and splitting them into four-foot lengths and piling them into a stack that stretched along the beach north of town.

The people, with some degree of experience with doctors, were suspicious of medical men, but a man who was out there all day long, six days a week, cutting wood . . .

He was somebody they could understand.

Doc defied "Authority."

And they loved him for it.

It wasn't so much the amount of wood he cut. He only did about two cords a day and there were men in town who could cut six cords a day. It was his cheerful disposition and his persistence. He kept at that wood pile for eight months . . . steadily knocking off his two cords a day . . . and the bigger the woodpile got, the madder Mike got . . .

And the more thoughtful Catherine got.

This was really some pile of wood.

If somebody were to do it today, it would look like the wall of China in downtown Seattle.

Piled to a height of six feet, it would stretch from today's City Hall in Seattle five blocks along Fourth Avenue to the Olympic Hotel. How many men would—or even could—cut that much wood without help and without a chain saw . . . beginning with huge trees . . . in eight months time?

For a woman . . .

The "Sidney Ducks," and other wild birds

In the traditional Seattle history books, the settlers arrived here dead broke and were able to sell piling to Captain Daniel S. Howard of the brig *Leonesa* for eight cents a running foot and cordwood for four dollars a cord. They put their backs to the task and pretty soon the original economy of the city was established. The folks quickly ran out of trees at Alki Point and started cutting at places like Gig Harbor . . . and, finally staked their claims across the bay where the city is today, because here the timber was thick and easily rolled down a steep hill to deep water.

The way the usual story goes is that Captain Howard appeared with money to buy piling for the San Francisco market as if "sent by a wise Providence." They knelt and thanked God.

It wasn't a wise Providence Doc Maynard thanked . . .

It was the "Sidney Ducks" and other wild birds who populated the rougher part of San Francisco at the time. The Sidney Ducks were a gang of convicts who had escaped from Sidney, Australia, and other men of their ilk who formed gangs like the "Hounds" and the "Regulators."

Thanks to the discovery of gold, San Francisco was a boom town in the early 1850s. As *Encyclopedia Americana* puts it: "The Argonauts appeared in such great numbers that supplies and services of every sort were quickly exhausted . . . Shiploads of merchandise were brought ashore and dumped on the beach for lack of storage. Buildings about the plaza were turned into gambling resorts and brought huge profits to their operators. Because everything was in short supply, prices rose to fantastic heights. Hundreds of buildings of canvas or wood were hastily erected to house stores, banks or offices, and when these were swept away in the frequent fires they were promptly rebuilt . . ."

All of which brings us to the gangs.

For a while these fellas just rolled drunks for their money, which was kind of a piecemeal, retail operation.

The big money lay in looting.

Well, murder offered an enterprising young man some incentive, but it was hard to tell in advance whether there were any real bucks in it.

But loot . . . that was a sure thing.

These entrepreneurs quickly realized that for any kind of a healthy economy in the looting business, it was necessary to have something to loot. And the best insurance for that was a fire. By the very nature of things, what with the population of San Francisco growing from 800 to 35,000 in a couple of years, fires were an enormous hazard. With the aid of the Barbary Coast gangs, they became a routine method of doing business.

Between 1849 and 1851 the town was burned down five times.

So, while the early settlers on Elliott Bay blessed The Lord for providing them with a solution to their economic problems, it really was The Devil.

The beneficent Captain Howard provided those original settlers at Alki Point with eight cents a running foot for pilings which he sold in San Francisco for a dollar a running foot.

Doc had plenty of opportunities to sell his woodpile for four bucks a cord, but he had a different proposition in mind. He didn't want a buyer. He wanted a partner. And finally, in the fall of 1851, he found the right man in Captain L. M. Felker of the brig *Franklin Adams*. Felker at first agreed to charter his boat to Maynard. The cordwood was excellent collateral. He would be paid when it sold in San Francisco. Felker so admired the doctor's persuasiveness that he subsequently went into partnership with him.

Doc accompanied his pile of wood to California and sold that 400 cords of wood in San Francisco for forty dollars a cord . . . *sixteen thousand bucks!* (The equivalent of $155,000 in today's money.)

That was the $16,000 which financed the invention of Seattle.

All's Weller that ends Weller

One of those quickie historians who zips around the world doing instant analyses of cities had kind of a lucky strike a number of years ago when he compared San Francisco to a man's mistress and Seattle to a man's wife. And without getting into the question of whether mistresses are more interesting people than wives, this small observation is a reflection of one facet of Doc Maynard's personality.

He was the first one to toss the pebble in the still lake of the virgin territory, and the waves he made have been making a widening circle ever since.

His association with John Weller is a case in point.

Weller performed a great service to the doctor when the latter was deeply distressed at home. He got the doctor out of the house and into politics, and if he had won the gubernatorial campaign, Doc might have gone to Columbus instead of Oregon. Weller, who had four wives and thought the doctor was out of his mind to attach that much importance to any one woman, was the catalyst who got the doctor away from Cleveland . . . although Maynard wasn't *going* anywhere.

He was a fugitive *from* somewhere.

It was a part and parcel of the doctor's character, however, that he felt some kind of moral obligation to Weller . . . so when Maynard arrived in San Francisco and sold his firewood, he took the time to trundle over to the goldfields and what turned out to be his final meeting in Sacramento with his old friend.

In a classic sense, Weller offered the ultimate bribe. He pointed to a chest of gold in his tent and told the doctor he could keep all that he could carry away. The powerfully built doctor who just had completed eight months of hard labor in the woods had a fortune at his fingertips.

When Maynard smiled and declined the offer, Weller knew that their close association was a thing of the past, and, like any good politician, accepted the decision with grace; and the conversation drifted into other channels. But the life in California was distasteful to Doc. While he was in Sacramento, five men were killed in one nearby camp and several others killed in the neighborhood. At the time he was in San Francisco, the town established some kind of a record with 1,000 murders a year.

Weller suggested that Maynard get into the lumber business. In those days you could buy all of the machinery necessary for a sawmill for $15,000. "Give up your profession," Weller said. "Get the machinery for a sawmill. In selling us lumber you'll make a hundred dollars for every one you may possibly make in doctoring and you'll soon be rich."

But the doctor wasn't interested in making small pieces of wood out of big ones.

He'd got a bellyfull of that in the past eight months.

And the wheels within the wheels of Fate were meshing for him even in his visit to California. Weller informed him that a couple of fellow Ohioans, John Stroble and Henry Yesler, had purchased the machinery necessary for a steam sawmill. Weller had heard from Yesler's wife, Sarah, who had arranged the financing. The machinery was en route to San Francisco. Mrs. Yesler had written everyone she knew—including Weller—in search of her husband. She was afraid the machinery would arrive and be sold for freight charges. And Yesler was missing.

When last heard from, the two men had investigated Marysville,

California, for a mill site and were headed to the Pacific Northwest. Weller suggested that the doctor might want the mill in the town he was proposing to build on Puget Sound.

The doctor was well aware of the importance of having the first steam sawmill on Puget Sound in his town. Most existing Seattle histories hold that Yesler talked Maynard out of the land for his sawmill.

The truth is the exact opposite.

The land was waiting for Yesler before the doctor ever met him or Yesler ever put in an appearance on Puget Sound.

Weller's final contribution to the construction of Seattle fell into place when he introduced the doctor to one George N. McConaha, another Ohioan. McConaha, like Maynard, had been summoned by Weller when the latter decided he wanted to become the first United States senator when California became a state. And McConaha had performed well on Weller's behalf. As a member of California's first state legislature, he had lobbied through Weller's nomination and appointment to the Senate by that body.

At the time the doctor was in Sacramento, McConaha was serving as the prosecuting attorney for the city of Sacramento.

Within six months, he would be at Doc Maynard's doorstep.

Out of loyalty, friendship or whimsy, Doc Maynard named one of the streets in his original plat of Seattle after his friend, Weller. Today, the bottom of that street originates in one of the facilities in the Kingdome Stadium . . .

And the least we could do is name it the "John Weller Memorial Men's Room."

Doctor, Lawyer, Merchant Chief

Things were clicking into place with uncanny precision while Maynard was in California.

When he returned to San Francisco from Sacramento, it was to find Captain Felker waiting for him along with what today would be called the world's biggest garage sale. There were more than 500 ships laying abandoned in San Francisco Bay as a result of the fact that the crews left them for the gold fields as soon as they hit dry land. A lot of them still had their cargoes on board.

And, for pennies on the dollar, the doctor purchased enough merchandise to load Felker's brig to the gunwales. When they started north, the doctor had enough in the way of goods to start two or three general stores . . . and he was only out five hundred bucks.

In those days, the going rate for starting a town was $3,000 . . . What you could buy for the three thousand was a fishery, a barrel factory, the necessary equipment for cutting piling and shingles and for hewing timbers. It also included the necessities for opening a general store.

Felker figured the doctor was some kind of a genius.

Maynard had enough capital to start *five* towns!

Felker went into partnership with the doctor.

And an excellent plan it was. The doctor could produce the cargoes for San Francisco on Puget Sound. Felker could provide merchandise for the store in the Bay City . . . and they could split the profits on both. Felker's role in the founding of Seattle always has been passed over as amounting to very little when the truth is that his was a key position from the beginning.

As the saying goes, "when you're hot, you're hot . . ." And, as the two partners made the turn into the Strait of Juan de Fuca at Cape Flattery, the Makah Indians were about to dispose of the contents of a wrecked ship along with the passengers and crew.

Felker had a little brass cannon on the bow of the *Franklin Adams*. A few well placed shots dispersed the Indians and saved the people and the ship's cargo. The people were Canadians. Felker and the doctor took them and their possessions to Victoria where the authorities rewarded them with enough cash and goods to start yet another town.

Doc Maynard kept the little brass cannon as a souvenir . . . and during his lifetime—perhaps even longer—it was fired on the Fourth of July and other civic occasions.

But when they got to Olympia, the doctor encountered a revolting development.

God help us all!

So much of what happened during the invention of Seattle baffled the pious part of the pioneer community, it ended up crediting the creation of our town to a little bit of Divine Intervention here, and a smidgin over there. The whole thing gets dropped into the lap of The Lord on the grounds that He moves in mysterious ways to do His thing.

If He was responsible, the Lord sure did it the hard way, because what happened was that while Doc Maynard was in California, a young fella went south with $60,000 belonging to Mike Simmons and kept on going. On November 18, 1851, Mike ran an ad in the *Oregon Spectator* reading:

"Notice—My late partner, Charles Hart Smith, having absconded with several thousand dollars belonging to me, and having besides defrauded every other person in this vicinity whom he could, under false pretenses, persuade to credit—this is to notify the public that the partnership lately existing under the name of Simmons & Smith is hereby dissolved, and all persons are warned not to trust the said Smith, under any circumstances, whatever. M. T. Simmons, Olympia, Lewis County, O.T., November 18, '51."

You'll notice the ad didn't say anything about the sixty thou. And the chances are that at that stage of the game Mike didn't know that he had one foot on a banana peel and the other on financial oblivion. At any rate, he sure didn't show it in regard to the romance between the doctor and Catherine Broshears. And, of course, he had all of the help he needed from the eligible bachelors around the Pacific Northwest who descended on Catherine like a bunch of bees attracted by the honey

Prosch says, "Notwithstanding the newness of things and their primitive character, life at the upper end of Puget Sound was not uninteresting to the widow." (After all, she was thirty-two, going on ninety-six, a well-preserved hunk of woman.) "Men were many enough compared to women, there probably being three or four to one. Women were correspondingly in favor. Nothing was too good for them. They could have what they wished for the asking.

"Mrs. Broshears soon found herself to be in high favor with the bachelors and widowers, and she was evidently regarded by them as a 'catch' of the best character. Her people speedily saw the direction of things, and they tried to direct it into quarters to suit themselves and their own ideas of propriety and desirability. They found out that the beginning of a romance had developed on the plains, east of the Rocky Mountains, and that it had attained with the passage of weeks and months such life and strength as to be quite serious.

"Knowing that Dr. Maynard was a married man, from his own admissions, they disapproved the bent and inclination shown by him and their widowed sister. They made suggestions of other men, introduced them, and did what they could to break up the alliance between Maynard and Mrs. Broshears. They restrained her somewhat of her liberty, and prevented her from going with him when they could.

"More than once they were on the verge of stopping by force the marriage."

Do you think Doc Maynard took this lying down?

Hell, no!

Instead of going on to Seattle, he set up shop in Olympia.

And that really did screw up the works in Mike's clock. The doctor introduced a totally new concept to the Mike Simmons monopoly.

It was known as "competition."

Doc Maynard had bought and equipped a general store for ten-cents on the dollar. What he did was start selling stuff for the same prices merchants were getting for it in San Francisco, Portland, Oregon City and Salem. Catherine would say later that his action created "quite a disturbance in the trade," and she was right. Mike previously had been getting ten times the going rate for his products.

But with Smith gone . . . And the $60,000 gone . . . Charging ten prices for things was not a luxury, it was a necessity. The Simmons Empire teetered on the brink of collapse. With Doc Maynard's store in town, Mike's financial demise was guaranteed. If he went under at the hands of the doctor, the family pressure against Catherine's marriage to Maynard would become unanimous and irresistible. And suddenly Catherine was on a very hot seat indeed. Her "go away, stay" attitude toward the doctor suddenly was crystallized out of the solution and into direct action.

"If you leave," she said, "I'll marry you."

To the family, she said, "It's going to be David Maynard or nobody."

A few months later, one G. A. Barnes set up what he advertised as a "Cheap Store," and broke Mike Simmons.

But by that time, Doc Maynard was long gone.

The return of the Native

While all this was going on, Chief Seattle was hopping around on one foot and the other like he had to go to the bathroom. He had the greatest grapevine on the Sound and knew that the doctor's primary interest in life was a hunk of land at the mouth of the Duwamish River.

The Chief had been in the doghouse with the members of his tribe ever since he had opened his big mouth about protecting the Nisquallies from Patkanim four years earlier. They were in pretty good shape as long as they stayed at Suquamish, which is on the west side of Puget Sound, but the fishing there was lousy. And, with Patkanim threatening to wipe them out if they came near their favorite camping ground at the mouth of the Duwamish, their traditional fishing ground had become a precarious place indeed.

They had to sort of "sneak" the fish out . . . ready to beat a strategic retreat when Patkanim came thundering down on them from his headquarters at the mouth of the Snohomish River.

For all of his bellering and bluster, Chief Seattle was *that* close to a recall election. His hopes were raised in the winter of 1850 when Doc Maynard survived one of Patkanim's cheap excursion trips around Puget Sound. And his native intelligence told him there was something in Doc Maynard's little black bag which commanded Patkanim's complete respect.

Respect?

Patkanim was scared to death of that bag.

Maynard, who was not unaware of the Indian Political Climate, had a whole bunch of merchandise on his hands . . . and Felker was off some place like San Francisco. What he needed was some cheap transportation to Elliott Bay with the ingredients for his store.

And it was a lot of stuff.

There were, for instance, several barrels of whiskey . . . brandy . . . rum . . . nearly two tons of molasses . . . half a ton of hardtack . . . three tons of flour . . . a box of pots and pans, axes, tobacco, raisins, shoes, boots and medical supplies . . . a quarter-of-a-ton of sugar . . . several dozen hickory shirts . . . a dozen window sashes . . . a box of eight-by-ten-inch window panes . . . a case each of mustard . . . salt . . . pepper and pepper sauce . . . a dozen grindstones and a half-dozen each of files and crosscut saws . . . several roles of calico and a bale or two of domestic—and more brooms than the chief had ever seen.

That was mid-March, 1852.

For the first time in four years, Chief Seattle and his tribe were returning to their Duwamish fishing ground in time for the spring run of Chinook salmon.

Opening day at the Seattle Yacht Club when thousands of boats of one kind and another pass through the Montlake Cut and into Lake Washington past a reviewing stand is a pretty and impressive function in our town annually . . .

But it never could equal the triumphant procession which marked the return of Chief Seattle and the 200 members of his tribe to the mouth of the Duwamish River and the home of his ancestors.

The sun could have been shining.

The sun had to be shining!

The sun was shining in Chief Seattle's heart—regardless of the kind of climate that The Lord visited upon that part of the earth around Alki Point on the particular day in question.

The chief lined up a flotilla of floating craft, the like of which never had been seen before in the town of Olympia . . . canoes . . . scows . . . sailing vessels—the works.

They departed Olympia on the morning of March 23.

With all that crowd it took 'em nine days to reach Elliott Bay.

What a triumph for Chief Seattle, Chief of the Suquamish and Allied Tribes, Chief of the Duwamish and Allied Tribes, High Muckamuck of the Most Exalted . . . returning in triumph from exile. There he was in full regalia at the head of the procession, lolling in the stern of the lead canoe . . .

Beside him was the impeccably clad Dr. Maynard with his broad-brimmed fedora . . . immaculate white shirt, black tie, flowered vest and flowing cape . . .

And his little black bag.

Unlike opening day at the yacht club when everybody is having a great time, there were mixed feelings among the folks on shore. There was, of course, the irrepressible Charlie Terry, looking like the Cheshire cat that just has swallowed the canary . . . he only recently had stolen the location from under the noses of the people from Cherry Grove and had named it New York after his native state.

Also there, however, were the people who had lost the battle for ownership of the new town on Elliott Bay. They weren't on speaking terms with the ones who had won the townsite. Some of them weren't even on speaking terms with one another. There was, for instance, the forthright young Louisa Boren, who had been trying for forty-five days to get the menfolk in her group off their duffs and moved over to a town-location which they had staked out at the head of the bay five miles away. Some of these people were sick of one another and the others were just plain sick . . .

But the sickest of the shore bunch was Patkanim.

That was *his* canoe Chief Seattle and the doctor were riding in!

Doc Maynard, not unmindful of the political situation between the two Indian Chiefs, and appreciative of the efforts to which Seattle, his new whipping boy, had extended himself, decided to make the Chief's day complete.

"What I'm going to do, Chief," he said, "is name the most important town in the world after you."

"Besides," he reflected, "it sure will tick off Patkanim."

And so Seattle was named.

Bye bye mudhole

You don't have to dig deep or read far to find out that a bunch of teetotallers from a presently non-existent town called Cherry Grove, Illinois, landed at Alki Point on November 15, 1851. The folks had had a terrible time coming across the continent . . . what with Indians and all like that.

By the time they got to Portland, half of the party wasn't talking to the other half, and they split up—one half remaining in Portland and the other half heading for Puget Sound. Leader of half the party was John Denny.

The other half was headed by his son, Arthur Armstrong Denny, who was sick with malaria at the time and sent his younger brother, David, to explore the Puget Sound country. When Arthur was well enough to come, he brought his half of the party with him . . .

Only to find himself euchred out of Alki Point by the brothers Charlie and Lee Terry. And here the party split again into two non-communicating groups.

What they knew for sure was that they were broke. And what they found out was they could get eight cents a running foot for piling. So, what they set about doing was finding the best place to get piling.

In the process, they went up and down the Duwamish River a few times—never noticing a particularly obnoxious mudhole at the mouth of the river. On February 15, 1852, four of the folks who were speaking with one another, Arthur and David Denny, William N. Bell and Carson Boren, paddled around Elliott Bay and found a place where it was easy to cut trees and roll them down a steep bank to deep water where they could be loaded aboard ship.

Here, they staked adjacent claims that ran from approximately the Kingdome to the Space Needle. David was too young to stake a claim. Arthur took the center cut, which was thick with beautiful, straight piling material, and they handed the bottom of the barrel to Carson Boren, Denny's brother-in-law, who was only there because his wife told him he had to be. What Boren didn't like was his wife. What he did like was hunting and fishing . . .

So *what* if he got the mudhole?

When Doc Maynard appeared on the scene, Arthur Denny was laid low again with malaria and the doctor was summoned to ease his pain a little . . .

During the course of which time Maynard maneuvered a little in a most un-medical manner. Today, the Hippocratic Oath hanging in his office would be ripped up and he would be stripped of his medical buttons by the Committee on Medical Ethics of the King County Medical Society.

The sick man bemoaned the fact that Charlie Terry had done him in. He felt awful. When they landed at Alki, it had been raining. The women and children had been in tears and now everything was going to hell in a handbasket.

The doctor administered some soothing syrup which consisted largely of alcohol into which opium had been dissolved. And as the elixir took hold of the patient, the doctor ventured the opinion that he was looking around for a hole in which to go fishing. He mentioned diffidently that he had a full-scale general store.

The place that interested him a little . . .

For a fishing camp only, you understand . . .

Was the punker part of Boren's claim.

That was the part that was under water when the tide came in. However, the Indians had been using this fishing camp on the point.

Boren's claim! Denny perked up.

Here was a chance for a country boy to take in the city slicker.

It could be arranged for the doctor to have that hunk of property. Denny felt that he could induce his brother-in-law to give a little. The doctor demurred. He wasn't at all sure this was what he was looking for.

Denny pointed out how welcome the doctor and his store would be.

The doctor relented a little . . .

Well, maybe.

Denny swiftly closed the deal.

He did not learn until later . . . much later . . . that, teetotaller or not, he'd been on an opium jag and given away downtown Seattle . . . on April 1.

Doc Maynard got busy.

The town is born

Two days later, Dr. Maynard and his crew of Indian volunteers hauled the ingredients for his store and the goods of the Boren and Bell families to the new location. Bagley writes: "On April 3, Bell, Boren's family and Doctor Maynard moved from Alki to their claims, leaving behind A.A. Denny who was too ill with the ague to come over until a house could be built. At first Bell camped on the north side and Boren on the south side of the claims continuing thus until they could build cabins . . ."

The doctor, who had other eggs to lay and other fish to fry, lacked their degree of leisure. Bagley covers this phase of our founding with: "Maynard's official entry named April 3, 1852 as his date of settlement. With his accustomed energy he at once set to work to provide himself with a store building, availing himself of white and Indian labor, and in a few days was selling goods in it. It was eighteen feet wide and twenty-six long, with an attic in the front half of it. The walls were of logs and the roof of shakes, the usual name for split boards about four feet long. It stood at the northwest corner of First Avenue South and Main Street. The unbroken forest was a few feet away on the east and the steep bank above tidewater on the west. The stores of that period included under one roof the necessaries of pioneer life as far as attainable, clothing, hardware, groceries, tools, ship chandlery, and Maynard's was the first of its kind in Seattle although Low and Terry had conducted a similar business at Alki."

The doctor called his store the "Seattle Exchange."

It was the first structure of any kind, size, or shape in our town and, as such, we ought to know what it looked like.

The top side of each log was hewn into a triangular shape and the bottom was notched to accept it. About eight feet from the ground, the logs were continued up another four to six feet, but in shorter lengths that created a peaked roof. Rafters about four feet apart extended from one end to the other and were covered with cedar shakes, which were fastened with wooden pins. The logs then were chinked with clay, which was plentiful in Seattle's birthplace. And this in turn was covered with slats inside and out.

Doc had plenty of cedar to work with. This was split and formed into a puncheon floor with an adz that in the hands of a good workman could be as smooth as a modern kitchen floor and just as waterproof. The cedar also was fashioned into tables, benches, stools, and a door which was made with an upper and lower section, with hinges and bars that defied all ordinary attempts at breaking it open. A bar served as the lock. Pivoted at one end, it dropped into a slot. At this end, a leather thong from the bar led through a hole above the door. In peaceful times, the thong was not drawn at night, giving rise to the phrase, "the latch string is always out."

The double door had a double purpose. When the upper section was open, it provided both light and ventilation, while the lower section kept out dogs, chickens, pigs—and, hopefully—unwanted Indians. There usually was an opening six feet square left in one wall, which led to a fireplace built outside of the cabin.

Lighting at night was provided by tallow candles or fish oil placed in a shallow bowl with a cotton wick in it . . . and by the open hearth. Wooden pins driven into the walls supported shelves made of split cedar. Uprights driven into the floor supported a platform that was covered with fir bows to serve as a mattress on which blankets were spread for a bed.

In this 18x26-foot-square structure, Doc Maynard housed the town's first combination hardware, drug, grocery and clothing store. It also served as the first hospital, polling place and meeting hall. And a few months after it was built, it became the first restaurant in town.

Doc Maynard was a one-man band.

I'm drawing on Bagley for a good deal of this information in spite of the fact that his history of Seattle was paid for by the people whose biographies appeared in it. In the biographical sections, the families controlled exactly what was said. But Bagley was too much of a reporter to saccharinize the historical truth in the non-biographical section.

He wrote: "Among his other activities (the doctor) immediately set to work to put up salmon for shipment. That season he sent to San Francisco nearly one thousand barrels of salmon. The barrels were made on the ground where they were packed, though where he got the coopers is not recorded. Procuring the fish was a simple matter, as the Indians supplied him with all he could use. On its arrival in San Francisco most of the shipment was found to be spoiled, and his venture proved almost a total loss.

"During this time he had men skilled with broadax squaring timbers, and others cutting piles and shaving shingles. A cargo of these was shipped to San Francisco on the brig *Franklin Adams*; 12,000 lineal feet of squared timbers, 8,000 lineal feet of piles, 10,000 shingles and 30 cords of wood. All of this found a ready market at good prices and from it he more than recouped the loss on the salmon."

As it was, he lost about $700 on the salmon deal . . .

And made about $20,000 on the "wood goods" in the same shipment.

Of course, all of the above is just something the doctor got under way in his first month in the new town. The chances are that if he had given the salmon packing deal a little more of his personal attention, it wouldn't have gone bad on him.

But, he had bigger fish to fry.

There were monumental enterprises afoot like getting a new territory started north of the Columbia River and, of course, obtaining a divorce from the Territorial Legislature. A man or woman with the right connections in the legislature could have a bill passed granting him or her a divorce—without ever bothering the other party to the marriage.

And to get the ball rolling, he had to help elect his friend, Isaac N. Ebey to the Oregon Territorial Legislature.

IV

The Great

Magoozle

Except for the people who live in the fourth and ninth grades where the teaching of Washington history is required by law, and those getting a master's degree in history, there aren't many people around who give a good goddam how Washington got started as a separate entity. Well, the people who write history books have got to know something about it, too . . . and for the most part, their attempts at figuring it out have resulted in a great deal of confusion for the people who are sentenced to nine months of Washington History in the fourth and ninth grades.

But in Doc Maynard's time, the creation of Washington Territory was BIG.

To be or not to be a new territory was the burning question of the day. It wiped all other news like who shot whom and where off the front pages of the paper . . . and it was the main tavern topic from the Canadian to the California borders. They even knew clear back in Washington, D.C. that there was some kind of a rumble going on in the northwest corner of the country.

The reason for all this was that the folks living south of the Columbia River got more money from the federal government than the folks living north of the Columbia River. And the question was, could everybody get more money from the federal government if there were *two* territories out here in the northwest corner instead of one. Or

would Congress just continue with the same appropriations for both
. . . which would result in the folks south of the Columbia getting less
money.

And that's how Doc Maynard got into the Great Magoozle.

(A magoozle, for the benefit of those who have retired or not as yet
awakened, is a method by which we get things done in America. It's
neither legal nor illegal, but it gets the job done.)

Everything always happens at once, and, naturally, the Great
Magoozle was coming to a head right at the time the doctor was
starting Seattle, which was why he couldn't fool around with a lot of
vacillating opinions about what the town should be named or where to
locate the downtown business district. He moved some of the
dissidents to the new location on April third, and he had to get going
on the magoozle by May third.

The doctor had participated in many a magoozle in the past, and
would engage in his fair share of magoozles in the future . . .

But this one was the GREAT Magoozle.

In it, he created Washington Territory . . . and won King County as
kind of a booby prize . . .

And they were only incidental to his real objective.

The light that failed

It takes a little doing to follow this, which is why the people in the
fourth and ninth grades flounder a lot on the question of what happened when and where, but I'll try and ABC it. While the doctor was
cutting his woodpile and the Denny Party was watching another
Indian bite the dust on the Oregon Trail and Mike Simmons was the
big frog in the small pond, some fellows tried to get the new territory
going.

At the Annual Fourth of July picnic in Olympia in 1851, one J.B.
Chapman made a big pitch about the creation of a new territory north
of the Columbia. This was nine months before Doc Maynard moved
the folks from Alki Point to his new town. Mr. Chapman really didn't

care much whether there was a new territory or not. It was just that his brother was big in the development of Portland, and J.B. wanted the folks back home to know that he was just as big of a shot as his brother.

To that point, Mr. Chapman had a singular record of failure.

He had tried to get a town going on Grays Harbor. It was one of the other twenty-five towns that advertised as being the terminus of the transcontinental railroad. That one never got beyond the planning stage. So, he tried to get another one going farther up the Chehalis River and that one went belly-up, too.

So then he got thinking that Lafayette Balch, who had started Steilacoom and advertised it as the terminus of a railroad that would come through Naches Pass, had the right idea. Balch called his place "Port" Steilacoom. Chapman started a town across the street and called his place Steilacoom "City."

This move annoyed Lafayette Balch all to pieces. He had tried to get going in Olympia, but Mike Simmons, with his monopoly going full blast, had thwarted the attempt. So Balch loaded his general store back on his boat and moved it a few miles north. Now, the shoe was on the other foot. He was getting a competitive store right across the street.

But Chapman was a pretty good con man, and he suckered both Balch and Simmons to back his plan for the new territory on the grounds that if they could get it, there would be enough in the deal for all of them.

So, they joined forces with him and kicked off the campaign for the new territory at the Fourth of July picnic in Olympia.

And Doc Maynard, who took to politics like a big dog takes to steak, interrupted his wood-splitting to get into the act. At the picnic, Chapman called for a thing that has come to be known as the "Cowlitz Convention." This was held at Cowlitz Landing on the Cowlitz River, which probably is why it was known as the Cowlitz Convention. At any rate, Chapman, Balch and Simmons ran the Cowlitz convention.

Right into the ground.

For a while there, Doc Maynard thought it was legit.

Then he realized the trio in charge couldn't have cared less whether or not a territory was created. Chapman's real problem was that he needed a job. If he could make a big enough name for himself, then the Oregon Territorial Legislature would name him as prosecuting attorney for the Puget Sound District. What Balch wanted was for Chapman to get the job as prosecuting attorney so he'd get the hell out of Steilacoom City and leave Port Steilacoom alone. And what Mike Simmons wanted out of it was an entity called "Simmons County."

Maynard first tumbled to the truth in the fall of 1851 before he took his load of wood to California. The way he found out about it was that Isaac Ebey told him. And the reason Ebey told him about it was that Ebey also wanted to be the prosecuting attorney for the Puget Sound District.

And when those two got together, the other guys didn't have a chance.

Doc scooted back from San Francisco in time to attend the session of the Oregon Legislature in Salem in the winter of 1852—before he moved to Seattle. When Chapman showed up with fifty-five signatures calling for the creation of Simmons County, the doctor and Ebey lobbied around the legislative halls and got things changed around some. The county was created all right. But the name was changed from "Simmons" to "Thurston," which is the way it is today.

Then came the matter of prosecutor for Puget Sound District. Chapman got two votes for the job. Ebey got fourteen. But there still was a small detail that had to be corrected. The new prosecutor had not as yet been admitted to the bar in Oregon Territory. So what they did was hurry on up to what we know of today as the Jackson Courthouse (which still is extant south of Chehalis) and get Judge William Strong to admit Ebey to the practice of law.

Balch was the only one of the original three who got anything out of it.

Chapman's Steilacoom City folded.

But, before all of this happened, the doctor had made the concluding speech of the Cowlitz Convention and in it he had caused an interesting paragraph to be inserted in the petition to Congress. The insertion notified Congress that if something wasn't done about creating the new territory by May 3, 1852, we'd hold another convention . . . and at this convention we would form our own state. And, if we formed our own state, the next time they heard from us, we'd be seeking admission as a state, not a mere territory.

That's where things stood when the doctor initiated the construction of Seattle.

And, that's why he only had thirty days to do it.

Strong Medicine at Saunders' Bottom

One of the first people that Doc Maynard met when he came to Oregon with Catherine was J. R. Jackson, proprietor of the establishment which has come to be known as the Jackson Courthouse. Jackson, a one-eyed man who disputed Mike Simmons' claim of being the first man to settle north of the Columbia, was married to the best cook north of the Columbia River. He also was sheriff of Lewis County when it extended all the way from the Rocky Mountains to the Pacific Ocean and all the way north to Alaska. His establishment became a place where, for a fee, you could get citizenship papers. You also could get other kinds of justice.

The Jackson Courthouse was located about ten miles south of Saunders' Bottom, (named for the muddy condition at this spot of the trail between Cowlitz Landing and Olympia). Ten miles north was S.S. Ford's farm, where the circuit court also held sessions.

Judge Strong was strong in the judging business at the time, although he was even stronger in the gambling business. Judging didn't pay well in those days, so he had a line of gambling paraphernalia which he sold from the "bench" when court was not in session. And here, the profits were enormous. The big item, of course, was the playing cards. He bought them at a penny-a-deck in New York, had them shipped here at government expense by the gross . . . and sold them for $1.50 per deck.

He was not a medical man and the title to this segment does not refer to anything connected with the human body. However, it had a great deal to do with Saunders' "Bottom" and the creation of the new territory in which Doc Maynard became deeply involved.

A month or so after the adjournment of the Cowlitz Convention, the judge was called upon to do his thing in Lewis County. At that time, there was no county seat and, acting under procedures adopted by the legislature, the county commissioners were authorized to set the location for the sessions of the circuit court. Intensely aware of the road conditions at Saunders' Bottom, the county commissioners cannily set the site for the court at Sidney Ford's. But Judge Strong, whose appreciation of the road conditions in Saunders' Bottom equalled that of the county commissioners, had other ideas. He peremptorily ordered the jurors to appear for court at J. R. Jackson's. Bancroft notes that the jurors refused to do so "on the ground they had been ordered in the manner of slave-driving, to which they objected as unbecoming to a judge and insulting to themselves. A public meeting was held, at which it was decided that the conduct of the judge merited the investigation of the impeaching power . . ."

There were other irritations involved, but this was the one that launched the second attempt at dividing the territory north of the Columbia from the rest of Oregon.

For reasons of his own, Doc was in the thick of it.

And this time, the First Team got into the act.

George N. McConaha, the "rail sitter"

Fate has methods of moving people around for reasons not available to the normal man . . . but all as a part of the Grand Plan. And such was the case with George N. McConaha, who got moved around more than most.

McConaha, who became Doc Maynard's lawyer, was born on January 4, 1820—making him twelve years younger than Doc. He studied for the bar in Cleveland at the time that Doc was doing his thing in that town. And they may have met then, but they most certainly met when Doc was in California.

In 1850 McConaha defended a man in a murder case and got an unexpected windfall of $750, which he used to join Weller in California.

McConaha always comes off as a big hero in Seattle history, but that's not the impression you get from some of the California papers at the time he departed from that scene. He was billed as a degenerate alcoholic who consorted with prostitutes and other people of low character . . . and presumably was run out of Sacramento wearing a coat of tar and feathers and riding on a rail.

He arrived at Doc Maynard's doorstep six months after they had met in California. Doc greeted him with open arms. By that time Doc had given up the notion of by-passing the intermediate "territorial" step and now he proposed to petition Congress to become a territory. However, that territory would need a delegate to Congress. And he saw no reason why McConaha wasn't the man for the job.

Doc also had an immediate and urgent need for a personal attorney. The city of Seattle was under way by then, and how would McConaha like a nice corner lot at First Avenue South and Washington Street (where the Maynard Building is located today)?

McConaha shook hands on the deal . . .

And the creation of Washington Territory took another step forward.

Fun and games at a Fourth of July picnic

If you think you're confused by all of this, think of the hapless historians who have spent the last century-and-a-quarter trying to figure the whole thing out themselves . . . and then explain it to the millions of fourth and ninth grade students.

No wonder the kids hate history.

But now everything will be made clear.

On July 4, 1851, J. B. Chapman, for his own special reasons, initiated a movement to create a separate territory north of the Columbia River. This was followed a couple of months later by the Cowlitz Convention at which Doc Maynard got carried away by his enthusiasm for the project and obtained passage of a resolution that if Congress didn't get off its ass and give us a territory by the following May, we would meet again, form our own state and request admission to the Union. I doubt if Doc really thought that would happen, but he figured it was good pressure politics.

A month after the Cowlitz Convention, Doc trundled off to California, sold his pile of wood and met McConaha. He returned in January to help Ebey into the prosecutor's job and thwarted the effort to name it Simmons County. (Mike's dislike of Maynard became more pronounced.) That was in January, 1852.

In March of the same year, he arrived in Seattle, looking for a new place to live with Catherine.

In May, they were supposed to have another convention and form a state, but by then everybody'd had time to think things over and they decided it was better politics to take another run at creating a new territory instead.

Meanwhile, McConaha appeared on the scene and took on the responsibility—among other things—of doing the doctor's legal work.

That's when the Great Magoozle got under way.

The movement which resulted in the creation of Washington Territory was initiated at another Fourth of July picnic in Olympia a year after Chapman had taken his run at the project and had fallen flat on his face.

One D. R. Bigelow, who had been making Fourth of July speeches all over America for years, had arrived in the Pacific Northwest eight months earlier, and the backers of the movement recognized that he was an expert in the field. Subsequent historians have remarked at the fact that, unlike Chapman, Bigelow did not call for a convention to draw up a memorial to Congress requesting a separate territory. To date, historians have pointed with pride that Bigelow's speech sparked the grass roots movement which became a prairie fire . . . sort of a spontaneous combustion.

But "grass roots" movements don't grow on trees.

Somebody has to plant 'em.

Bigelow's job was to raise the flag and see who saluted. He was to leave the rest of the operation to the guys in the smoke-filled room backstage. The most-often quoted part of his speech goes like this:

"We are now assembled on the verge of United States soil—no monumental shafts erected on the revolutionary battlefields meet our eyes to stimulate our patriotism and awaken our sympathies. We are far removed from all such scenes, farther than the most enthusiastic actors in those scenes ever expected the results of their labors to extend. But the scene exhibited here today shows that the great national heart sends its pulsations, actively, healthfully, patriotically even to this distant extremity. We see the flag of the Union waving over us, and we feel that beneath its ample folds we are at home . . ."

There were half-a-dozen principals in the backstage operation, of whom only Doc Maynard and his friend, J.R. Jackson were holdovers from the participants of the previous year's convention. They had at least the tacit backing of the two legislators from north of the Columbia, F.A. Chenoweth and Isaac N. Ebey. In addition, they brought in R.J. White, Quincy A. Brooks, Charles S. Hathaway and F.A. Clarke . . .

And, of course, Doc's attorney, George N. McConaha.

What the fellas did after the speech was take a reading of the reaction to the speech. They knew going in that they had the people around Puget Sound in the palm of their hand. What they had to find out was whether men living along the Columbia River like Seth Catlin and F. A. Clarke figured they were close enough to Salem to get what they wanted without all the bother of creating a new territory. These two men represented the preponderance of the population and if they didn't choose to go along, the whole project would be dead.

It was no different in those days than today. The people along the Washington side of the Columbia River owe a greater allegiance to Portland and Salem than they do to Seattle and Olympia.

The men in leadership positions along the Columbia didn't respond with what could be called overt enthusiasm. But, at least, they wouldn't oppose the movement. And Chenoweth even agreed to active participation in creating the new territory.

Anyway, it was enough to spend a few bucks on.

The first thing they needed was a newspaper with which to beat the drums for the project, and McConaha, who saw himself becoming the first delegate to Congress from the new governmental unit, talked his law partner into starting the first weekly publication north of the Columbia. I'm sure that the doctor, who always put his money where his mouth was, participated in financing the venture.

At any rate the first issue of the *Olympia Columbian* appeared on the newsstands on September 11, 1852. It was dedicated to the principles of the Democratic Party and to the creation of what they hoped would become the new territory of "Columbia."

The first issue of the paper carried the full text of D.R. Bigelow's speech.

The object of their affection

The magoozlers knew they could convince the folks living north of the Columbia of anything they thought might bring in more federal money. The folks south of the river could tumble one way or another . . . also depending on who got how much money and when. The seat of power was in Salem, and there were no public opinion polls.

Well, that wasn't entirely true.

There was Joseph Lane, Oregon's delegate to Congress. If they could find out which way he blew, they would know the direction of the political winds. Lane had been governor in 1849-50. Under him, the territorial legislature had sent a memorial to Congress asking for a railroad and telegraph to the Pacific Northwest although, as Bancroft put it, "there were not enough people in all Oregon to make a good sized country town."

"There was an ingenuous vanity about his public and private acts, a happy self-confidence, mingled with a flattering deference to some and an air of dignity to others, which made him a hero of certain circles in Washington as well as the pride of his constituency."

It was this quality that enabled him, as a Roman Catholic, to be elected as delegate to Congress from a territory primarily nested by Methodists. The fatal error committed by Chapman, Simmons and Balch had been that they didn't clear with Lane before firing their memorial off to Congress. This was accompanied by the fact that they made their try during his first session as delegate. And he followed the precept that in case you're not sure what to do, the safe route is to do nothing.

So the first step was to find out which way Lane blew.

Lane allowed as how he could go for the deal if they could drum up support among the constituency north of the Columbia. He had produced money for Oregon before and assured the folks south of the Columbia that the creation of a new territory north of the Columbia would mean double the federal funds in the Pacific Northwest. They wouldn't lose money on the deal because they could spend the entire amount they got south of the Columbia without those folks north of the river yapping about it.

Lane told the magoozlers that if they could draw up a resolution and get backing for it, he would drop a memorial from a "citizens' group" in the hopper on the opening day of the session and do his level best to buck it through. He cautioned them not to make the mistake that the Chapman axis had made the previous year. Chapman had made a big point of the fact that there were 3,000 people living north of the Columbia.

"Without at least 10,000 people, Congress won't even think about you," he cautioned. "Let me see some signs of activity before I leave in mid-October."

Hail Columbian!

The heavy artillery was initiated by the *Columbian* on September 25 with specifics like calling for the name of "Columbia" for the new territory. The paper pointed out that the area north of the Columbia River was five times the size of Missouri . . . six times the size of Illinois . . . seven times larger than the state of New York and five times the size of all of the New England states put together.

Here's a sample of part of an editorial:

"That a country of such vast extent, so geographically situated, and of such great prospective importance, should remain under one territorial government, constituted as it is at present, is, we believe, destructive to our own interest as citizens, and injurious to those of our general government. Nature has pointedly divided the territory by the Columbia River; that portion to the south has hitherto (received) all the fostering care of, all the benefits arising from the act of Congress approved August 14, 1848, establishing the Territorial Government of Oregon . . . while that portion north of this river . . . has been utterly neglected . . . "

The editorial pointed out that we had a sufficient number of legal voters to be entitled to four out of twenty-five legislators, but until recently had only one . . . petitions for improvements invariably have been disregarded . . . funds from Congress for public buildings have been expended only in southern Oregon . . . sales of public lands have been for improvements south of the river . . . the surveyor general and superintendent of Indian affairs never came north of the river . . .

In the same issue of the paper, there was a letter signed by "Elis" suggesting that there be a meeting on October 25 at the home of J. R. Jackson where preparations could be made for the election of delegates to a convention at Monticello a month later where duly-elected citizens would draft a memorial to seeking a division of the Oregon Territory.

Those were busy days for Doc Maynard and his young attorney, George McConaha. They had a lot of legal and political material to put together before the meeting at J. R. Jackson's. By mid-October, the arguments for division were completed and carried in the *Columbian* so that the folks who gathered at J. R. Jackson's on the 25th would know what they were supposed to do . . .

And Lane would have them all done up in a nice package with a blue ribbon around it.

Because of its historical significance, the resolution is repeated here:

"1. The present Territory of Oregon, containing an area of three hundred and forty-one thousand square miles, is entirely too large an extent of territory to be embraced within the limits of one state.

"2. The said territory possesses a seacoast of six-hundred and fifty miles in extent; the country east of the Cascade Mountains is bound to that on the coast by the strongest ties of interest; and, inasmuch as we believe that the territory must inevitably be divided at no very distant day it would be unjust that one state should possess so large a seaboard to the exclusion of the interior.

"3. The territory embraced within the boundaries of the proposed "Territory of Columbia," containing an area of about thirty-two thousand square miles, is about a fair and just medium of territorial extent for one state.

"4. The proposed "Territory of Columbia" presents natural resources capable of supporting a population at least as large as that of any state in the Union, possessing an equal extent of territory.

"5. Those portions of Oregon Territory lying respectively north and south of the Columbia River, must, from their geographical position, always rival each other in commercial advantage, and their respective citizens must, as they now are and always have been, actuated by a spirit of opposition.

"6. The southern part of Oregon Territory, having a majority of voters, have controlled the Territorial Legislature, and Northern Oregon has never received any benefit from the appropriations made by Congress for said territory, which were subject to the disposition of said Legislature.

"7. The seat of the Territorial Legislature is now situated, by the nearest practicable route, at a distance of five hundred miles from a large portion of the citizens of Northern Oregon.

"8. A great portion of the legislation suitable to the south is, for local reasons, opposed to the interests of the north, and inasmuch as the south has a majority of the voters, and representatives are always bound to reflect the will of their constituents, we can entertain no reasonable hopes that our legislative wants will ever be properly regarded under the present organization.

"9. Experience has shown that in states having a moderate sized territory the wants of the people are more easily made known to their representatives and there is less danger of conflict between sectional interests, and more prompt and adequate legislation can always be obtained."

The arguments for division also made note of the fact the land north of the Columbia was rich in natural resources and presented unparalleled inducements to emigrants who would swell the *present large population* (italics mine) and that the population was rapidly increasing and required the attention of a separate and independent legislature.

"Present large population . . ."

That was the great masterpiece of overstatement.

Oregon made it into the ranks of the territories with a mere 10,000 white residents for the good and simple reason the United States didn't want the land to fall into the hands of the British. But the proposed new territory—even taking in all the land from the Pacific Ocean to the summit of the Rocky Mountains—had fewer than 4,000 and the vast majority of these were living along the north bank of the Columbia River. The total population of the Puget Sound basin ran around 200—and they were the ones who really wanted the new territory, not the people living along the river. Future territories wouldn't make it with less than 50,000 to 60,000.

When Joe Lane trundled off to Washington City with the petition from the settlers, it carried eight signatures. For four of the eight the signatures on that document it was their only appearance in Washington history. They were at the right time and the right place to put their names on a piece of paper . . . then they disappeared into the rain and mists.

Let's see how it added up: George N. McConaha (they spelled it McConaher in the *Congressional Globe*) had only been around for three months. R.J. White was listed as secretary. That was his only appearance in our history books. And apparently he was only here for a day or so because future correspondence was carried on by Quincy A. Brooks. The other one timers were Charles S. Hathaway, C.H. Winslow and F.A. Clarke.

The only two signators whose names also had appeared on the Chapman petition of the previous year were J. R. Jackson and D. S. Maynard.

America in action . . . "grass roots" department

Joe Lane left for Washington, D.C. sometime between the middle and tail end of October, with the memorial seeking the division of Oregon Territory as it subsequently appeared in the *Congressional Globe*, predecessor to the *Congressional Record*, safely tucked in his pocket.

Now all the magoozlers had to do was get the citizens to go along with what already had been written.

And so it was with this in mind that the *Columbian* began to "hype" up the Monticello Convention.

On October 23, the *Columbian* pointed out that the only solution to all of the wrongs that had been visited on the people north of the Columbia River was a "LEGAL DIVORCE FROM THE SOUTH—the formation of a new territory north of the Columbia, with full power to legislate for ourselves, and be entitled to all the rights and privileges which such separation may guarantee, as allowed to territories in general."

The editorials touched all of the emotional bases in the book. "Are we, as American citizens to be thrust aside as unworthy to be the recipients of national bounty, and with none so poor to do us reverence?

No, fellow citizens, such is not, cannot be the spirit and intention of our government, but we are in the hands of the Phillistines, and it depends upon ourselves to put a stop to their boastful language, 'we shall rule and you shall in thralldom serve . . .' "

The *Columbian* promised that with the territorial status would come steam sawmills . . . roads . . . mail routes . . . postoffices . . . courthouses . . . a university.

On November 6 the paper took a gratuitous shot at the Chapman-Balch-Simmons axis with, "Let us take warning, at this stage of our proceedings, and profit from the former abortive movement for bringing about the results which we now have in view . . ."

One of the great gimmicks utilized by the magoozlers was the business of making the delegates to Monticello "official." Here's a sample of what the newspaper pitched: "LET ALL THE DELEGATES BEAR IN MIND TO PROCURE CERTIFICATES OF THEIR APPOINTMENT FROM THE OFFICERS OF THE GENERAL MEETINGS . . . REMEMBER THE DELEGATES ARE TO MEET AT MONTICELLO, (mouth of the Cowlitz River) THE LAST THURSDAY IN NOVEMBER . . ."

I loved the parentheses above.

Monticello has come down to us in our history books as the spot where the spirit of the people attained some kind of spontaneous combustion that blossomed into a new U.S. territory.

But the guys operating the magoozle believed in killing flies with sledgehammers. They knew that half the delegates would get lost if the location of the big event wasn't carefully spelled out. And, of course, they were right. Monticello was an extremely wet farm location owned by one H. D. Huntington. (It periodically flooded out until 1923 when capitalist R. A. Long built a big dike around the place and built a town called Longview.)

So, every news story carried detailed instructions on how to get to Monticello.

The Monticello Convention—a master magoozle

I've heard it said that if the news media had reached the present state of its art a couple of hundred years ago, the fellas never would have been able to put the United States together. A television reporter poking around among the delegates to the Monticello Convention would have blown the whole operation before it ever got started.

The way the magoozlers had it set up was that if Lane would drop the resolution in the hopper at the opening session of Congress, they would produce a grass roots movement with enough bodies to impress Congress before the matter came up on the floor for debate.

Key to this phase of the operation lay in the opening words of the resolution: "The memorial of the undersigned, *delegates of the citizens of Northern Oregon, in convention assembled . . ."*

I've italicized portions of the above to draw your attention to the fact that the organizers of the convention wished to leave the impression that each of the delegates to the convention had stood for election in his own community and represented a whole slew of other people residing back there in the underbrush someplace and whooping it up for territorial status. The newspaper did nothing to disillusion either Congress or the other delegates on the subject. Nearly every issue of the *Columbian* for a matter of two months emphasized the importance of holding elections at the precinct level and arming the delegates wth official credentials signed by the chairman of the grass roots meeting.

But it didn't always work precisely that way.

And the matter of Edward J. Allen is a case in point.

On May 19, 1852—six months before the Monticello Convention, Edward J. Allen, who was twenty-two years old and had not as yet cast a vote of any kind in any election—departed from Pittsburgh, Pennsylvania, for Oregon. Allen was a sickly young man; his doctors had informed him that if he remained in Pittsburgh he wouldn't live to vote for anybody.

If the truth be known, he was considerably more interested in the state of his health than in the state of the Union. Right off, he sprained his ankle on the Oregon Trail. He had to walk on that ankle several hours a day and the resulting pain left him with insufficient sleep. The trail, itself, left him with insufficient food and water.

Allen reached Portland in October and got himself a job in a sawmill where he worked twelve hours a day, six days a week, trying to recover his health and put together a grubstake to continue his journey to his destination on Puget Sound. He had reached Cowlitz Landing on the Cowlitz River on November 24, the day before the Monticello Convention. At the time, he had about as much knowledge of the Pacific Northwest as a native of New Guinea.

Allen tells us in his memoirs that he was preparing to initiate the long walk to Olympia when he met a group of men heading down river in the other direction. Because he previously had met Quincy Brooks, one of the group, back in Pittsburgh, he fell into conversation with the men in the group and they informed him that they were headed for Monticello.

"What," he asked, "is Monticello?"

Monticello, they told him, was the location of the convention.

"What convention?"

"To form a new territory."

"What territory?"

One of the men said he thought it was going to be called "Columbia." Whatever the name, the people north of the river wanted to be separated from the people south of the Columbia.

The idea intrigued Allen but, as he noted in his memoirs, he'd only been in this part of the territory for a couple of days . . . represented no constituency . . . had no credentials.

"What the hell," somebody rejoined. "Your credentials are as good as some of ours."

Going to Monticello seemed like a good idea at the time, and Allen had nothing else to do, so he headed back down the river with his new-found friends. Some fifteen of them were put up in the loft of a barn where they drank and sang and played mumbletypeg all night.

The next morning, a sleepy, hung-over and bewildered Allen was approached by somebody whose name he couldn't remember and informed that he was a member of the committee to draft a resolution to Congress requesting the creation of a new territory north of the Columbia River.

Happily for posterity the complete text of the proceedings at Monticello were printed in the December 11, 1852, issue of the *Columbian*. And this was one "railroad" that ran on schedule. The entire operation previously had been scripted. It proceeded with the precision of a well-oiled grandfather clock.

The story noted that "Pursuant to a resolution adopted at a meeting of the citizens of Northern Oregon, held on the 25th and 27th days of October last in the courtroom for Lewis County (J. R. Jackson's log cabin) a convention of delegates from the different precincts and settlements of Northern Oregon assembled in the town of Monticello (Huntington's farm) on the 25th day of November, 1852."

One W. W. Plumb called the convention to order.

This was Mr. Plumb's first mention in Washington history.

It also was his last.

The newspaper reports that thereupon "Mr. G. N. McConaha was chosen president by application," and "on the motion of Quincy A. Brooks, Dr. R. J. (or R. V., nobody ever got that straight) White was unanimously chosen Secretary." (This mention at the Monticello Convention was Dr. White's only appearance on the stage of Washington history.)

The convention operated without a hitch.

McConaha took the chair, giving his grateful thanks for the distinguished honor they had conferred upon him and adding, "I can assure you gentlemen, that this distinction has been as unexpected by me as it was unsolicited. I am proud to have been chosen of so large and intelligent a body of men." He suggested that they had over-rated his abilities. However, he was "cheered by the hope that whatever errors I commit, they will receive immediate correction by your generous cooperation." He said he would not presume to dictate what should be done at the convention. He noted that it was the job of "all of us." It was their job to carry out and perfect the instructions which the delegates had received from their constituents.

He added:

"You come fresh from the people with positive instructions, knowing their grievances, and cannot, therefore, fail truly to reflect the popular will . . ."

After a certain amount of additional butter in the same vein, Quincy A. Brooks arose to name a committee of thirteen to draft a memorial to Congress. He then proceeded to nominate himself, Doc Maynard, J. R. Jackson, William Plumb, Alfred Cook, E. L. Finch, A. F. Scott, F. A. Clark, C. S. Hathaway, E. H. Winslow, Seth Catlin, N. Stone, and E. A. Allen.

For eight of the thirteen, it would be their only appearance in Washington history. Where they had been before nobody knows. And they disappeared without a trace after the convention. Like E. A. Allen—who is not counted among the eight—they just happened to be at the right place at the right time.

Well, that was the end of the morning session.

Two hours later, at two o'clock, they reconvened and, *voila,* there was the memorial from the Monticello Convention all printed up and ready to go.

Two hours to create a new territory.

No fooling around like they do nowadays.

The pioneers did things fast.

Actually, the whole thing was like being against sin and in favor of motherhood. The fellows voted for everything that was presented to them. The newspaper report reads, "On motion of Dr. Maynard, the report of the committee was taken up and considered *seriatim.*

"The various portions of the memorial were discussed and adopted without a dissenting vote.

"Before taking the final vote on adoption of the memorial the convention was addressed by Messrs. PLUMB, CATLINE (misspelled) MAYNARD, JACKSON, MILES and others." Quincy A. Brooks then gave a speech that the secretary said was too long to record. Brooks then sought and got a resolution that they would meet again the third Wednesday of May, 1853, at Olympia so they could take further action if Congress had not acted in the meantime. He also introduced resolutions urging that the memorial be sent to Delegate Lane and to all newspapers locally and nationally.

Having endorsed and signed the memorial to Congress, and arranged for its dispatch to various and sundry places, the delegates got down to the real point of the convention.

They voted to send D. S. Maynard to Salem with a copy of a petition asking the Oregon Legislature to endorse the proposed new territory.

They didn't know this was the point of the convention.

Only the magoozlers knew that.

The doctor thanked them for putting their trust in him on this important mission. He then introduced resolutions that were unanimously endorsed thanking the president and secretary for their services and F. A. Clarke for his kindness and attention and the use of his "hotel."

Mr. Clarke responded to the doctor's kind words and moved for adjournment.

The Monticello Convention was history.

(Historians, and the poor kids who have to try to understand what they wrote, have had a terrible time with the Monticello Convention. The convention adjourned on November 28, 1852. There was no possible way a memorial passed at that convention could reach Washington, D.C., on December 6, eight days later. Bancroft took the easy way out. He said the convention was held on October 25. When Meany wrote his *History of Washington* in 1909, he went along with Bancroft. But after thinking about it for thirteen years, he did a piece in the *Washington Quarterly* in 1922 in which he opined that Lane "must have acted on his volition or *upon initiative from some other source.*" (*Italics mine.*) Snowden took the position that Lane must have used the memorial that had been sent the previous year by the Cowlitz Convention. But that was not the case.

Arthur Denny, who must have been aiming at being named the father of Seattle for a long time, saved every mention of his name that had ever been printed. The copy issued to those in attendance at Monticello was one of them. In 1889, when statehood came to Washington, he was giving reporters the low-down on the important role he played, but somebody noticed his name wasn't on the list of petitioners in the *Congressional Globe* . . . only Doc Maynard's—on the memorial Lane had taken back with him before Monticello.

The doctor—long dead—had done it to Denny again!

Dissolution of marriage—1852 style

From the pure standpoint of physical exertion, the creation of a new territory in the United States did not require the same amount of muscular strength as cutting a pile of wood containing 400 cords. And, I might add, the doctor enjoyed the magoozle with a greater degree of enthusiasm than was his in the cutting of the woodpile.

But he did it for Catherine just the same.

She was having all the trouble she could take care of with her family the way things were . . . without finding herself named as correspondent in a court divorce case . . . or without having the doctor's name spread all over the pages of the newspapers with the juicy material he had to produce in order to get a legislative divorce.

But the doctor was a big man in the territory at the time and just imagine what the newspapers could do with this kind of "privileged" news in today's media marketplace . . . His petition read:

"To The_____

"The Legislature of the Territory of Oregon. The undersigned Your Petitioner Humbly represents to Your Honorable Body, that he was Lawfully married to Lydia A. Rickey in the State of Vermont on the twenty eighth day of August A.D. 1828, that the undersigned and his wife Lydia continued to reside in the State of Vermont until the Autumn of 1834 when they removed to the State of Ohio in which State Lydia still resides.

"And Your Petitioner further represents to Your Honorable Body that he and his aforsaid companion continued to live together as man and wife until the Spring of 1841, that in the month of April of the year last aforsaid on returning home from visiting a patient at about the hour of ten o'clock in the night found his wife lying with a certain John Hemrick in an obscene manner. That the undersigned had previously doubted her chastity but had never before seen anything positively confirming his suspicions, at which time the usual relations between man and wife ceased.

"And Your Petitioner also represents to Your Honorable Body that his wife has had two children, The Eldest a Son Born in The Year 1830 named Henry C. Maynard and The Youngest a Daughter Born in the Year 1834 named Frances J. Maynard, which Said Children still reside in the State of Ohio, That Your Petitioner verrily believes said children to be his own, and that he desires to bring them to Oregon where the undersigned has permanently settled.

"And Your Petitioner further represents to Your Honorable Body, That until of late Your Petitioner had not determined ever to making application for a Divorce on account of the tender regard which he had for his Children. But that time and the advice of friends has in that respect worked a change in the mind of Your Petitioner. And further that Your Petitioner has written to obtain testimony from Ohio but owing to emigration from that country and other causes set forth by Correspondents from Ohio, he has not been able to obtain testimony of Material Witnesses. And Your Petitioner represents that his Correspondent in Ohio informed him by letter that it will be impossible to obtain positive testimony until persons in California can be found which said letter will be laid before Your Honorable Body.

"Finally, Your Petitioner would Humbly represent to Your Honorable Body, that as it is impossible that he and his wife can ever again live together, and as it is at present and perhaps ever will be out of the power of Your Petitioner to procure the testimony which might be required in a court of Chancery to entitle the undersigned to a Divorce from his said wife, And believing that his sufferings of mind have been born long and patiently and believing before God and Man, that he is justly entitled to the relief which he seeks, has as a last resort appealed to the wisdom and magnanimity of Your Honorable Body.

"It is with Great reluctance that the undersigned presents his petition to the Peoples Representatives. He deeply regrets to consume one moment of their valuable time. And the undersigned will here state to Your Honorable Body that he has always provided for, and kept his wife in a comfortable living until he left Ohio for Oregon Territory. And that at the time of leaving for this Country, he left her provided with a comfortable Home and a means of living independently at which home the undersigned will further State That he never Quarreled with or abused his wife, Either before or after the discovery of her unfaithfulness.

"Wherefore Your Petitioner believing that he is without other remedy Humbly prays Your Honorable Body to pass a law Divorcing him from the Bonds of matrimony now existing between him and his wife. And as and for such he will ever pray,

D. S. Maynard"

"personally appeared before me Samuel Parker a justice of the peace fore the county of marion David S. Maynard and after being duly sworn says that the facts set forth in this petition is true to the best of his beliefs. Sworn to before me S Parker J.P this the 10 day of december A.D 1852

Samuel Parker J.P"

Doc Maynard came close to tossing in the sponge on this next one, but his attorney, McConaha, who had been through the mill on this kind of thing many times before, reminded him that, "If you don't make your case, they'll throw your petition out."

So the following letter dated August 4, 1852, also was put into the record . . .

"Dr. Sir   I reed yours of the 25th of May and was much grattified to learn that you were in good health I also seen and read your letters to Payne and Grimshaw and they both requested me to say to you that they regarded it as impossible to git the evidence which you desire unless you were here in person Your many acquaintances here are unanimous in the desire to aid you in procuring the evidence which you desire but Candor compels me to say to you that I do not believe that if you were here yourself that you could succeed in procuring the evidence of a positive character as to the incontinency of your wife.

"I have seen and talked with Sprague Brown and others on the subject and whilst we all agree in opinion that your wife has been in time past and still is addicted to the habits of adultery yet this is only our opinion it is true that it is the belief of the community generally that she is unchaste.

"Yet how can her want of chastity be proven Who will sware that he had carnal connections with her Ormsby says to me in confidence that he could sware to her want of chastity but that he would flee his country or die in jail before he would tell what he knows & say that he well knows that you deserve a divorce in every sense of the word but that he cannot and will not divulge anything that he knows on the subject & so say the others.

"I saw her a short time since and asked her if she had got any letters from you She said no but that you wrote regularly to Henry She said she had written one letter to you since you had gone to Oregon just to let you know that she was as independent as ever & declared that she was much happier in your absence than she had ever been in your society said you had been jealous of her for many years and she hoped you would remain in Oregon for the remainder of your life

"I asked her if you had ever mistreated her She said no, not in any other way than by your jealousy & indifference Said she knew people had talked about her but disregarded it

"I spoke with Wilson as you directed me but he thinks that your only chance of succeeding will be before the Legislature. He says that that public Rumor without Specific proof offered of some want of chastity on her part will not be sufficient on your part before a court.

"The truth is Doctor that people here are unwilling to give evidence in the matter She is shrewd and sly & keeps good lookout & another thing her friends & relatives here are respected very much and on their account people hate to say what they know or believe about her.

"William Craig is in California. also Harper & Miles If you could only find where abouts they are you might readily procure the desired proof Craig you know is a man that will neither lie or flinch & if you could find him he would testify that he caught her and Ormsby *kissing* and that too in the bushes—but persons here who are known to her misconduct are loth to communicate what they do know for the reasons which I have before stated

"Doc, I trust that you know that I desire to serve you if in my power and indeed I believe that there is not one of your acquaintances in this community but deeply sympathises with you in your unhappy Situation It is true as you say in your letter you have suffered long and patiently and God knows you ought to be relieved— My family are all well & Sarah sends her best regards to you Your son Henry has a situation on the railroad and says he is resolved to come to you next spring

"Frances is at school She is a lovely girl but I will come to a close hoping that you will write again ere long Yours in truth
C_____.

W. G. Oliver

"To Dr D. S. Maynard

"P.S. McNair and Sarah Stevens are married at last after their Seven years Courtship."

The above, along with signed affidavits of a bunch of other prominent men in the Territory stating that the doctor was a moral man who richly deserved the divorce, could have been just the meat of such newspapers as the *Oregon Spectator* which carried the story that McConaha had been ridden out of one town on a rail . . . had consorted with pimps and prostitutes and spent his time in low company in the saloons of Sacramento while his wife and children languished at home.

As it was, the doctor's plan worked.

Through his friend, Isaac Ebey, a petition asking for support from the Legislature for the division of the Territory was dropped in the hopper in Salem on December 6, 1852.

This was the same day the companion piece was dropped in the hopper in Washington, D.C., by Lane. (A service to the community which moved Doc to provide his town with the name of Lane Street six months later when the plat of Seattle was filed.)

Doc Maynard slid his divorce petition right in behind the petition for getting the Legislature's aid in securing the new territory. And sure enough, the newspapers were baying down the trail of the new territory.

There wasn't word one about the doctor's divorce . . .

It has remained in the Archives of the Oregon Historical Society for the past 126 years.

The perfidy of Isaac N. Ebey

The doctor didn't come out of it without a scare, though, and it was well he had followed McConaha's advice to let it all "hang out."

The scare came from his friend Ebey.

Going in, Ebey had introduced the doctor's divorce petition and accompanied it with an affidavit stating that he had met the doctor two years earlier and believed him to be a moral man, well thought of in his community and someone who had a divorce coming. That was on December 10.

On December 15, Ebey came up with this: "Mr. Ebey's Report From the Minority of the Committee On D. S. Maynard's Bill for Divorce." It started out: "The minority of the select committee, to whom was referred the petition of D. S. Maynard, praying the Legislature to dissolve the bonds of matrimony existing between him and his wife, beg leave to submit the following as some of the reasons that have led him to dissent from the decision come to by the majority of the committee:

"Without entering upon the consideration of the facts connected with this case, it will be sufficient in the opinion of the minority of said committee, to state the general principles of law on which he predicates his opinion that the prayer of the petitioner should not be granted.

"The position assumed by the report of the committee in favor of the prayer of the petitioner, is, in the opinion of the minority, not tenable, either upon the principles of sound morality or law . . ."

In the shocker that followed, Ebey wrote a complete brief on the concept that marriage was a civil contract that only could be changed through the courts. The Legislature couldn't just write a new law and knock out the contract . . .

Especially without consulting with the other party to the original contract.

Doc Maynard, who had helped Ebey get the prosecutor's job and then had functioned as Ebey's campaign manager when he was elected to the Oregon Territorial Legislature six months earlier, was not appreciative of Ebey's concern with the theory of law in this instance.

But Ebey had his own guilt complex to deal with.

He'd been married for six years, himself . . . and four of those six years he'd been peregrinating around the west while his wife languished at home in Missouri wondering if, as, or when she'd get a notice like the one Lydia was about to receive—telling her that her husband had found another woman. She had but recently arrived in the Pacific Northwest with her two kids, only to find she saw almost as little of her husband as she had when the two of them were separated by most of the continent. To top all of this off, she was terminally ill with tuberculosis (although nobody knew what tuberculosis was at the time).

When she heard her husband was sponsoring the doctor's divorce, she blew her cork.

"Look, Doc," Ebey said, "I've got to keep the home fires burning. You're going to get your divorce, but this minority report gets me off the hook with my wife."

The doctor's failure to appreciate this caused Ebey to sweeten the pot. "I'll tell you what I'm going to do. You've got a nice little town going up there. How would you like to have a county to accompany it?"

Well, the doctor's divorce was granted on December 21.

The next day Ebey introduced a bill creating King County and naming Doc Maynard's store as the County Seat.

Doc Maynard high-tailed it for Olympia . . .

And Catherine.

"The bells are ringing for me and my gal!"

Thanks to the kindly ministrations of her family, Catherine's opinion of herself was at a low ebb . . . and one of the poultices that seemed paramount to her ego was a church wedding. It was an emotional condition of which the doctor was completely aware. And while a Justice of the Peace could have made her marriage with the doctor as legally binding as any performed in a church, she wanted that show of respectability.

The Reverend Mr. Benjamin Close recently had been named to represent the spiritual needs of the people in northern Oregon by the Oregon and California Conference of the Methodists.

On January 15, 1853, Dr. and Mrs. Maynard were married by Mr. Close at the home of friends in Bush Prairie. Those in attendance were Catherine's brother, A. J. Simmons; a brother-in-law, Joseph Broshears, and his wife, and Mr. and Mrs. Gabriel Jones.

Conspicuous by their absence were Susanna and Samuel Rider, and Mike and Elizabeth Simmons.

Catherine and the doctor spent the five days of their second honeymoon traveling from Olympia to Seattle . . . where together they would share the further invention of our town . . . with the joint ownership of 640 acres of land.

Nor did Mr. Close go away empty handed.

When he attended a meeting with his bishop, E. R. Ames, he would have his own brand of contribution to the continued mission of the church.

The second paper recorded in King County was a conditional quit claim deed from David S. and Catherine Maynard to the Methodist

Episcopal Church dated July 15, 1853. What it did was provide the church with a beautiful piece of property overlooking Elliott Bay from the top of what we know as Yesler Way.

Thirty beautiful acres in what the doctor faithfully promised Mr. Close would be the biggest town in the Pacific Northwest.

The condition of the conditional quit claim deed was that the church must do something—anything, toward the development of a school of higher education with it no later than the end of March, 1856.

V

Madam Damnable &
The Stout-hearted Men

An integral proportion of Seattle's creation evolves from and reverts to Madam Damnable's whorehouse, and those idiots in charge of writing our history left her out of it completely.

I can't believe it!

Oh, yes, I can. And the Divine Comedy herein lies in the fact that she functioned in the finest structure in the entire town plat. Nowadays only the rich own view property. But back then Madam Damnable's was the only house in town with a view . . .

There's a picture of her house in every history book.

They left out her occupation.

When I try to pass along to you the essence of our beginnings, I can do no better than quote a man who talked about the beginnings of Charleston, South Carolina: "From the beginning, the people of Charleston were different. They drank. They dueled, gambled, raced horses, wenched, baited bulls, pitted cocks, pulled geese, sailed yachts. They were a grand lot and quite different from the blue-nosed Puritans who settled the up country."

In our case, the Blue-Nosed Puritans were only four or five blocks up the street, but they successfully isolated themselves from the essence of the town . . . and then would have us believe they *were* the

MME. DAMNABLE

HER MANSION ... HER CLIENTELE

essence, when all they really did was run around the outskirts of the action wringing their hands and wondering how they could curb it.

One wonderful irony which illustrates the point lies in the fact that the much-touted "White Church" in our town went belly up during its first year of operation . . . and stayed empty for the next four years while the white house of Sin rose to dizzying heights of glory, famed throughout the world during this same period of time.

David Swinson Maynard was not about to have a whorehouse in his town that was just like your average, run-of-the-mill whorehouse in the usual seaport town. He had to have the best, and only the best. There never was one like it before and none since.

The doctor, directing the destiny of our town with Machiavellian skill—and a will of steel—was essentially a moral man. He knew, on the other hand, that if Seattle were to fulfill the destiny which he had in mind for her, the oldest of all professions must be integrated into the scheme of things. While he ran the show, Madam Damnable's—like the animals permitted on the Ark—was the only example of the species permitted in the place. He required that it be operated with finesse and discretion. Madam Mary Ann Boyer, the diminutive lady who operated the place, crossed him only once . . . to her everlasting regret.

Doc Maynard recognized the need for this kind of facility but he was not about to have a Barbary Coast like the one in San Francisco take root in his town. Court records show that in later years more prostitutes per square inch were arrested in Seattle than any other town in the Territory . . .

But not while Doc Maynard was running the show.

Discretion was the order of the day.

Dignitaries rested their tired bodies in Madam Damnable's luxurious public rooms, probably without even knowing about the function of the place—unless, of course, they responded positively to the question, "And what is your pleasure?" Madam Damnable's functioned with such discretion that the United States of America felt perfectly proper in holding federal court sessions in the structure. And, as a matter of fact, the only encounter with scandal came when Judge

Strong essayed the sale of his gambling equipment from "bench" when his circuit court was not in session.

Doc Maynard thought about that one for a while and concluded that the game was worth the cards.

Doc Maynard gathered around himself a group of men who could understand the importance of Madam Damnable's presence . . . and it was on this basis that he fulfilled the words of the famous song about "Give me some men who are stout-hearted men and I'll soon give you ten thousand more . . ."

The "mew" with the view

A century or so ago, the Voelker family of Bavaria moved to Pennsylvania to participate in the development of a section of this country populated by what have come down to us as the Pennsylvania Dutch. Most of them became Quakers or continued as dedicated members of the Lutheran Church . . .

While they were in Pennsylvania they opted to change the family name to Felker.

And it was inevitable that in the prodigious reproduction process that was popular in those days the family would spawn a few black sheep who at the age of twelve ran away to become cabin boys on sailing ships. At any rate, one of them did and ended up important in the founding of Seattle.

Thanks to the sanctimonious souls who got into our history business early on, Captain Felker has been virtually deleted from our history books . . .

Except for that one picture of Madam Damnable's piece de resistance.

Pioneer National Title Company records show that Doctor Maynard sold all of block four to Leonard M. Felker for $350 on August 24, 1853. This was three months and one day after the doctor had filed the plat of what would become the central business district of the city of Seattle for the next fifty years.

It was the biggest real estate transaction in our town to that date . . . thirty-five times what the average lot was selling for in the average town in the Pacific Northwest and 280 times what you could buy land for from the federal government at the time.

It was the choicest piece of property in town.

And at that, more than half of it was under water at high tide.

Until the landfills were made that created our present industrial district and Harbor Island beginning in 1895, this piece of property was known as "Maynard's Point," midway between Jackson and King Streets on the west side of First Avenue South.

In those days Seattle was shaped like a teardrop, beginning at sea-level at First Avenue South and Washington Street and running south to a bluff twenty-five feet high above the Duwamish River which was a healthy stream forty yards wide at First Avenue South and South King Street.

One of the great tributes to Doc Maynard's sagacity—and a little trick he had picked up during his years in Cleveland—was the existence in all his deeds of sale of the proviso that "a substantial building be constructed on the premises within three months." The doctor has come under some scrutiny as an "unscrupulous" real estate man—our city's first, by the way—for selling the same lot several times to different people.

But this was his reason:

It discouraged land speculators and brought in the kinds of people he wanted for the construction of a major city. He appointed himself as the sole judge of what constituted a "substantial" building . . . and he sold lots for as little as ten dollars to somebody with the skills needed to make ours the major town on Puget Sound.

Felker was such a man.

What he did was provide Seattle with a Southern Mansion.

The front entrance of the two-story structure was flanked by the square columns of the period and supported the traditional second-floor veranda. There were the four customary "nine-on-nine" windows (nine panes of glass above and below) on each floor, with the door centered in the structure. Entering the grand, eight-foot front door with ornamental lamps on either side, one faced the broad bannistered staircase which parted into two smaller ascending sets of stairs on either side about halfway above the first floor.

On either side of the front entrance hall were magnificent paneled rooms with fireplaces, an architectural design to be found throughout the South in those days that was duplicated on the second floor. In the fashion of the time, there were wide floorboards cut from southern pine and imported from Baltimore as were tongue-and-groove boards of the white exterior. An addition in the rear that was perpendicular to the main structure housed the kitchen and what would have been the small cubicles designed for servants in the South.

There were no slaves in Seattle, however . . .

And the services provided in the small rooms were of far greater economic impact on the embryo town than those provided by the negro servants as cited in *Gone With the Wind*.

The exercises conducted in the upstairs rooms were enjoyed by men who were gone with the wind, but it was the kind of wind that propelled the ships which came to our town in huge numbers and spread the fame of Seattle throughout the world . . .

Especially the fame of one Mary Ann Boyer—nee Conklin. Mary Ann was known by sailors in the far corners of the earth as "Madam Damnable" (a name that was altered by our historians to "Mother" Damnable) because "she swore like a trooper."

That's the one that really bugs me.

A musical comedy with the title, "Call me Madam!" makes sense . . .

But, "Call me *Mother?*"

Naval engagement at Madam Damnable's

Thomas S. Phelps, who became an admiral in the United States Navy, was a mere lieutenant on board the sloop-of-war *Decatur* on

January 26, 1856, when a ragtag bunch of desperate Indians made an abortive assault on the town of Seattle.

Lieutenant Phelps was pretty partial to the United States Navy, which he credits with saving Seattle in its hour of desperate need—but he also had a sense of humor that was overlooked by our first historians. Phelps was the kind of a man who kept copious notes of the interesting things that happened in his career. And the so-called "Battle of Seattle" was one of them. Some seventeen years after the fact he revisited the town and the local folk persuaded him to assemble his notes in some kind of permanent form. And in 1881 the notes appeared in an article—along with a map of Seattle as it was at the time of the Indian Rebellion—in a Navy publication called *United Service*.

The servicemen were steeled for an encounter with savage Indians.

But they weren't prepared to meet Madam Damnable.

Six days after the Battle of Seattle the Navy strategists sat down and determined upon a program for the future defense of the city. Essentially, it consisted of burning anything that stood in the line of fire between the Navy's cannon and the potential approach of hostile Indians.

Indians loved to creep through the bushes.

So the Navy burned down the underbrush in town . . .

Except for the bushes around Madam Damnable's whorehouse. Madam Damnable figured that they were *her* bushes on *her* property. The success of her entire operation hinged on privacy. And if the United States Navy burned *down* the bushes, they burned *up* the customers. If they burned up the customers they wouldn't attend her services and she couldn't pay the rent to Captain Felker.

Phelps' description of the scorched earth policy resembles the operation of a present-day real estate developer. He wrote: "Both officers and men entered upon the work with a spirit worthy of the occasion, and the stumps too large to be extracted with levers were burned, the fires being kept alive night and day till reduced below the surface, when ax and shovel completed the rest, and in a few days, South Seattle assumed the appearance of a well laid-out town."

Except for Madam Damnable's.

That still was surrounded by bushes.

Phelps again writes: "On an elevation near the southwest point of the peninsula was situated a large boarding house, kept by a stout, coarse Irishwoman, who, for some reason, was called Madam Damnable, perhaps in consequence of her masculine build and the vile language constantly flowing from her lips, or it may have been from her resemblance to her prototype of that appellation, a famous French woman, formerly residing in Callao (the principal seaport of Peru)."

Phelps was under orders from his commanding officer, Guert Gansevoort, to burn down Mary Ann's bushes.

Mary Ann, who understood exactly what was going on, hated Gansevoort with a passion which transferred itself to everybody in the commander's crew. Phelps noted that she was a terrible woman, and a terror to the members of the crew who found her tongue more to be dreaded than the entire Indian army that the sailors and marines had faced a week before.

The problem lay in the fact that the commander insisted that roads be built in what today is the Pioneer Square Historic District so that if the

Indians attacked again there would be easy lines of communication within the perimeter of the town. This meant clearing the brush off First Avenue South as far south as Madam Damnable's mansion and then clearing them east along Jackson Street, which was thirty yards north of the mansion. What the commander really wanted to do was denude her property so it would stand out like a sore thumb on the landscape, exposing all of the sinners who approached the place to the eyes of the clucking Puritans up the street.

Work parties were sent out from the *Decatur* every day but each party "sedulously" avoided the part of the project near the "female dragon's house" until the rest of the landscape was the ideal of a developer's dream and as bare as a baby's posterior . . .

Phelps wrote: "Every imaginable device was adopted to complete this road, but the moment our men appeared upon the scene, with three dogs at her heels, and an apron filled with rocks, this termagant would come tearing from the house, and the way stones, oaths and curses flew was something fearful to contemplate, and, charging like a fury, with the dogs wild to flesh their teeth in the detested invaders, the division invariably gave way before the storm, fleeing, officers and all, as if old Satan himself was after them."

These were the same guys who had stood up to the horde of a thousand attacking Indians only a week earlier.

Phelps reported that Captain Gansevoort had on a number of occasions been the victim of her most intense vituperation . . . and being averse to facing her, himself, "satisfied his conscience" by ordering his subordinates to "do their duty." Phelps comments at this point that these orders were all well and good, but the big question was *"how* to do it." The first and second divisions mounted assaults on the premises and were driven off. And it became Phelps' turn to face the inevitable.

"Plucking up all the courage we could muster," he wrote, "and with trembling knees, we essayed the task set before us. For once, the house seemed deserted, not a sound issued from behind its silent walls; not even a dog could be seen or heard; and thus encouraged, we sprang to our work with all the energy of desperate men. The road rapidly progressed, the house reached and nearly passed, while our spirits rose with the joyful thought that the old dragon was either absent or overcome with constant vigils, had at last succumbed to exhausted nature, and when on the eve of relieving our suppressed feelings with congratulatory shouts, the door flew open, and this demon in petticoats, who had bided her time, shot out upon us like a bolt from a catapult, and, to our astonished senses, the very air seemed filled with sticks, stones, curses and dogs, and the division, a moment before so firm and hopeful, now, blanched with fear, first wavered, and then broke, and incontinently fled in every direction to escape this whirlwind of passion.

"It is, perhaps, needless to remark that I did not volunteer to again undertake the completion of that road . . ."

For the next twelve days, the military strategists developed and rejected plans for storming Madam Damnable's. They tried doing it under the cover of night, but the dogs were alert and roused Mary Ann. They tried the diversionary tactic of sending half the crew in small boats to approach from the water side of the structure while the other half of the crew attacked the garden. This, as Phelps reports, "fell to the ground."

Finally, Captain Guert Gansevoort summoned the entire ship's company for a frontal attack . . . and put Phelps in charge.

A hundred and fifty men armed to the teeth with hand guns, bayonets and howitzers . . .

Against one woman.

It was a greater concentration of fire power than had been applied in one location against the combined armies of the eastern and western Washington Indians.

Gansevoort, of course, was safely back on the poop of the sloop, three blocks away.

There is no telling what mayhem Madam Damnable might have visited upon the honor and prestige of the United States Navy and the Marine Corps combined if it hadn't been for Quartermaster Sam Silk. Phelps reports that Sam, "a veritable old-time salt," ventured the opinion that he might be personally acquainted with this lady. He couldn't tell from a distance of thirty yards because his eyesight was failing. But close up, he could tell for sure . . .

And so it was that Sam Silk and Midshipman Francis G. Dallas advanced under a flag of truce.

Mary Ann, with a billet of wood in hand and ready for action, eyed the two approaching men suspiciously. As they got closer, Silk began chuckling. "It's Annie," he told the nervous midshipman by his side. "I used to know her when she operated a whorehouse at Fell's Point in Baltimore."

Sam Silk approached Mary Ann with extended arms, "Why what do you mean, you damned old harridan," he said affectionately, "raising hell this way? Don't you remember the good old days at Fell's Point?"

He told her the United States Navy was not trying to put her out of business, just clear a temporary road for military purposes.

"For old times' sake, Annie?" he pleaded.

With Mary Ann, the customer was always right.

"Very well," she responded, "for old times' sake."

She dropped her sticks and stones, called off her dogs and went back into the mansion.

Sam Silk was the hero of the day.

With liberty and justice for all

What with Madam Damnable's mansion being the fanciest structure on Puget Sound, it was no more than natural that it serve as the first courthouse as well as whorehouse. Doc Maynard had himself named as the first court clerk and it was a simple matter for the clerk to make the necessary arrangements for the administration of justice in a spot where his friend, Felker, could pick up a few extra bucks.

And fancy prices, indeed, were charged for the use of one of the first-floor parlors during the daytime—Monday through Friday—leaving the premises upstairs available for other enterprises on the weekends when the loggers and other men came to town looking for fun. In the first ten-day session in October of 1854 when Washington became a territory, the territory was charged $25 for use of the parlor, plus an additional $4 for the use of the furniture . . . an outrageous $10 for use of some of the rooms in the "slave quarters" for the use of the jury and an additional $66—at a shocking fifty cents apiece for the meals of everybody concerned with the operation. (A full course chicken dinner only cost two-bits.)

The young prosecuting attorney protested the exorbitant prices levied against the territory by the landlady, but she laid her sticks and stones bit on him and he backed down.

In those days the Duwamish River debouched upon 1,500 acres of tideflats that subsequently have become Seattle's industrial district. The course of the main channel was shunted north by three low-lying islands with the imaginative names of "Island Number One," "Island Number Two" and "Island Number Three." The river flowed north along the base of Beacon Hill on what subsequently became (1) the River Road, (2) Duwamish Way and now (3) Airport Way, flowing west between what today is the Kingdome Stadium and the Pioneer Square Historic District . . .

And past Maynard's Point, where it dropped into deep water.

All traffic to and from the Duwamish Valley passed through Doc Maynard's claim . . .

And Luther Collins generated most of that traffic.

In his own way, Luther was as great a promoter as the doctor. He set about single-handedly to populate the Duwamish Valley with farmers—having jumped somebody else's claim to get his own. And as a result the valley became the breadbasket of the Puget Sound basin. He and the others boasted cabbages that weighed forty-seven pounds and turnips weighing twenty-nine pounds . . . four-pound potatoes . . . twenty-nine-pound beets . . . two-pound onions, and apples and peaches sixteen inches in circumference. By 1855 he had 200,000 apple, peach, pear and cherry trees for sale in his nursery. Truck gardening vegetables of all varieties were raised here and shipped around the Sound, along with chickens and eggs, pigs and dairy and beef cattle.

The farmers came to Seattle to sell their products and to buy their supplies.

All of this contributing to the economic growth of Seattle.

When the doctor obtained his divorce from Lydia, Luther signed an affidavit that Maynard had sufficient cause for complaint and it was evident to him "that the Evil disposition of his wife had caused him to seek peace (in Seattle) where we have Every Evidence he intends to spend his days."

In return for the favor, the doctor had Luther appointed as the first commissioner of King County.

From time to time, however, the doctor had his hands full taking care of Luther, who was his own kind of a wild man. He was in continual court ruckuses with his neighbors over one thing and another.

Luther was what you would call an "active" man . . . and the court dockets are loaded with many of his activities . . . as attested to by the following which are taken verbatim from the archives:

"October 13, 1861. This day came Diana Woodbridge, and made oath, that on the day and date above written Luther M. Collins did come to her house and strike her on her shoulder and her arm three times and threaten to shoot her and further that the said Luther M. Collins was armed had his pistol in his belt and his rifle gun in his hand cocked and that he commit [sic] this violence and made these threats on the complainants premises in King County."

The same day one John Martin came before the court with the charge that Luther did "willfully and maliciously and with premeditation commit an assault with intent to kill him the said John Martin with a revolver pistol first and then afterwards with a rifle gun . . ."

When the judge got it all sorted out he found that one Joseph Farris had stolen two of Luther's hogs of the "aforesaid L. M. Collins, which hogs were worth twenty dollars."

Luther, taking the law in his own hands and hunting for the thief, shot up the neighborhood, scared the hell out of all the neighbors and got himself thrown in the clink.

Luther was a wild man, all right.

But Doc Maynard was his principal protector . . .

And on one occasion that protection turned out to be *real* important to Luther.

Luther was hauled into court on a charge of defacing his own property. What he had done was tack several Indian scalps on his fence. The prosecutor admitted that one or two scalps was within the bounds, but a dozen or more was tacky.

Luther countered by stating that he had taken the scalps only from "unfriendly" Indians. He said he kept them tacked up on the fence posts as "good luck charms . . ." pointing out that he lived some distance from town and he never knew whether the Indians who appeared at his place were friendly or not.

Luther also pointed out, for example, that he was very friendly with his Indian mistress, a young lady of handsome proportions who drew official attention to her boy friend on two subsequent occasions. Once was during the Indian Rebellion, when all friendly Indians were supposed to have moved to the west side of Puget Sound. Indians who remained behind were presumed unfriendly. Commander Gansevoort lodged a complaint charging Luther's girl friend with being a hostile Indian and Luther won the case by pointing out she was the friendliest Indian he had ever met . . .

Which brought up the second court case on the subject.

Luther's wife, Diane, divorced him, on the grounds he was too friendly with this friendly Indian.

Luther's most interesting date with a judge came on Friday, October 27, 1854. The handwritten court record reads: "Comes now into open court Luther M. Collins in the custody of Sheriff Thomas Russell . . . Frank Clarke prosecuting the cause of the Territory . . ."

"The charge?"

"Murder."

So there was Luther behind bars.

And there was the doctor on the outside of the bars saying, "Luther, what am I going to do with you?"

"I have faith, Doc," Luther pleaded. "Get me off the hook!"

The record doesn't show how the doctor did it, but when the court reconvened ten days later, the prosecuting attorney appeared before the judge and "begged leave to no longer prosecute said cause . . . " Luther was set free to carry on a rigorous life that ended abruptly a few years later when he drowned near Orofino, Idaho, where he had gone during a gold rush.

If you have ever wondered whether or not the present county commissioners are setting precedent by getting away with murder, you can rest your mind.

They've been getting away with it from the beginning.

Crazy like a fox

The thing to keep in mind about that complicated human being we know of as David Swinson Maynard is that he liked living high on the hog, and used the real estate which he owned as his primary source of income. He and Catherine had twice as much land as any of the rest of the married couples.

His idealistic objective was the construction of the greatest town in the territory. And he played chess with that real estate until the day he died. There are those who have made the point that Seattle's development has been the result of a series of gigantic real estate promotions . . . which isn't far from the truth.

As usual, Doc was the one who established the formula.

In this connection—what with one reason or another—some 80,000,000 cubic yards of earth were moved in this town . . .

Before the freeway was cut through.

The doctor had got his training in the importance of landfills in Cleveland. Cleveland, in turn had gotten its from Boston, Boston from London, London from Paris, Paris from Venice, Venice from

Rome—or in some such progression of real estate promotions. The other settlers thought he was out of his mind, for instance, because he was willing to stake his claim on land, half of which was under water when the tide came in. He didn't intend for that land to stay under water for any appreciable length of time. One can safely say that the idea of the industrial landfills south of the Pioneer Square Historic District were the product of his original plan. This would include the construction of Harbor Island . . . and in its own way the construction of the Lake Washington Ship Canal. In the original instance, the plan was to construct that canal along Spokane Street. Even today on the side of Beacon Hill, you can see the hole where the digging of that canal was initiated.

In those early days, the doctor was too busy putting together a city to run for public office. But he did have need of a few jobs that were interconnected with his real estate transactions and he had himself appointed as a Justice of the Peace, Probate Judge and, of course, Notary Public. But the neatest of all his magoozles on this front was the appointment he secured for himself as the Clerk of the United States District Court.

We were a little low on federal judges in those days, and the circuit court judge only came to town when his judgment was needed. He left the details of arranging things up to his clerk, who was happy to take the responsibilities off of the judge's shoulders. (Knowing how justice was rendered in those days, I have to admit to the possibility that the Doctor cut the judge in for a few bucks just for the privilege of handling the details of justice. After all, one of the travelling judges sold gambling equipment when court was not in session . . . and when the court was in session, it was in the leading whorehouse in the Pacific Northwest.)

To understand the depth of the doctor's magoozle on this front, we have to keep in mind that there once were a couple of mountains in the heart of our town. One was called the Jackson Street hill. When we first were trying to figure out what to do with the Jackson Street hill, the plan was to put a tunnel through it like the tunnel through Twin Peaks in San Francisco. To obtain a mental picture of that hill, just imagine that an eight-story building constructed on the freeway at Jackson Street today would just have reached the top of that hill.

In later years, that mountain was dumped into Elliott Bay to give us the land on which the International District and the Kingdome Stadium rest today.

Then there was the Denny Hill.

Part of it was used to fill in the waterfront from the Pike Place Market down to Pioneer Square.

The major part of it, however, was moved to create the Denny Regrade . . .

By taking it out and dumping it into Elliott Bay . . .

Millions of tons of it . . .

Dumped in Elliott Bay.

Keeping all of this in mind, we go to the very first sale of the very first piece of real estate in what has become the city of Seattle. On May 16, 1853—seven days before the doctor and Arthur Denny filed the first plats which created our town—Maynard sold two lots for a grand total of ten bucks.

They were, unobtrusively enough, lots three and six in block two of the doctor's donation claim.

At any rate, the very first land sale of any kind by anybody to anybody else was made by the doctor to Felker a week before the original plats of the town were filed. The two lots were immediately north of the doctor's store on the northwest corner of First Avenue South and South Main Street . . .

And one of them was under water at high tide.

And that's the one that was worth the money . . .

A hundred times the money.

The early court records show that on a number of occasions, ship captains were hailed into court on a charge of dumping ballast in the harbor. Most of the cargo obtained in Puget Sound by the early sailing ships consisted of piling, hewn timbers, shingles and oysters and salmon destined for the San Francisco market. Therefore, the captains came north weighted down with ballast. They dumped this wherever they could.

Doc Maynard took advantage of the fact that there are a lot of harbors in the United States which can't take dumping of ballast. So the doctor had a nice federal law against indiscriminate dumping of ballast going for him.

He also had a lot of holes in his donation claim that needed filling.

So, there he sat in court. A captain would be hailed before the District Court judge on a charge of dumping ballast. Actually, all the judge did was issue warnings that this was illegal. The alert court clerk cornered the captains outside the court room and informed them that he had a nice spot, handy to everything, where they could dump their ballast.

For a mere five bucks a ton.

Felker was one of the captains.

His appreciation of the doctor's ingenuity was heightened when he learned where ballast could be dumped . . .

On lots three and four in block two. What with being the owner of lot three, Felker was the happy recipient of half the take . . . well, maybe not half. The judge must have got his cut.

Anyway, this was the first landfill in the city of Seattle. In the next forty years, enough ballast was dumped at this spot to form what was known in the 1890's as "Ballast Island." Somewhere between 30,000 and 40,000 tons of rock from Telegraph Hill in San Francisco were dumped and the island subsequently was filled in completely and today is engulfed by added fill. And the Alaskan Way viaduct runs over the whole thing.

While the doctor didn't live long enough to see it, his entire donation claim has been filled today, creating the land for the Kingdome Stadium and the industrial district of the city south of King Street.

On the other hand, the doctor and Felker—and maybe the judge— got their fair share of that first 30,000 to 40,000 tons that were dumped . . .

At five bucks a ton.

Doc Maynard—matchmaker

Although he was largely omitted from Seattle's original history books, it is impossible to underestimate the importance of Charles Plummer in shaping the destiny of this city. Bagley lists him as second only to Doctor Maynard . . . saying of him, "Next to Doctor Maynard in the activity of his business enterprise came Charles Plummer. He came to Seattle early in 1853 and continued in the mercantile business until his death (August 29, 1866.) Plummer was full of energy and enterprise and from time to time widened his activities wherever he saw an opportunity."

Bagley concludes with: "The writer regrets that more information regarding him is not available."

In one respect, Plummer comes in third . . . being ranked after Felker. Felker was the first man with a considerable amount of capital that Doc Maynard was able to interest in his town. Felker invested heavily in the doctor's enterprises with the construction of Madam Damnable's house and as a partner in the doctor's fishing enterprises. Felker also provided the doctor with a shipping advantage to San Francisco. But Felker never lived here . . . and disappeared from the Seattle scene sometime within the first decade of the town's existence.

Plummer, on the other hand, not only saw eye to eye with the doctor on how the town should grow, but established himself here—and above all had a lot of money to throw into the pot. The doctor always overextended his capital in the development of the town. And he might not have made it without this man. Plummer developed the town's first brick yard. He bought a lumber mill and coal mine on the Black River which fed into the Duwamish and provided the original industry of what now has become the industrialized Duwamish Valley. He provided the first water system in town, the first public pier, the first dance hall, bowling alley, billiard parlor and saloon.

His was the second store in town—directly across the street from the doctor's Seattle Exchange.

And he was the second postmaster.

He and Charlie Terry were the strong men of the first board of Town Trustees . . . and together, they invoked the doctor's policies with a degree of ruthlessness that routed the Prohibitionists completely and at least for the first half-century of the town's existence.

We don't know where Plummer came from, but early histories refer to his "Yankee" ingenuity. And we don't know how old he was although a logical educated guess is that he was about Charlie Terry's age, which puts him at about twenty-three years of age when he arrived on the scene. The chances are that he left New England in 1849 to participate in the California gold rush and that he hit it fairly big there, because he had that most priceless asset in the Pacific Northwest at the time . . .

Cash.

The doctor was stuck with Arthur Denny, who was upright and uptight, but he chose as his friends men like Plummer in shaping the personality of the city. And the logical conclusion is that Plummer, like the doctor and the others who constituted Seattle's first "establishment" found California a little too wild and raw. Unlike Arthur Denny, who stumbled upon the place, Plummer came here on purpose and put his shoulder to the wheel because he liked the way the doctor was mounting his metropolis. They were men to whom the molding of the city was a matter of choice rather than accident . . .

And they prevailed.

The statement of today that the United States is on a tilt and all the nuts roll down to California was as true in those days as it is now. You had to climb uphill to get to Seattle.

Plummer appeared on Puget Sound some time in 1853.

He had cash and every town proprietor on the Sound wanted it and him. It is known that he visited Olympia, Steilacoom, Port Madison, Port Gamble, Port Townsend, New York-Alki and Bellingham. He almost staked a claim in the latter place, where coal already was discovered and being mined.

But Doc Maynard got him with one of the slickest tricks of his career.

The doctor introduced him to Ellender Smith.

Maynard previously had enticed Dr. H. A. Smith, a fellow practitioner from Ohio, to Elliott Bay. The two men agreed that Elliott Bay would be the terminus of the transcontinental railroad. And they worked together to bring it here. They disagreed only on where the actual terminus facilities would be located. Maynard figured they would be on his claim at the south end of the town. Smith thought they would be at the north end. So, he staked his claim at what we now know as Smith Cove.

As it was, both of them were right.

Today we have railroad yards in both places.

Smith, who was twenty-two years younger than Doc Maynard, came close to being a carbon copy of this town's founder. Young Smith completed his medical education in Cincinnati, Ohio. He set forth for the California goldrush with his mother and his sister, treated cholera en route and for some reason was diverted to the Willamette Valley . . . the only difference between the two men being that Doc Maynard was diverted by a dame . . .

And Smith was just diverted.

Smith, who couldn't make up his mind whether he wanted to be a doctor, a writer or an orchardist, left his mother and sister in Portland when he fell into the hands of Luther Collins, who was pitching the orchard business with every ounce of energy he had. Smith arrived on Elliott Bay with Luther in the spring of 1853, but neither Luther nor Doc Maynard was able to sell him on locating along the Duwamish.

However, as it turned out, the timing was perfect for the future of this city.

Smith completed his log cabin at Smith's Cove in the spring of 1853 and sent for his mother and sister that summer . . . the two of them arriving about midsummer . . . to be greeted by Doc Maynard, who was not so antiquated that he failed to note that Ellender Smith was a comely young maiden indeed.

Plummer showed up in late July.

Sly old Doc Maynard introduced him to Ellender, and while Plummer still was in a bemused state, the doctor took step number two . . .

On August 6, 1853, he *gave* the young man lot four in block eleven, the second best piece of view property in town. It was on a bluff overlooking the Duwamish River and the Cascade Mountains at what today is the northeast corner of Occidental Avenue South and South Jackson Street

The doctor wanted Plummer so badly that he might have given him the property at the Point . . . but he already was negotiating with Felker for that one for hard cash. If he was going to give away some property, it wasn't going to be the best piece he owned. Or, the chances are even more likely that he knew, with Ellender in there to sweeten the pot, he didn't need to. Whatever it was, he knew what he was doing . . .

Because it worked.

The doctor inserted his usual "condition" about constructing a substantial building . . . and Plummer, eager to impress Ellender, went into competition with Felker to provide the finest structure in town. By the fall of 1854—when other towns around the Sound were lucky to get log cabins—Doc Maynard had under construction in his town two mansions that would be in the mansion class even by today's standards.

As Justice of the Peace, the doctor performed the ceremony by which Charles Plummer and Ellender Smith were married in January of 1855.

The doctor, who was an eminently practical man when he chose to be, provided the happy young couple with some brooding hens along with a rooster or two as a wedding present . . .

And Plummer, being the kind of operator he was, constructed a chicken house as big as the average settler's cabin.

Doc Maynard, the Plummers' friend

On January 16, 1854, Doc Maynard sold Plummer lots two and seven in block three—directly across Main Street from his own store. And it was here that the young man established the second store in the town. Two years later, he sold him the two lots immediately south—giving Plummer the four lots at the north end of block fronting on what today is First Avenue South and South Main Street. And here Plummer subsequently would build what has come down to us as both Plummer's Hall and Snoqualmie Hall, the main tourist attraction—outside of Madam Damnable's—in town. All in all in the first two years, the doctor sold Plummer forty lots in the heart of the business district . . .

And Plummer used every inch of land to help develop the town.

Plummer developed the Duwamish Mill Company, which brought both lumber and coal down the river and past the main entrance of the town. He built the town's first brickyard along the banks of the river and the record shows that at one time he shipped a single cargo containing half a million bricks. Plummer at times had two different partners in the mercantile business, H. A. Stone and S. B. Hinds. And, in combination with the doctor's store, the waterfront at First Avenue South and South Main Street became the original heart of the original business district.

Thanks to the machinations of the doctor, the county seat was located in his store. All business conducted by anyone with the county had to stop at Plummer's pier and the latter ran an overhead water system from a stream on the side hill a dozen or more blocks away. He also laid in a supply of cordwood for the propulsion of the new steamers that were beginning to appear on the Sound.

Within a short time, every ship of any kind which visited Puget Sound found it necessary to stop at Plummer's pier . . .

Up to and including the mailboat.

But here, they ran into a little problem.

Arthur Denny had somehow wangled the postmaster's job without the doctor's knowledge. And, naturally, he had located the post office in his little log cabin way to hell and gone north of Plummer's pier in the wilderness at First Avenue and Madison Street—nearly a mile away and with no docking facilities. All of the mail landed at Plummer's pier and had to be hauled to Denny's cabin and then hauled back again to the center of town where the business was being conducted.

"It doesn't make sense to me," Plummer said.

"No sweat," the doctor replied.

The Democrats were in charge of Washington Territory and of Washington D. C.

Denny was a Whig.

And the doctor informed his friends in key positions that Denny not only was a Whig but an offensively partisan Whig. It was a statement as easily confirmed as the nose on your face.

Three months after Denny got the postmastership, the rug was jerked out from under him. In due course, the job was awarded to Plummer.

East side, wet side, all around the town

While Leonard Felker and Doc Maynard constituted the team that put Seattle together in the original instance, Felker never did take up residence in our town . . . and as time went by his presence here became less frequent until he finally disappeared from the records about 1860. But the doctor moved Charles Plummer into a key position so smoothly that Felker's absence never was missed. And, beginning in 1854, the two men became Seattle's second Establishment.

And their first problem was Prohibition.

Neither the doctor nor Plummer wanted a wide open town. Madam Damnable—alone and away out there on the Point, which was a block away from the nearest store or restaurant—ran an unobtrusive operation. Actually, she was six blocks or so from the nearest resident Bluenose . . . and they just pretended she wasn't there. On the other hand, the doctor and the Plummer had no intention of letting the Prohibitionists turn Seattle into a closed town.

Things came to a head early in 1854 when the county government was created and Plummer got the first liquor license in King County. Plummer immediately put the license to work in his store at First Avenue South and South Main Street.

He installed the city's first saloon, a place with a honky-tonk piano, relatively ornate bar and a couple of pool tables. He didn't do much business with the Christers who lived north of Yesler Way, but the sailors and miners, and fishermen and loggers came to Seattle in droves on the weekends. And Plummer did a roaring business— below the line (the line for the next half-century or so being Yesler Way.)

During April of the first session of the Legislature in 1854, a bill patterned after the Maine Liquor Law was introduced. Maynard and Plummer, with their Masonic and Democratic connections in the legislature, saw to it that the bill got short shrift. But the next year, the women's groups pressured the legislature into passing a liquor law.

The Wets countered that move by arranging for the first referendum vote of the people in the history of the territory. The vote was 564 in favor of Prohibition and 650 against . . . a difference of eighty-six votes. The Drys hollered "fraud" on the grounds that ballots which were not marked one way or the other were counted as being against Prohibition. But they never were able to make anything come of it.

And that was the closest the territory—as such—ever came to enacting a ban on the manufacture and sale of alcohol during the lifetimes of Seattle's founders. From then on the Drys made a lot of noise, and occasionally they would elect someone to office—but it never mattered much until the debacle of 1909 when the Blue Laws were passed.

The Blue Laws making anything that was any fun illegal.

From 1854 on, licensed premises proliferated in Seattle and within a decade we had "squaw" saloons, regular saloons, cheap saloons and classy saloons with such wonderful names as the Dolly Varden . . . the Gem . . . the Snug . . . the Alhambra . . . Oro Fino . . . Bank Exchange . . . Billy the Mug's and such colorful spots as the Sample Room and the Collar & Elbow Room.

In 1859, the stout-hearted Plummer built the forerunner of Seattle Center when he established the finest entertainment spot on Puget Sound and called it "Snoqualmie Hall." He put a bowling alley in the basement, moved his pool tables and bar to the first floor and added a dance hall and meeting room on the second floor.

It was here that all of the major indoor entertainment of the town was brought for about a decade . . . exhibitions . . . magicians . . . elocutionists . . . instrumental and vocal concerts . . . lecturers . . . dancers . . . comedians and meetings . . .

Yes, meetings.

This was Seattle's first convention center.

And one of the more amusing events evolved when the hall upstairs was rented for a convention of the Order of Good Templars. The Order of Good Templars was an international temperance organization. Snoqualmie Hall was the biggest place in town and that's where they heard the temperance story and sang the temperance songs like "Come Sign The Pledge," "Some Poor old Mother at Home," and "A Picture from Life's Other Side" . . .

While on the floor below, a bunch of drunks trying to keep time with a tinny piano were hollering at the top of their lungs such popular pieces as "Turkey in the Straw," the "Arkansas Traveler," "Oh! Susanna," and "Wait for the Wagon!"

Plummer played both ends against the middle.

Seattle's first "Lady?"

Nobody knows and the record doesn't show when Madam Damnable died, although it was some time prior to 1863. But she was just as colorful here in the "hereafter" as she had been in the "here."

Doc Maynard, who provided cradle-to-grave service for the people who came to his town, had designated land for a cemetery along the banks of the Duwamish somewhere in the vicinity of Fifth Avenue South and South Jackson Street. When Mary Ann died, she was buried in the doctor's cemetery.

Then, they needed room for the first gasworks in town and it became necessary to remove the bodies. David Denny offered some of his land up where Denny Park is today at Dexter Avenue and Denny Way. By that time, there were 223 bodies and the gas company contracted with a gentleman to move the bodies to the new location.

When they got to Madam Damnable, they found to their astonishment that the coffin weighed about five hundred pounds . . . and when they opened it, they discovered that due to a judicious mixture of seawater and limestone, she had turned to stone in her grave.

There's no record of whatever happened to her body, but the rest of the bodies were moved to a new location on what was a view spot on an area known as Denny Hill.

All seemed well for a while, but then the folks decided to remove Denny Hill and the process had to be repeated . . . with the final destination of the first 223 people who died in town being what we know of today as Lakeview Cemetery.

The digger with the contract for moving the bodies did a sloppy job and when the steamshovels started biting into the hill, they came up with a miscellaneous collection of shinbones, skulls and ribs. This, in turn, resulted in a great hue and cry about the desecration of the graveyard. In response to the screams of the proletariat, the ingenious contractor disposed of that hill between midnight and eight o'clock in the morning . . .

Giving rise to the first use of an expression in current use today: "The graveyard shift."

Seattle's first fish factory

Fish-packing always has been up there in the top ten basic industries of our town. And Doc Maynard, who fell in love with the flavor of salmon on the Oregon Trail, was the first person in town to try and preserve it.

Among the twice-told tales of Seattle history is the one about the doctor's original experiment with the preservation of salmon. The way it reads in our traditional history books is that the doctor was a dumb cluck who tried to salt salmon down for the San Francisco trade. The salmon spoiled and he lost money on the deal . . .

The way it's put is "Doctor Maynard had this wonderful scheme about preserving salmon," as though he were out of his tree.

The facts are that the Hudson's Bay Company had been engaged in this kind of salmon packing for twenty years before the doctor showed up. It cost a dollar a barrel to salt the salmon down. They sold for twenty-dollars a barrel in San Francisco. The doctor, who was elsewhere at the time, contracted with someone else to salt down a thousand barrels, a shipment on which he and his partner, Leonard Felker, stood to net $19,000 from an investment of $1,000.

The salmon spoiled.

Each of them lost $700.

But in the same shipment were piling, shingles, squared timbers and cordwood on which they made $20,000.

They learned from the "fish fiasco" and after that they, and everybody else in the business on Puget Sound made money on salted salmon . . . until the mid 1860's when somebody figured out how to can salmon . . . and then it became one of the major factors of this city's economic growth.

But that wasn't the entire story.

And Bagley provides us with additional details . . .

After pointing out that Dr. Maynard was the first person in Seattle to get into the salmon trade, Bagley says: "During the next twenty-five years, the fishing industry on the Sound depended on its revenue upon salted fish and fish oil . . . San Francisco offered a good market for this salted fish, also for the oil which was expressed from the lower grade fish and offal."

But even that wasn't the whole story and Bagley covers that one, too, with: "Maynard's salmon enterprise carried with it another important industry, that of barrel-making. In pioneer days, the cooper made all his barrels by hand and of wood. The hoops were of split hazel or small vine maple, shaved on the inside, notched at each end on the lower side in a way that the notches would engage. These hoops were strong and endurable. They continued in use into the '70's when iron hoops superseded them. Salmon, beef, pork and later lime were all put in barrels and kept large numbers of men busy in making them."

"Hoop making was an art in itself. Men went into the woods and cut straight hazel or vine maple bushes from six to ten feet long and an inch in diameter at the top. These were carried to a shed or central station and there split and shaved, tied into bundles and carried . . . to the riverside and taken to town. Contracts for 100,000 or more to be sent to San Francisco were not unusual . . . "

Fortunes were made in this business.

And the meat of the coconut lies in: "When ready for market they (the hoops) were put in big canoes or bateaux and brought (to town) by way of Lake Sammamish and river, Lake Washington, Black and Duwamish rivers . . . "

All of them past Maynard's Point.

All of them contributing to the growth of Maynard's town . . .

"Everybody makes mistakes. That's why they have erasers on pencils."

In *Sons of the Profits*, I wrote about Henry Yesler under a chapter entitled "The Bastard," and there's nothing during the intervening ten years that either I or other researchers have come up with which changes the context of that designation.

The sawmill which he brought to Seattle always has been billed as the most important industry in town at the time . . . the basis of our whole industrial complex.

Well, God help us if all of our industries were run the way Henry's was!

On the other hand, no one can deny that in the field of bastardry, he was the most stout-hearted man we had.

The doctor brought Henry Yesler into the act in the original instance because he needed the publicity for his embryo town. He didn't care whether the sawmill ever amounted to a tinker's dam—as long as it was in his town. Every town north of the Columbia River—and there were a dozen or more trying to survive—needed a steam sawmill worse than it did anything else on earth. Prior to that time there only had been hydraulic mills which couldn't cut boards straight enough to compete in the San Francisco trade. The town that could get the mill as its basic industry could, like any other basic industry, attract satellite industries like shipbuilding, metal-working, housing, and shipping.

It was the general consensus that the town which got the first steam sawmill would have an unassailable advantage over the other towns.

The doctor handed Henry ten half-lots in the platted portion of his donation claim (two of which were under water at high tide) and persuaded Boren to give Yesler three times as many in his claim in order to get the first mill in Seattle. Charlie Terry, who was beginning to have doubts about his location at Alki at the time, offered Yesler the whole town. Yesler also was offered whatever he wanted in Olympia, Steilacoom, Port Townsend and Bellingham Bay on Puget Sound and in the incipient town of Charleston in Grays Harbor as well as as many free lots as he wanted in Portland.

But the doctor got him.

And, the doctor exercised a not inconsiderable influence in the *Olympia Columbian,* which was the only paper north of the Columbia River. And on October 23, 1853, the following item appeared:

". . . there is a new steam sawmill in process of erection by Mr. H. L. Yesler at Seattle, north of the Duwamish River, and which, we are told, will be ready to go into operation early in November, next and no mistake. Huzza for Seattle! It would be folly to suppose that the mill will not prove as good as a goldmine to Mr. Yesler, besides tending greatly to improve the fine town site of Seattle and the fertile country around it by attracting thither the farmer, the laborer and the capitalist."

To approximate that announcement today, you'd have to be watching John Chancellor on the national news announcing that the Boeing Company had landed a billion dollar contract with Pan American World Airways. In this respect, Yesler's mill was a major shot in the arm for the incipient city.

Within a month the doctor was mighty glad he'd only given up five-and-a-half lots to this intellectual imbecile.

Henry had served his purpose.

From then on, he was only a headache for Doc Maynard.

Henry Yesler's wife, who was really a very nice person, had made the arrangements with a friend in Massillon, Ohio, for the $15,000 that Henry needed to build a sawmill. And had arranged to have the machinery shipped to San Francisco. Henry had worked as a carpenter back in Massillon and had come west with one John Stroble who had been in the sawmill business in Ohio. Henry didn't know beans about building or operating a mill. And he really needed Stroble to get it all together.

The newspaper article noted that the mill would be in operation in November, yet, when the doctor showed up with Catherine in January, he got a rude awakening. Catherine later told a newspaper reporter that Stroble prepared her first breakfast in Seattle, and was a man with whom she formed an immediate friendship. (She told the same reporter she always felt that Yesler was a "worthless fellow.")

Anyway, it was during that breakfast that Stroble dropped the news on the Maynards that he and Henry had quarrelled and that he was headed back to Ohio. As it turned out, there was nothing the doctor could do to patch up the quarrel and Stroble departed, leaving Henry in charge of the operation.

For purposes of understanding the subsequent events, it is necessary to know that all of those little sawmills in the early days were relatively simple to put together. When Cyrus Walker, the Puget Sound manager of the Pope & Talbot Company put that company's first sawmill together in Port Gamble later in 1853, it was exactly one week from the time the machinery arrived to the time the first lumber was cut.

It took Henry *five months!*

And that was only the beginning of his troubles.

Henry never did make money on that mill.

Yesler was pointed out as a perfect example of total inefficiency.

Commenting on the *Columbian's* prediction of Yesler's "goldmine," Thomas R. Cox says, "Yet a goldmine it was not." He goes on to say that some mills suffered from poor management, others from faulty equipment . . . Henry's suffered from both. He notes that: "Henry Yesler's mill in Seattle, the first steam sawmill in what was to become the State of Washington, is an excellent case in point. One of the partners . . . commented 'Yesler has disappointed us in nearly everything . . .'"

Doc Maynard couldn't have said it better.

Pausing a piece for Snoqualmie Pass

Snoqualmie Pass was then, is now and probably forever will be the lowest and best pass through the Cascade Mountains, which separate the wet from the dry side of the state of Washington. The mountains have an hour-glass shape, being 100 miles wide at the Canadian and Oregon borders and fifty miles in the middle.

The pass runs through the middle and is about a thousand feet lower in elevation than the next nearest pass.

The Puget Sound basin is eighty miles long and eight miles wide and so deep you wouldn't believe it unless you saw a model of it at the Pacific Science Center—which is where you can see a model of it. But to relieve you of suspense on the subject, it runs to depths of 900 feet . . . with some of them right up to the shoreline. Seattle is in the middle of the east shore of this inland sea and, as a crow or an airplane flies, Elliott Bay is the nearest and best harbor to the lowest and best pass.

The Indians have known this for something like 5,000 years. The Hudson's Bay people had known it for a quarter of a century before Doc Maynard appeared on the scene. And with all that knowledge floating around, I can tell you one thing for guaranteed sure, the doctor found out about it fast . . .

And did some worrying about it.

In his day, there were no highways through the forests, except those provided by the rivers. And the river out of Snoqualmie Pass is rather reasonably known of as the Snoqualmie River . . . which, in turn, has three forks in the mountains—known with deadly logic as the "North," "Middle" and "South" forks of the Snoqualmie River. These converge above Snoqualmie Falls and at that point, the river flows abruptly north where it combines with the Skykomish River eight miles east of Everett to form the Snohomish River, which in turn empties into Port Gardner, where the city of Everett is located.

When the doctor explored Puget Sound in the fall of 1850, he had intime' chats with various and sundry Indians, trappers, prospectors and inquisitive men who just like to explore things. They gave him the lowdown on the eleven rivers which flow into Puget Sound and where they originate . . . and the various and sundry bays into which these rivers empty.

His problem was whether to opt for the mouth of the Snohomish where the harbor wasn't one, two, three with Elliott Bay, and be sure the trans-mountain traffic was coming his way . . . or to go for the best harbor and hope to abort traffic to his town above the falls. Accordingly, and although Catherine doesn't evidence the slightest notion of why they were doing this, she and the doctor spent weeks prowling around the rivers that came down out of the mountains and into the Duwamish. The thing she does remember is how nice the trees were around one of the rivers and its source, and how, to please her, the doctor named them Cedar River and Cedar Lake.

But Doc Maynard wasn't merely on a sightseeing trip.

He was trying to find a way of hooking up Snoqualmie Pass to the Duwamish River and consequently to his town on Elliott Bay. What he did was find just that. And he did a great deal more. He became the first person to traipse across the pass, meet wagon trains at the Grand Ronde, and lead them back to his town through Snoqualmie Pass. He later headed up the committee which raised the funds to build the first wagon road through the pass.

And, don't think he was without competition.

Lafayette Balch was doing the same thing with Naches Pass, giving away free lots in Steilacoom to people who came over that pass and settled in his town. He was fighting a losing battle. Some of the more traumatic experiences of the early days are related by the poor pioneers who took his advice. Today, as anybody around these parts knows, Naches Pass is closed in the winter. Even with all of our heavy snow removal equipment, we can't keep her open.

When Governor Isaac I. Stevens won the appointment to survey the northern route for a railroad from the head of the Missouri to the Strait of Juan de Fuca, he took on the 2,000 miles across the Rockies and assigned his good army buddy, George B. McClellan, to find the lowest and best pass through the Cascade Mountains. Stevens, who read omnivorously of the western explorations, had a pretty good hunch Snoqualmie was the lowest and best pass.

McClellan, on the other hand, knew which side his bread was buttered on . . . and that was on the side of Jefferson Davis who was at the time the Secretary of War. The war between the states was shaping up. He had strong southern leanings and he sure as hell didn't want a railroad built across the northern tier of states.

That would just tap a whole lot more land that would become anti-slavery and lend more support to the cause of the North. He rightly figured that the government probably only would give full financial support to one transcontinental railroad. If it did, he wanted that road to run through the southern states.

So Stevens would order McClellan to find Snoqualmie Pass.

But the big boss simultaneously would quietly countermand Stevens' order and require that McClellan *not* find Snoqualmie Pass.

They couldn't beat the physical evidence of the existing geography and soon the whole United States would know that Snoqualmie was the lowest and best pass to the most commodious harbor on Puget Sound.

What follows is the story of how that happened.

Doc Maynard meets the tiny bandy-legged tyrant

Isaac Ingalls Stevens was the kind of a guy of whom it could be said, "to know him was to hate him." His secretary, Elwood Evans, later a prominent historian in our state, was in an eminent position to make a judgment when he succinctly described his former boss as a "tiny bandy-legged tyrant." I presume that Evans was close enough to him over a long enough period of time to write with authority about his bandy legs, because there are no pictures of Stevens which show his body below the waist. That's because he would smash the camera of any photographer with the temerity to shoot the lower part of his anatomy.

There was, however, an additional reason for Stevens' ban on full-length photos . . .

Washington's first governor was only five feet, three inches tall.

He might have topped Madam Damnable by an inch.

These days, he couldn't have made it into the sacred walls of the United States Military Academy, because even on tip-toes he couldn't reach the physical entrance requirement. In those days, he not only made it, but became the valedictorian of the class of 1839. And, despite his physical stature, he looked down on anybody who (1) wasn't a graduate of West Point and (2) wasn't the valedictorian of the class of 1839.

In his heyday, he successfully provoked quarrels with the President and the Congress of the United States . . . the Secretaries of War and Interior . . . Great Britain . . . the Governor General of British Columbia . . . the Chief Justice of the Supreme Court of Washington Territory . . . the Washington Territorial Legislature . . . the Commanding General of the United States Army on the Pacific Coast . . . all the members of his immediate retinue . . . and a whole passel of Indian Chiefs in a hunk of ground that reached from the California and Canadian borders and the Pacific Ocean to the summit of the Rocky Mountains.

The only guy he never could get in a fight with was Doc Maynard.

Yet every time he entered into a confrontation with the doctor, he ended up on his tokas—without ever understanding how he got there.

Stevens' first encounter with Doc Maynard came on January 10, 1854. We're indebted to David and Catherine Blaine, Seattle's first full-time Methodist minister and wife, for the date. The Blaines were prolific letter-writers and somebody at the other end saved the letters for posterity.

Under the date of January 11, 1854, David Blaine wrote: "I have just seen Governor Stevens. He came to Seattle last night; is expecting to go up our river tomorrow to visit our coal mines and make arrangements for the exploration of our country back to the pass in the Cascade range, with a view to ascertaining the most feasible situation for the terminus of the Pacific railroad. Many in this territory are sanguine in the opinion that this terminus will be at some point on Puget Sound. This place (Seattle), in view of the natural easy route hither and our excellent and commodious harbor, said to be the best on the Sound, will probably be the place."

That was the week that was for Seattle.

On January 1, the Governor had set sail in a small sailing craft, the *Sarah Stone,* with his ethnological advisor, George Gibbs for a visit with James Douglas, the head of the Hudson's Bay Company in Victoria, and a quick look at Pacific Northwest Indians . . . but mostly in search of the terminus for the transcontinental railroad. He had left the upper waters of the Missouri River some six months before with instructions to survey the route of a "Pacific Northwest Railroad." With a crew of 175 technicians, mule drivers, etc. he had surveyed a swath of land 200 miles wide and 2,000 miles across untracked wilderness.

Now he had to determine on the terminus.

His orders were to locate it on the closest feasible spot to the Strait of Juan de Fuca. That he had anticipated it would be considerably closer to the Strait than Elliott Bay is indicated by the fact that he later bought land in Anacortes. But, on January 10, he fell into the hands of Doc Maynard.

The doctor met him at Plummer's pier along with Plummer, McConaha, W. J. Wright, who had replaced Arthur Denny as postmaster, Luther Collins and one William Heebner. These gentlemen escorted him to the most luxurious accommodations he yet had encountered on Puget Sound, a second-floor suite at Madam Damnable's, who was, among her other attributes, one of the finest cooks in the Pacific Northwest.

The next day, the Committee, with Chief Seattle's men providing the paddle power, escorted the governor on a tour of the backcountry . . . a trip that involved heading up the Duwamish and Black Rivers to a place which we know of today as Renton where the governor was shown a functioning coal mine with easy access to tidewater. It was some of the finest coal on the Pacific Coast and later would make King County the most important coal-producing county on the coast.

He was introduced to Seattle's prolific hinterland en route, showing the Duwamish and Kent valleys as the bread basket of Puget Sound . . . and then taken up the Cedar River (which entered Lake Washington a hundred yards east of the Black River . . . and then taken between Rattlesnake Mountain and Mount Washington to the confluence of the north, middle and south forks of the Snoqualmie River).

As an experienced engineer, he was fully cognizant of the fact that he had been taken through what could become an easy, low-level railroad route to Elliott Bay, and what obviously was the best harbor he had seen since his arrival in the Puget Sound country.

Six days later, on January 17, Catherine Blaine penned the following: "Our governor is now arrived and we are to have a Territorial Legislature. The members are to be elected next month. The governor's home is at Olympia at present. He was down last Friday with Governor (she meant "Judge") Lancaster, the nominee for congressman. They both addressed the people here . . . They gave very good satisfaction. I did not see the governor, but the judge called on us twice. He appears well, has the reputation of being a fine man, a Christian.

"The governor is as rough in his appearance as any of our back-woodsmen. They say he wears a red flannel shirt, no white one, coarse clothes and unshaven beard . . . He unhesitatingly declares the advantages of the northern route and thinks, as we all here know, that if such a route is ever built, its western terminus will be somewhere on the Sound . . . He pronounces himself pleased with the country, considers its resources abundant, and says he is astonished at the degree of intelligence he finds wherever he goes ."

Chief Seattle and the other Indians, as well as the members of the committee, who had explored the pass themselves, assured him that the valley where the town of North Bend is located today, was connected by gradual grades with the lowest pass in the Cascades. It was a conclusion the governor had reached during previous interviews with Hudson's Bay people, trappers and Indians on both sides of the mountains.

The governor was impressed.

Under normal circumstances, the governor would have followed the Snoqualmie River to its mouth. That would be the natural flow of traffic. On the other hand, he hadn't even seen the Snoqualmie River until after he had been shown an alternate route aborting the natural flow of traffic to Elliott Bay. The doctor casually reminded him that the mouth of the Snoqualmie was thirty railroad construction miles north.

At $60,000-a-mile.

To a man fighting the overall construction costs and under an injunction to reach tidewater and the best harbor by the "*shortest* and most feasible route." the doctor's argument was persuasive. The problem was that the governor's trusted Lieutenant, George B. McClellan, had informed him that Snoqualmie Pass was impassable in the winter.

"My man Tinkham will be trying to come through that pass any day now," the governor informed his hosts. "If he confirms what you say, you have a railroad terminus."

"We'll have some Indians meet him when he comes through," the doctor replied.

Under the doctor's instructions, Chief Seattle appointed some of his most knowledgeable braves to see to it that the governor's man was met as he came through. Under normal circumstances the man would follow the course of the river to its mouth. The doctor impressed on Seattle the importance of intercepting the explorer and showing him the easy route to Elliott Bay.

Unbeknownst to any of them, George B. McClellan, who had explored and *not* found Snoqualmie Pass from eastern Washington, was exploring and *not* finding the pass from the west side . . . at the very moment the doctor was showing the governor the same river.

How they missed one another at Snoqualmie Falls is one of the great mysteries of mischance in history.

But, at that same moment, one A. W. Tinkham, who had ranged far and wide seeking the best railroad route in the governor's survey party across the continent, was approaching Snoqualmie Pass from eastern Washington. And the diary he kept of that exploration is the most critically important document that has been neglected in Seattle history to date:

"On the 7th of January, with two Wallah-Wallah Indians, I proceeded up the Columbia till it receives the waters of the Yakima River, and then taking the latter stream, turned westwardly to trace its waters to their source, in the close vicinity of which also spring the headwaters of the Snoqualme [sic] and White Rivers, emptying into Puget Sound."

He then goes into a considerable description of the Yakima valley, the terrain, Indians and Roman Catholic missions. On January 17, Tinkham reached what he spelled as Kle-al-um Lake and found the snow to be two feet deep. He described the approaches to the pass as being favorable to a railroad line, noting that the valley rose gradually on either side of the river, adding that "Here, too, commences the wooded region extending to the shores of the Pacific, and where exhaustless stores of firs and cedars will not only furnish the building material for a railroad, but will, from its resources, with suitable means of transportation, supply the wants of the country east of it, lacking in timber and fuel."

On January 20, he camped on the edge of what he spelled as Lake Kitch-e-lus. He continues with: "Wishing to know the real difficulty to be apprehended from the passage of these mountains in the winter season by railroad trains, I gave particular attention to the measurement and examination of the snows on the route. From Kitch-e-lus Lake to the summit, some five miles, and where occurs the deepest snow, the average measurement was about six feet, but frequently running as high as seven feet . . . The whole snow was light and dry . . .

"These snows present little obstruction to removal in comparison with the compact, drift snows of the Atlantic States, and would cause very little detention to the passage of trains. Passing on to the western slope of the Cascades, the snow rapidly disappears; fourteen miles from the summit there was but eight inches of snow, and gradually it fades away as the approach is made to the shores of the sound."

Tinkham points out that "It should be borne in mind that this examination was made in mid-winter, from the 20th to the 25th of January, and in a winter known to be one of unusual cold, and that the accumulated snows of the winter were but six feet in their greatest depth, and this only covers some half dozen miles of route . . . "

Tinkham arrived in the general area of North Bend on the twenty-sixth or twenty-seventh and was met by Chief Seattle's Indians. He notes that: "Without giving the details of the remainder of my journey to the sea-board, which in a more extended report may be noticed, I reached the vicinity of Seattle, under the guidance of Indians, on the night of January 27, tracing a very excellent railroad connexion [sic] from the valley of the Snoqualme [sic] to that commodious and beautiful harbor."

Where he spent that night in a commodious and beautiful bed at Madam Damnable's.

That was twelve days after Governor Stevens had spent a comfortable night in the same comfortable bed.

Of course, during the intervening period, the bed had been kept busy . . . and they *did* change the sheets for Tinkham.

Convention city

Seattle became the convention city of the Pacific Northwest in that same happy January . . . and if ever the Lord intervened on the doctor's behalf, that was the month he did it. Come to think of it, the Devil demanded equal time of the doctor's soul and there was all hell to pay for a while there.

It started with George B. McClellan, the guy that Secretary of War Jefferson Davis ordered *not* to find Snoqualmie Pass. With Fate intervening in successive waves, McClellan spent New Year's Day with one of our old acquaintances. And, if I hadn't seen it in McClellan's own report, I wouldn't have believed it. As it was it bade fair to knock me off my perch.

He spent New Year's Day with Chief Patkanim at the mouth of the Snohomish River. McClellan wasn't very good with the Chinook jargon, but he sure learned quickly how to speak Patkanim. What he did was use "sign" language.

Dollar sign.

He explained to Patkanim that the Great White Father in Washington, D.C., wanted him to go up the Snoqualmie River and look for Snoqualmie Pass. But that the Great White Father also had ordered him *not* to find Snoqualmie Pass. By this time, what with his experience with Doc Maynard a few years earlier, Patkanim concluded that the white man was nuttier than any Indian fruitcake he'd ever met. But if the guy wanted to spend his money not finding some place, it was quite all right with Patkanim if the price was right.

So, what they did for the next nine days was take a leisurely trip to Snoqualmie Falls, arriving there on January 9 . . . a day on which the Lord smiled on McClellan's cause by dropping a load of snow on the pass that extended well down into Rattlesnake Prairie. If I know Patkanim, he took credit for the snowfall and charged extra for it. And if I know McClellan, it didn't come out of his pocket.

The federal government coughed up the extra charges for *not* finding Snoqualmie Pass.

And, man, did they beat a hasty retreat.

It took them nine days to go from what we now know as Everett to what we now know as North Bend.

It took 'em two days, the tenth and the eleventh, to get back down to the mouth of the Snohomish River again.

McClellan then proceeded with his usual speed, exploring bays and harbors of the coast in the general direction of Seattle. He found Elliott Bay on January 15 and probably spent the night at Alki Point, proceeding to take soundings in the bay that day and the next, arriving in Seattle on the night of the sixteenth.

To appreciate the picture, it is necessary for us to understand the activities of the Lord at this juncture. Stevens beat his way out of Seattle through snow, wind, rain and sleet, bound northward to find out if his hosts had indeed been telling him the truth about Port Gardner . . . and to look in on a few other places, like Fort Victoria on Vancouver Island. Snow, wind, rain and sleet were no deterrents to the complusive little tyrant.

But they sure slowed down McClellan.

And, as luck would have it, McClellan was wending his weary way from Alki Point to Seattle on the same day that the governor courageously sailed into the teeth of the weather headed past Smith Cove on his way to his appointment in the north. They passed one another without contact.

Imagine McClellan's delight at being met by a committee of genial men with a deep understanding of creature comfort, a bottle or two of Kentucky bourbon and the luxury of a hot bath at the finest hotel he had encountered since he'd left San Francisco more than six months before.

There was one discordant note in this symphonic paradise.

These guys guaranteed him a quick run up the Duwamish, Black and Cedar rivers and an easy trip to Snoqualmie Pass the next day. How in God's name would he avoid taking the trip with them?

This time with witnesses!

But the Lord let His countenance smile on McClellan.

George woke up the next morning to a spectacular view of Mount Rainier and to an even more awe-inspiring view of the Duwamish River which lay immediately below his second-floor room in Madam Damnable's establishment.

That was January 17, 1853 . . .

The coldest day in the memory of any human being on Puget Sound to that date.

The Duwamish River was frozen solid.

They couldn't make the trip.

Thank you, God!

The Saints and the Sinners

When you read the average history about the pioneers of our town—
they never were just pioneers, they were "hardy" pioneers—and they
needed to be hardy for reasons which shortly will be explained. But,
before getting into that, let me give you one of my favorite passages
from one of our history books.

After explaining that the efforts of our pioneers "required a fortitude
and staying power seldom equalled in the history of human effort,"
this book continues with: "But above all and beyond this, they carried
the profound convictions of Christian men and women, of patriots
and martyrs. They battled with the forces of Nature and implacable
enemies; they found, too, that their moral battles must be openly
fought year after year in the face of riotous disregard of the laws of
God and man."

Talk about the forces of Nature.

She, he or it, sure was doing her thing on that January 17, and
Catherine Blaine took occasion to write home about her hardships. To
appreciate the situation, you must understand that the Blaines had
brought formalized Methodist Episcopalian religion to Seattle a month
earlier. The Blaines came here under pressure exerted by Arthur
Denny. They didn't have a home of their own at the time, but as they
wrote to their relatives back east, "Brother Denny" found a place for
them in his little log cabin located where the Federal Building at First
between Marion and Madison is today. The Denny family huddled
into one room of the two-room structure, turning the other room over
to the newly wedded Blaines. The windows consisted of thin white
cloth.

Here's a verbatim excerpt from Catherine Blaine's letter:

"The present week is the coldest known within the memory of the
oldest white inhabitant. This morning it was ten degrees above zero.
Our room is so open that we can look through cracks in every
direction. It freezes within five feet from the stove where we have as
much fire as we can get into the little thing. I washed before school this
morning, standing over the tub with the shawl on and my teeth
chattering with the cold . . ."

And there was McClellan taking a bath in a big tub of hot water in Madam Damnable's whorehouse six blocks away with windows on the lines of a southern mansion . . . nine panes above and nine below the sash. Rainier, the mountain that the Indians called God, thrust its pristine glory into the azure sky. A crackling fire in the huge fireplace shone on the highly polished floor and reflected in the lath and plaster walls and ceiling. A bottle of bourbon sat on the night stand along with a pitcher of ice, if that should be his pleasure. From the kitchen below wafted the comforting aroma of bacon frying and hot coffee.

The river was frozen.

All was well with the world.

McClellan rang for room service.

The wages of sin . . .

On January 30 and 31 and on February 1, Stevens, McClellan and Tinkham wrote varying reports on the conditions in Snoqualmie Pass.

But they had one thing in common . . .

Total praise for the town of Seattle.

Stevens wrote: "Mr. Tinkham reached Olympia from Snoqualmie Pass, bringing information of the most important character; the snow deposited in layers of one or two feet, but six or seven feet deep for some six miles, and one and a half foot or more for only about forty-five additional miles, and undisturbed by wind, and offering not the slightest obstruction to the passage of trains. The grades good to Seattle, with a tunnel of considerable length. I herewith enclose a copy of Mr. Tinkham's report, and cannot too much commend the energy and judgement which he has shown in crossing, in mid-winter, the Cascade Range, and actually bringing to the Sound the route of the Snoqualme [sic] Pass, and thus accomplishing what had not be [sic] done by any previous labors of the expedition." (The last a reference to McClellan's failure to find the pass.)

McClellan ducked the pass issue completely, noting in his report:

"The result of my examination as to harbors is, that of all the harbors between the north end of Whidby's Island and Olympia, that of Seattle is by far the best, being well protected against the wind, having thirty fathoms of water, a most excellent holding ground, being easily approached from the Straits of Fuca, and having a good back country. It is, therefore, in my opinion, the proper terminus for any railroad extending to the waters commonly known as Puget Sound."

Madam Damnable's establishment had served the town well. And today we have McClellan Street just south of Doc Maynard's original claim.

Tinkham's copious report noted there were no substantial difficulties in crossing the mountains, stating, "It should be borne in mind that this examination was made in a winter known to be one of unusual cold . . ." and concluding with the words that were music to Doc Maynard's ears: "tracing a very excellent railroad connexion [sic] from the valley of the Snoqualme [sic] to that commodious and beautiful harbor."

That material went into the official reports which then were fed to the news media. And for the next twenty years, every newspaper in the country automatically referred to the Northern Pacific Railroad from some place on the Great Lakes "to the town of Seattle on Puget Sound."

Then, three months after Maynard's death, when Arthur Denny was in charge of the negotiations for making Seattle the terminus of the Northern Pacific Railroad, he got the now-famous telegram from the two representatives of the railroad:

"Kalama, July 14, 1873
"A. A. Denny, Seattle.
"We have located the terminus on Commencement Bay.
"R.D. Rice, J. C. Ainsworth, Commissioners."

Tacoma?

Nobody had ever *heard* of Tacoma before.

The man who traditionally has been referred to as the "father" of our town had blown the most important assignment of his entire public career. And it would be fifty years from the time that Doc Maynard sold the world on the importance of Snoqualmie Pass that it reached the full utilization that it enjoys today.

The Madam and the Master

Madam Damnable was the only one among those who knew what was happening who failed to appreciate the significance of the doctor's accomplishment. As far as she was concerned, all of this "pro bono publico" time she had been required to give to visiting dignitaries during the month of January was for the birds.

It cut into the profits something awful.

And when the Madam considered that something was awful, she let the world in general know about it . . . and the person who inflicted that something awful heard about it specifically and graphically . . . this time it was Doc Maynard.

He responded with the only incident on record in which he resorted to physical violence. What he did was turn Mary Ann over his knee and give her a good paddling on the "seat of learning."

Mary Ann promptly went to Justice Sam Holderness with a charge against the doctor of "Trespass against a person." Sam, who was well aware of the entire situation, found for the doctor and Mary Ann appealed the case to the Circuit Court, which showed up in the shape of Judge Strong in one of the Madam's parlors on the first floor.

This time she had enlisted the aid of Prosecutor Frank Clarke, who had changed the charge against the doctor to "Assault and Battery." The case came to trial on April 24, 1854. Judge Strong upheld the decision of Sam Holderness and added his own fillip to the proceedings. He levied court costs and lawyers' fees against the plaintiff.

Where Doc Maynard was concerned, Mary Ann was a good girl from then on.

VI

The Doctor and the Tiny Bandy-legged Tyrant

One of the little details that is largely overlooked in our history books is that under international law the United States had to figure out some kind of a legal gimmick to separate the land of the free and the home of the brave from its original occupants. It was a matter that caused a certain amount of friction then and is providing the legal profession with a field day right now . . . with the U.S. Supreme Court periodically being dragged into the fracas on account of trivia like who owns the state of Massachusetts.

Locally the conflict crops up from time to time in the headlines like when the state of Washington built a nice million-dollar bridge across a river in the Quinault Reservation and the Indians wouldn't let us hook up Highway 101 to either end . . . or when the Indians cast their fishing nets upon the waters of the Puyallup River in the town of Tacoma . . . and we had to call on the Tacoma Fire and Police Departments to try to quell the "rebellion."

Well, all of this stuff started back when Doc Maynard was inventing Seattle. You don't find much in the way of Indian trouble in Seattle for the simple reason that the doctor decided that the best way to avoid Indian trouble was to keep the Indians and the troubles with the Indians away to hell and gone out of his town.

He had a relatively fine needle to thread on this one because about ninety-eight per cent of the population felt the most efficient and economical method of solving the problem lay in the extermination of the aborigines.

The Methodist missionaries, who were big in the Pacific Northwest at the time, had an attitude on the subject which was reflected in a history of the missionary movement written by The Reverend Mr. Gustavus Hines and published in 1850 with a paragraph that reads: "The doom of extinction is over this wretched race, and the hand of Providence is removing them to give place to a people more worthy of so beautiful and fertile a country."

So, in addition to more guns, we had God.

Participating in the extinction of the wretched race was doing God's work.

On a more practical front, there was one Isaac Ingalls Stevens, first governor of Washington Territory . . . the principal exterminator . . .

Subsequently referred to by his disenchanted secretary as "that tiny bandy-legged tyrant."

Doc Maynard didn't believe that human beings should deliberately set about killing each other, regardless of whose side the Lord was on . . . so he found himself in a nose-to-nose confrontation with his peers in general . . . and the tiny bandy-legged tyrant in particular.

But he also had his own goal . . .

Creation of the world's greatest city.

How he coped is one of the great unsung songs of our history.

Give the little man a big hand

At this point, it is essential to regroup the sequence of events for the sake of understanding how they progressed. Stevens left the nation's capital for his transcontinental trip in about June, 1853. He arrived in Olympia late in November and initiated a number of enterprises . . . the assembling of the survey information on the railroad that would fill three volumes . . . issue the necessary proclamations for the creation of the new territory . . . find Snoqualmie Pass if he could . . . and, finally, try to find out what the Indian problem was all about.

On December 1, five days after Stevens arrived in Olympia, Secretary of War Jefferson Davis had dictated a letter to the governor telling him to forget the whole blamed railroad survey. The letter would take ten weeks getting here . . . and it was during that time the governor prowled Puget Sound seeking Indians and Snoqualmie Pass.

The record shows that he visited Seattle twice, once between January 10 and 15, 1854 . . . and then returned two weeks later to address some 2,300 Indians that Doc Maynard, with the aid of Chief Seattle, had summoned to Elliott Bay around and adjacent to Doc Maynard's store. This was the first meeting between Stevens and any substantial number of Indians.

And it was at this place and time that we get into what has come to be known as "Chief Seattle's Speech." (Written twenty-five years after the fact by Dr. Smith, poet laureate of the pioneers.) The gist of it was, "Take it easy on us, you guys. You're liable to be in the same boat we are some day, and the Lord will look upon you with a greater degree of compasssion if you behave like Christians." It was a speech of such mellifluence that Shakespeare might have been moved to comment, "Man, I wish I'd said that!"

The only problem is that Chief Seattle didn't . . . couldn't have said it. He not only didn't speak a word of English, he couldn't even converse in the trade language, Chinook, which was bastardized from several languages. He could speak only in his native Duwamish dialect which consisted at the most of about 800 words.

Dr. Smith, who was there, says that the meeting took place in front of Dr. Maynard's office at the foot of Main Street. The doctor got up and introduced Stevens as the Commissioner of Indian Affairs, and the man who held the destiny of the Indians in the palm of his hand. Doctor Smith describes the scene with: "The bay swarmed with canoes and the shore was lined with living, swaying, writhing, dusky humanity."

Stevens, who was a very short man, like five feet three inches, and conscious of his lack of physical stature, made up for it by being both overbearing and condescending. He talked to what he considered a bunch of ignorant aborigines in the kind of language he had picked up from a first primer of the *McGuffey Reader* . . . sentences like, "I see a cat," and "Oh, see Jane run."

And the Indians behaved like a group of frolicking first graders, chasing each other, talking among themselves and generally behaving in a manner calculated to give rise to the governor's gorge.

Then Chief Seattle stood up.

I have to give you some of Smith's prose because it's an image of the chief for whom our town is named filtered through his rose-colored glasses of a quarter of a century. He described Chief Seattle as broad-shouldered, deep chested and finely proportioned, where in most of the pictures and statues of the chief he really looks like kind of a dumb cluck. Here's Smith on the subject again: "His eyes were large, intelligent, expressive, and friendly in repose and faithfully mirrored the varying moods of the great soul. He was usually solemn, silent, and dignified, but on great occasions moved among the assembled multitudes like a Titan among Lilliputians; his lightest word was law."

If you want to get a picture of what the chief *really* looked like, imagine one of Seattle's mayors . . . any Seattle mayor. If he matches the above description, that's how close Chief Seattle matched it.

Here's Smith on Chief Seattle again: "When rising to speak in council or tender advice, all eyes were turned upon him, and deep-toned, sonorous and eloquent sentences rolled from his lips like the ceaseless thunders of cataracts flowing from exhaustless fountains, and his magnificent bearing was as noble as that of the most cultivated military chieftain in command of the forces of the continent . . ."

Not exactly the mental image projected by the chief when he spoke to the assembled Indians about Patkanim on Whidbey Island a few years earlier.

Anyway, in the 1881 edition of the affair, Dr. Smith has Chief Seattle, who was over six feet tall, arising "with all the dignity of a senator who carries the responsibility of a nation on his shoulders."

Stevens, who had arrived here thinking he was the star of the show, was ruffled by the fact that these rambunctious redskins had talked through his short dissertation. If Smith remembered correctly, the governor would have been even less impressed by what happened next. "Chief Seattle's trumpet-toned voice rolled over the immense multitude, like the startling reveille of a brass [sic] drum, when silence became as instantaneous and perfect as that which follows a clap of thunder from a clear sky."

What happened then wasn't in the script the governor had visualized when he first set up this session.

The chief thundered on for half an hour.

To the governor, who couldn't understand a word of what the chief was saying, it sounded like a demonstration by the winner of an Iowa hog-calling contest.

But that was only minor.

Chief Seattle raised his right hand to the sky . . . and that still was only part of it. He placed his left hand on the head of the little governor . . . and it stayed there for the duration of Chief Seattle's dissertation.

Five-foot-three Stevens, who never allowed a full-length picture of himself unless he was astride a horse, already had a low opinion of Indians.

Chief Seattle, with that graceful placement of his left hand, became the low man on the governor's totem pole.

Bad medicine at Medicine Creek

Governor Stevens' first meeting with any substantial number of Indians in Western Washington occurred in front of Doc Maynard's store in the latter part of January, 1854, when the doctor—through Chief Seattle—produced an estimated 2,300 members of that aboriginal race.

The second took place eleven months later on Christmas Day and the day following.

We all would have been better off if the governor had spent the holidays with his family.

But he didn't and we aren't.

Location of that second meeting with the Indians was at Medicine Creek where the first and worst treaty with the western Washington Indians was signed on December 26, 1854. Medicine Creek parallels the Nisqually River which, in turn, enters Puget Sound via the Nisqually Flats, a piece of geography located about halfway between Tacoma and Olympia, There were about 600 Indians present.

Governor Stevens' son, Hazard, whose version of the affair has dominated most of our history books, goes like this:

"The messages and exhortations of the governor, promising them protection, pointing out the way of bettering their condition, and even imitating the envied superior race, broke upon them like a lighthouse in a dark night upon the storm-tossed mariner, relieved their fears and anxieties, and gave them hope. They hastened to assemble at the appointed council grounds, eager to listen to the new white chief, and learn what he offered them from the Great Father for their benefit."

Judge James Wickersham, of the Alaska fame, provided a somewhat different version of the affair forty years later when he opined: "The treaties constituted a contract obtained through over-persuasion . . .

deceit . . . promises not on the record . . . contracts obtained by the strong, from the ward, by the guardian, the child from the parent.

"They were unfair, unjust, ungenerous and illegal."

Outside of that they were pretty good.

A sidelight was provided later by the chief interpreter, George Gibbs, who was taken by the fact that the governor was drunk . . . and at the same time lectured the Indians on the evils of alcohol. (Consumption of alcohol by Indians was prohibited in the treaties.)

To further set the scene, the brightest Indian of the bunch on hand for that treaty-signing was Chief Leschi, the richest and most influential of the associated Nisqually tribes.

The thing that must be kept in mind here is that the smart Indians in the Pacific Northwest had been doing business with the Hudson's Bay Company for thirty years—a whole generation. The Bay Company men were tough, but when they made a deal, it was a deal. If they bought a piece of ground from an Indian, they paid for it in cash or the equivalent in goods at a fair price. The same was true of furs. Bay Company rules against the sale of liquor or other crimes applied equally to whites and Indians. Bay Company people intermarried with Indians. And Dr. William Tolmie, the Bay Company factor at Fort Nisqually, had told Governor Stevens that Chief Leschi was an extremely intelligent Indian and a leader of the other Indians. "Get Leschi on your side and you've got a good head start," he said.

And so it was that the governor gave Leschi a slip of paper appointing him as a chief. (As there weren't enough recognized chiefs to go around, the government had to appoint chiefs so it could negotiate the treaties to make everything legal under international law.)

Here's how the governor approached what was probably the most sophisticated Indian in the Pacific Northwest:

"My children! You are not my children because you are the fruit of my loins, but because you are children for whom I have the same feeling as if you were the fruit of my loins. You are my children for whom I will strenuously labor all the days of my life until I shall be taken hence.

"What will man do for his own children? He will see that they are well cared for, that they have clothes to protect them against the cold and rain, that they have food to guard them against hunger, and as for thirst you have your own glorious streams in which to quench it. I want you as my children to be fed and clothed and made comfortable and happy . . . We want to place you in homes where you can cultivate the soil, raising potatoes and other articles of food and where you may be able to pass in canoes over the waters of the Sound and back in the mountains to get roots and berries . . ."

He then went into the subject of *The Great Father*.

Some of his quotes went like this: "The *Great Father* desires this . . . I want to know your grievances and report to the *Great Father* about you . . . I have been to the *Great Father* and told him your condition . . . I made a journey of fifty days to the *Great Father* on your behalf . . . I went to the great shores of the east to report to the *Great Father* . . . I told the *Great Father* I had traveled six moons in reaching this country and had never found an Indian who would not give me food, raiment and animals to forward me and mine to the great country of the west . . . I went to the *Great Father* and you all know I have come back."

The *Great Father* was Franklin Pierce . . .

The pro-slavery Democrat named on the forty-ninth ballot at the Democratic Convention.

"Take that . . . and that . . . and THAT!"

The governor then offered the Indians 4,000 acres of land that had been agreed upon in conference with his Indian agents in Olympia before he approached the treaty grounds. I'm sure that he was not there to deliberately insult the Indians, so it has to be presumed he knew absolutely nothing about the lands he offered the Indians at that treaty. This is further confirmed by the fact that nine months later he met with them and gave them exactly what they asked for in the first place.

But it was too late then.

A lot too late.

Congress, for once, had ratified the Medicine Creek treaty three months after it was made. The rest of the treaties wouldn't be ratified for four years.

Of all the treaties, this had to be the one they ratified fast. It was on this one the Indians based their subsequent actions.

The governor was totally unprepared for Chief Leschi's response. He apparently didn't know that the chief had farm and grazing land of his own that was greater than what the United States government offered to all of the Indians represented at the Medicine Creek treaty grounds. Leschi already was engaged in farming and knew the value of farm real estate. He also ran a string of some 150 horses . . . and the reports were that he had discovered gold in the Cascades. At the least, he was an extremely wealthy Indian. The other appointed chiefs signed, but Leschi's response was one of outrage.

The gist of his reply was: "You tell us you want us to be farmers. But what happens is that the white settlers grab off all the good farm land and you try to palm off this useless junk on us."

This was the last response Stevens had anticipated from an aborigine.

He blew his cork: "You'll take this ground and like it!"

Chief Leschi tore up his appointment as Indian "chief" and threw it at the furious governor's feet.

The chief then stalked away from the treaty grounds.

His last words were: "I'll fight rather than take it!"

For years an uneasy peace had been maintained between the whites and the Indians in the Oregon Territory—primarily through the efforts of the Indian superintendent, Joel Palmer—but now the news that spread like wildfire throughout the Indian nations was that the white man finally had shown his true colors. He was trying to steal the Indians blind.

The Pacific Northwest was a tinder box . . .

And what was this piece of land so despised that Chief Leschi would rather fight than take?

I hate to mention it because the people living there already have been put down often enough . . .

It was Tacoma.

Pop goes the weasel

If I had to nominate any one thing as the slickest magoozle Doc Maynard ever perpetrated on behalf of his incipient city, it would have to be the one he slid past everybody involved in the treaty at Point Elliott on January 22, 1855.

This one was Doc Maynard at his Machiavellian best.

To get the picture, please remember that one year earlier he had collected some 2,300 Indians to meet the new governor of Washington Territory in front of his store, the Seattle Exchange. Four weeks earlier the tiny bandy-legged tyrant had instigated the disastrous Indian Rebellion in the first Indian treaty at Medicine Creek. The signing of a treaty at Point Elliott was to be the second one attempted. And Point Elliott, for the benefit of those who never heard of it, is known today as Mukilteo, the spot just south of Everett where the ferry leaves for Columbia Beach on Whidbey Island.

Stevens had provoked an Indian rebellion liberating relatively few acres from the Indians during the negotiations at Medicine Creek. But now he was into the first major Indian treaty . . .

Extinguishing the Indian title to 5,177,600 acres of land . . .

King, Snohomish, Skagit and Whatcom counties.

All the land on the east side of Puget Sound from Seattle to the Canadian border . . . today the most valuable land in the state of Washington. And would you believe it, history records there were exactly the same number of Indians this time as had been in front of the doctor's store the previous year . . . four times as many Indians as had been at the signing of the Medicine Creek Treaty. This apparently was Doc Maynard's basic supply of Indians.

Governor Stevens, of course, was delighted at the turnout. But then, he was drunk again and really didn't know what was up from what was down. Ezra Meeker notes that the governor knew as much about the Territory as a passenger on a railroad train does about the foreign country the train is traveling through.

But Doc knew what the stakes were . . .

Another treaty like Medicine Creek and a massacre of the white population on Puget Sound would begin.

On the one hand, he had the governor to contend with . . . a man with characteristics described by Meeker with, "He would take no counsel nor brook opposition to his will . . . it may be said of his appointment of others to fill numerous offices were made to fill up a personal following rather than for fitness."

In those days men seeking to get into the Indian agent business would part with payola of from $500 to $5,000—just to get a job as Indian agent. Bancroft estimates that once they got it, eighty per cent of the money appropriated by Congress for the Indians slid into the pockets of some of the Indian agents. There were some honest Indian agents. General Joel Palmer was one. Mike Simmons was another. But for the most part they were a bunch of unmitigated crooks. It was a sorry chapter in our history. But the point is that there was nobody around the governor willing to brook his wrath or tell him something he didn't want to know . . .

Except, of course, Doc Maynard . . .

Who was a lot smarter than that.

The doctor had his own objectives here . . . and they were largely selfish objectives . . . but then again, he didn't want any killing and he was not about to light the fuse leading to a firecracker like Stevens.

A magoozle was in order.

The doctor's primary objective was simple . . .

As the only real estate man in Seattle, he already had sold a large section of the downtown business district to people he felt would help him construct the greatest city on earth. But there was a little problem here. The land wasn't as yet his to sell. It didn't even belong to the United States government . . . and wouldn't belong to the United

States government until this treaty was signed and the Indian title to it
had been extinguished.

Now we get into the complications.

Over 5,000,000 acres were at stake . . . but the doctor's interest lay
in a mere 54,790 acres. That was the amount of land he considered
as the ultimate acreage of the city he had in mind. It extended from
Point Pully on the south (known today as Three Tree Point), and a
place called Four Mile Rock on the north, a location directly west of
Lake Washington. The land then ran generally south along the west
side of Lake Washington . . . and then generally west again to Point
Pully . . .

In other words, Seattle's city limits today . . .

Well, not quite.

Our city today goes a mile or so north of what the doctor envisioned
and encompasses 58,603.84 acres, not the 54,790 acres he had in
mind.

The doctor's objective was to extract that 54,790 acres from the
5,177,600 at stake in the total picture at Point Elliott. He needed a
separate treaty to get it . . . and this is where Chief Seattle earned the
right to be the doctor's whipping boy. He stood up and was counted.
This was the territory that belonged to the Duwamish and allied tribes,
of which he was the supreme chief . . . and by God . . .

God?

Well, yes.

He had been converted to Roman Catholicism by that time.

Anyway, by God, he wanted a separate treaty, covering his allied
tribes.

Doc Maynard was condemned by his peers as an "Indian Lover," than
which there could be nothing lower . . . but there wasn't much love in
this deal.

Not when it came to the construction of his city.

So enter his second objective.

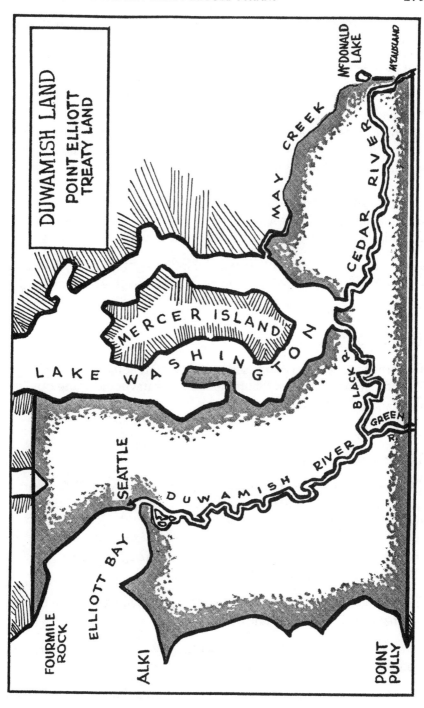

DUWAMISH LAND

POINT ELLIOTT
TREATY LAND

McDONALD
LAKE

McCLUSLAND

MAY CREEK

CEDAR RIVER

MERCER ISLAND

LAKE WASHINGTON

BLACK

GREEN R.

SEATTLE

DUWAMISH RIVER

FOURMILE ROCK

ELLIOTT BAY

ALKI

POINT PULLY

There was a need for Indian reservations . . . reservations with a lot more land than had been awarded the Indians at Medicine Creek . . .

But he didn't want them in Seattle.

As a matter of fact, it was far better that they be some place else. Everybody else may have been a little bit fuzzy about things, but Doc Maynard saw the picture with utter clarity. The Indians were safer some place else. So were the whites. And the development of the city was far more propitious if there were no Indian claims to cloud the title to the land. He magoozled a square mile for the Indians on some of the best property on Puget Sound, and some land elsewhere . . . the most significant of it being at Port Madison on the west side of the Sound where Chief Seattle had been born.

And, out of the Point Elliott Treaty the Indians got some 40,000 acres instead of the 4,000 that had been awarded them at Medicine Creek.

Oh, happy day!

Governor Stevens was surprised and delighted at the response he got from the Indians at Point Elliott, although he never did figure out why the Indian chiefs put in such a plug for Doc Maynard . . .

Up to and including Patkanim.

The process went like this:

Chief Seattle initiated the round of thanks by saying: "My heart is good toward Dr. Maynard. I want always to get my medicine from him." This sentiment was echoed by Chief Choitshoot who said, "My mind is the same as Seattle's. I love him (Maynard) and send my friends to him if they are sick." Chief Goliah brought Maynard up with "I shall be glad to have a doctor for the Indians."

Even Patkanim got on the bandwagon with: "We want everything as you have said, the doctor and all."

After each mention of Doc Maynard there was thunderous applause from the 2,300 Indians present.

And this goes to show you how little Governor Stevens knew about what he was doing. The Indians were thanking the doctor for providing them with a place where they could survive. Stevens thought they wanted a doctor to make house calls in their tepees.

His response was: "My friend Seattle has put me in mind of something I had forgotten. You shall have a doctor to cure your bodies and I trust your souls also."

From then on he provided for the inclusion of a white doctor in all of the Indian treaties . . .

A singularly bad move with the Walla Walla treaty.

The Indians over there had killed Dr. Whitman because they thought he was poisoning them.

But what a fine real estate deal it was for the doctor. The federal government paid the Indians three cents an acre for the Seattle townsite—and turned around and gave it to Doc Maynard for free. And he had no reservations on his land . . .

With the exception of mental reservations.

He already was selling that land at an average of $290.95 an acre.

You can fool some of the people

We have spent so many years busting our elbows patting our backs about the "Great Northwest" that we've come to the uneasy point of almost believing it. And most of the people writing most of the history books have contributed to our delinquency. But the truth is that we had a bunch of people here who weren't very nice at all.

Nationally, the Great Northwest had a bad reputation.

To begin with, you can't confine Seattle's history to the things that went on within the city limits. In 1852 and 1853 the folks back east didn't even know there was a city here—let alone a city limits. In more modern times, we've had incidents like the Watts riots in Los Angeles erupting between the white and black races . . . except that between 1852 and 1856 the race riots in the Pacific Northwest were between the whites and the reds. For comparison, you have to extrapolate the

Watts riots from a neighborhood in the Smog City to an area extending from California to the Canadian border.

Bancroft gives us a tip on what it was like in 1852, the year the folks were driving their stakes in the land that became our town: "With such a rough element in their country (The Rogue River in southern Oregon) as these miners and settlers, many of them bloody-minded and unprincipled men, and most of them holding the opinion that it was right and altogether proper that the natives should be killed, it was impossible to have peace. The white man, many of them, did not want peace. The quicker the country was rid of the redskin vermin the better, they said. And in carrying out their determination, they often outdid the savage in savagery."

On June 1, 1853, the *Yreka Herald* hit the nail on the head with, "Let our motto be extermination and death to all opposers."

In March of 1854 Major General John E. Wool, commanding army officer on the Pacific Coast, wrote a much-publicized letter to his superiors in the War Department charging that the settlers initiated a war against the Indians in order to bring in more federal troops . . . and in turn sell supplies at exhorbitant prices to the military. Federal soldiers, escorting an Indian to jail, fired upon and killed attacking miners who had killed their prisoner. Villages of Indians were massacred by the whites. And Wool wrote that he was forced to deploy his troops in the protection of Indians rather than the whites.

Bancroft writes of Indian women in the Rogue River fights risking their lives to provide water for wounded soldiers, adding, "I find no mention made of any such humane or Christian conduct on the part of the superior race." In another instance he tells of a treaty in southern Oregon acquired at gun point, "placing the conquered wholly in the power of the conquerors, and in return, for which they were to receive quasi-benefits which they did not want, could not understand, and were better off without."

The Rogue River War of 1853 cost the lives of a hundred white people and several hundred Indians at a cost to the federal government of $7,000 a day.

Bancroft referred to it as a "bloody carnival."

And don't think the hostilities were isolated to southern Oregon Washington became a territory that year . . . and got a new governor . . . and all of the residents of the Territory looked to see whether or not he would pour oil on troubled waters or use it to further the conflagration. Stevens didn't get here until December, 1853. He was back in Washington nine of the twelve months of 1854. His only conclusive action of that year was the totally unacceptable treaty signed with Chief Leschi and the chiefs of the upper Sound.

And Doc Maynard didn't need any diagrams to tell him what was happening to our town.

In 1853, concomitant with the joyous news that Washington had become a territory, the doctor sold eighty-seven lots in his new town.

In 1854 sales dropped to fifteen lots.

In the first four months of 1855—in spite of the favorable treaty signed at Point Elliott in January of that year—real estate sales dropped to zero. Charlie Plummer was the only investor who saw any future in Seattle . . . he bought a whole block on May 22 for $175.

The governor could fool some of the whites about his intentions . . .

But not the ones who put out money for real estate.

The easy route out

In those early history books about Seattle and/or Washington Territory, you get ten pages of who conquered what molehill and how. For a while there, the Indians were beating the pants off of the United States Army and the Volunteer Militia combined. And it was all very exciting when, after about four years, the "good guys" won. But in order to be the good guys, they had to win and win big against overwhelming odds. The script called for a pitiful handful of gallant settlers against the savage horde.

We needed the money.

And Congress was mighty suspicious.

But it wasn't until the 1890's that historians like Bancroft and Judge

Wickersham and Ezra Meeker began to blow the whistle on the operation. But by that time we had all the money we were going to get in war reparations. So it didn't hurt to let the folks know that once more history had been written by the big battalions. We didn't have any more brains, but we had a lot more firepower than the Indians.

It was not a heroic period for the superior race.

Among the things that came out later from his closest aides was the fact that Stevens upended a lot of bottles of booze during his negotiations with the Indians . . . and that he was, to say the very least, a difficult man when he had a load of corn on board. While the drys were in Olympia making King County alcoholically arid, the doctor was at Point Elliott watching Stevens. Here was a man whose sense of values was based on whether or not a fellow officer had graduated from the United States Military Academy at West Point. The aborigines were located on the scale of living things in about the same category as any other kind of rodent.

How he must have *loved* Chief Seattle's hand on his head!

The doctor was a witness to the two sides of Governor Stevens. A year earlier he had been on hand when Stevens, the engineering genius, had conquered the vast wilderness of America and carved out the route that would be followed when the first transcontinental railroad was constructed to the Pacific Northwest. At Point Elliott, he saw the face of hate based on fear . . . which is the most virulent there is.

It was disguised by the mask of the *Great Father* who had been nominated on the forty-ninth ballot at the Democratic convention. But I wonder how many people it fooled, up to and including the Indian Chiefs who got up and put the arm on the doctor by thanking him for the role he'd played in the negotiations.

Doc Maynard was the only "outsider" on hand.

The rest of the negotiating team was subject to the whim of the governor.

The doctor had obtained what he came after—the land for his city. But he also was the same person who had stuck with a shrewish woman for nine years when it would have been the easy route out for him to be a hero and join the army in the war against Mexico. He was the same man who had witnessed the killings in California and, as Prosch said, "it was too much like a continued battle to please the peaceable physician." Now, he was faced with the same prospect in his own home ground. And it wasn't just Stevens. Stevens rapidly was moving into the position of the chief executioner, but the growl of public opinion was with him.

Which brings us to the key issue.

As a matter of convenience in Washington D. C., the local Indian superintendents were asked to gather as many Indians as possible into big reservations. The prospect of keeping books on a whole bunch of different tribes loomed as horrendous in the nation's capital. So Stevens' instructions read like this: "In concluding articles of agreement and convention with the Indian tribes in Washington Territory, you will endeavor to unite the numerous bands and fragments of tribes into tribes and provide for concentration of one or more of such tribes upon the reservations which may be set apart for their future homes."

These were standard instructions to the Indian superintendents, and the key word above is "endeavor" to locate the tribes on one big reservation. Stevens, who was a thoroughly literal man, took these instructions literally.

Superintendent Palmer, who had the same instructions and tried to carry them out when possible, also knew what the circumstances were locally and knew how to yield.

Bancroft explains: "But the opposition made by all natives to being forced upon the territory of other tribes, or to having other tribes brought into contact with them, on their own lands, caused Palmer to select, an alternative to the first proposal of putting incompatible groups of natives on one reservation." Governor Stevens, who had negotiated with Indians for fewer months than Palmer had years, possessed no such insights.

Bagley sums up the fatal flaw of the Point Elliott Treaty. He points out that the Tulalip Reservation, occupying a whole township north of Everett, accorded the Indians in the Point Elliott Treaty, gave considerably more satisfaction than the Medicine Creek Treaty, but adds: "But Governor Stevens made the serious mistake of, also, ordering the Duwamish Indians and allied bands to be moved thereon within a year. This included the Indians inhabiting the upper White River and other streams forming the Duwamish.

"The Snoqualmie and Snohomish were allied tribes under the leadership of Pat Kanim, [sic] a wily, turbulent and dominating personality, who terrorized over the smaller and weaker tribes living in the vicinity. The latter had good reason for refusing to be placed on a reservation with semi-hostile tribes under such leadership, and leave their place of abode, hunting grounds and fisheries where their forefathers had dwelt for centuries."

The governor reached his decision to consolidate the tribes at the end of the Point Elliott Treaty-signing . . .

And nothing could induce him to change his mind at that time.

The die is cast

Doc Maynard may have susained some hope that Governor Stevens would not plunge the new Territory into war—until about mid-May, 1855. After all, the governor's instructions from the Bureau of Indian Affairs were specific on one front. Except around existing settlements, he was to take it easy on the Indian treaty business.

The actual wording of his instructions were supposed to have left him with no leeway: "You *will* at present conclude treaties with such tribes *only* as are located immediately adjacent to the settlements of the whites, and between whom and our citizens animosities prevail, or disturbances of the peace are apprehended." And to further put the emphasis on the above, the department added that it was "*desirable* that the stipulations to be fulfilled annually on the part of the United States be few in number." (Italics mine.)

The "will" and "desirable" above provide totally different emphasis. They go along with instructions that the governor should "*endeavor*" to unite tribes on one reservation. Treating with the Indians near the settlements only was an order. Uniting them on one reservation was a suggestion.

Stevens, of course, read it the way he wanted to read it.

The whole Indian question was a chance for Stevens to make a big name for himself. He was legit when he went from the Point Elliott Treaty to another at Point No Point a few days later. There were lumber mills functioning at Port Madison, Appletree Cove and Port Gamble. And he was acting within reason when he treated with the Clallams and Makahs on January 31. Port Townsend already was a functioning town.

But he went away out in left field when he tried to treat with the Quilleutes along the coast.

He had struck out with Chief Leschi. Doc Maynard had saved his bacon at Point Elliott. Then he completely and unnecessarily blew it with five tribes at the Chehalis Treaty grounds in February.

James Swan, who was there, corroborates this with: "The governor certainly erred in judgment in attempting to place these five different tribes on the same reservation; but his motive was, that as they were so few, being mere remnants of once powerful bands, it would be better to have them concentrated at one point. They, however, did not think so; their ancient prejudices were as strong as ever, and they well knew that they never could agree to live together."

The tenuousness of his position would have given pause to a more reasonable man . . . together with his specific instructions to consolidate his gains around land that already was settled. And further evidence was available to the governor. Two Roman Catholic priests familiar with conditions in eastern Washington warned the governor and other U. S. authorities that their part of the country was a tinder box. The weight of Superintendent Palmer was added to that of the priests. No treaty had even been attempted with the warlike Indians in either eastern Oregon or Washington.

But all of this came to naught when General Wool suggested that eastern Washington be declared off limits to white people until the tribes could be brought under military control.

If Wool was against it, Stevens was for it (this is where you get into one of those incredible situations which change the course of history. General Wool and a bunch of his army buddies were swapping lies that had been irrigated by corn whiskey in a bar in San Francisco and Wool, who really did have a lot to do with it, opined that he had won the battle of Buena Vista in the Mexican War. The general was in his seventies and headed for retirement at the time, and whether they agreed with him or not, the other fellows went along with the gag . . .

But not the tiny, bandy-legged tyrant.

He *had* to tell Wool that Zachary Taylor was the commanding general at Buena Vista, and *he* was the one who won the battle.

And, in his own inebriated state, Stevens had to rub it in by pointing out to the assembled group of army officers that Wool wasn't even a West Point graduate.)

Stevens dispatched Indian agents to Walla Walla to initiate the treaty-making process . . . and on May 12, 1855, left Olympia—with his teen-aged son accompanying him—for Walla Walla.

No bunch of redskins was going to intimidate him!

George Gibbs tried to warn the governor not to get into the Walla Walla Treaty. Recalling it later he wrote: "All that summer, rumors came in of the intention of the Indians to break out. Indian women living with white settlers warned their husbands to take care of themselves; but these reports were disregarded, because we had so long slept on the volcano that we did not believe it could burn . . ."

"That the governor's treaties had a great deal to do with fomenting this war there is no doubt. Those on the Sound were much too hurried, and the reservations allowed them were insufficient; but his great blunder was in bringing together the Nez Perces, Walla Wallas, Yakimas and others into one council, and cramming a treaty down their throats in a hurry."

The governor did not take readily to advice, which is why he totally disregarded an important piece of information supplied him by Bishop A. M. A. Blanchet, who had been dealing with eastern Washington Indians for nearly a decade.

Blanchet condemned A. J. Bolon, the governor's appointee as Indian agent for eastern Washington.

He said that in visits to the Yakima Indians, Bolon had shown a complete incapacity for his job as Indian agent. He "has, 1. Associated with and given all his trust to that which is the most vile in this nation; 2. He has made himself, by his acts, the initiator of games of chance prejudicial to the Indians; 3. He has carelessly rewarded thieves, and by doing this has incurred theft among the Indians; 4. He has shown with regard to the missionaries of this nation a vile conduct which the missionaries would never have expected from a government agent; 5. He has by his general conduct, lost the trust of all that is good among the Indians to the point that in my opinion Mr. Bolon can no longer perform in this nation the good that the government expects of its agents in the midst of them. [The Indians.]

"For these reasons I think it my duty to solicit his changement (Removal.)"

It was advice that fell on deaf ears.

The governor initiated the treaty-signing on May 21, 1855. The big chiefs of the eastern Washington tribes didn't even show up at the treaty-grounds for a week. Where treaties were completed in a matter of a day or two in western Washington, it took nearly a month to get the signatures at Walla Walla.

There were about 100 whites present . . .

And 5,000 warlike Indians.

During that summer, gold was discovered near Fort Colville and a lot of miners headed into the war zone. The Indians said that somebody among them "outraged" one of the women of the Yakima tribe.

Make no small plans

The future of Seattle was bleak indeed in the summer of 1855 . . . no matter which way the inventor of the place looked at it. A majority of the people of the Pacific Northwest looked at extermination of the Indians as a great idea. They would have preferred to just wish the problem away, but it wasn't going to disappear that easily.

But all that was needed was a leader and a spark and the superior race would dispose of the inferior.

Looking at it from both sides, the doctor could see that Chief Seattle in particular and the other Indians on the west side of the mountains were between a rock and a hard place. There was no safety for them. The whites were itching to shoot them. The warlike Indians in eastern Washington promised them that if they sided with the whites, they would be considered as the enemy. The men would be killed . . . the women and children taken as slaves.

There were between 6,000 and 7,000 Indians in eastern Washington . . . Between 8,000 and 9,000 in western Washington.

The doctor had one thing going for him.

Stevens was in eastern Washington . . . and would continue to be away from his post as governor in Olympia for the next six months, because after he finished treating with the tribes in eastern Washington, it was his intention to head east of the Rockies and treat with the Blackfoot tribes at Fort Benton. And while the governor was away, Charles Mason, Secretary of State, acted as governor.

Mason was in his early twenties, and a contemporary described him as well-equipped by "education, by temperament and by mental calibre for the duties devolving upon him. He was possessed to a great degree of that rare faculty of listening patiently to counsel . . . then to weigh it and act upon his own judgment, while throwing all prejudice aside. He was a courteous gentleman, not headstrong, but firm; not opinionated, yet self-reliant; easily approached, nevertheless dignified in his bearing, while not in the least self-conscious as to his own importance in the difficult position in which he was so suddenly and unexpectedly thrust."

Following the governor's departure in May, Doc Maynard approached the acting governor with a proposition that was too reasonable to be ignored. The instructions from the Bureau of Indians Affairs clearly stated that the principal thrust was the separation of the Indians and the whites around the various settlements. Stevens was spending all of the money allotted for Indian Affairs in the purchase of presents and financing the payroll for the eastern Washington treaties.

What the doctor would do was take over the role that was supposed to have been played by the United States government. He would, in effect, get the children off the streets in the event of war.

But he didn't have the immediate cash.

What he proposed to do was sell the land in Seattle which he and Governor Stevens had agreed would become the terminus of the railroad.

You can see that land today.

It's where the passenger terminals of the transcontinental railroads are located on South Jackson Street at Fourth and Fifth Avenues South.

Mason responded well to the suggestion.

He didn't have the cash, himself, but there were a couple of other guys in the administration who did. They were Major H. A. Goldsborough, the territorial tax collector . . . and James P. Tilton, surveyor of public lands.

On August 4, 1855, Dr. Maynard consummated the largest and most important real estate transaction in Washington Territory to that date—with a consortium composed of Mason, Goldsborough and Tilton.

He sold the terminus of the transcontinental railroad . . .

For $2,400.

He used the money to buy one sloop and charter another belonging to Luther Collins . . . and bought the supplies necessary to sustain about twenty-five percent of all of the western Washington Indians for a period of four or five months.

Mason did his part by negotiating with another man whose role in Washington history has been sadly neglected, one John Swan. Swan, an Olympia resident, saw eye-to-eye with the doctor and Acting Governor Mason on the necessity of isolating Indians near the settlements in the event of war. He would try and locate another contingent of Indians on Fox Island, near Steilacoom.

The doctor sold ten lots in the heart of the town and 121 lots covering all possible railroad approaches to the town—as they would come in on stilts across the tideflats.

At that point his total real estate sales—from the time he disposed of his first lots to Henry Yesler in January, 1853—consisted of some thirty-acres of the 640 he had obtained for nothing in his original donation claim.

All hell breaks loose

It would be erroneous to presume that Doc Maynard thought of himself as some kind of a hero in the events of the next few months. Unlike a number of the others involved, who collected and preserved every scrap of paper they could lay their hands on, Doc Maynard didn't save anything . . . didn't record anything that was not absolutely essential. His wife, who was not the brightest lady who ever came down the pike, didn't even know what he was up to half the time. A lot of other people resented what he was doing and wrote letters to the editor about it, but the doctor was too busy keeping his town from going belly-up to notice.

Except on two noteworthy occasions—once against the Indians and once against the Methodists—he didn't even lose his sense of humor.

And his strength during this stressful period did more to set the character of the city of Seattle than anything else which he had done to that point in our history.

At about the time that Doc Maynard completed his transaction with the consortium in Olympia, word reached civilization, after an Indian maiden was "outraged" by gold seekers, that the Indians in eastern Washington would deal "peremptorily" with prospectors. It was one of the many pieces of clear evidence that the vaccination of the Walla Walla Treaty had not "taken." Indian agent A. J. Bolon proceeded to the country with the objective of trying to reason with the toughest chief of the bunch, Kamiakim, head of the Yakimas. He last was seen alive on September 18, 1855 at a Catholic mission near the present site of the town of Yakima.

That was one-and-a-half months after the doctor's real estate sale. A few days later, Bolon's body was found.

Somebody had shot him in the back, then cut his throat, then burned him and his saddle bags and his saddle and his horse.

Somebody was sure sore at Bolon.

There were any number of reasons such as the five that Father Blanchet had outlined in his letter to Governor Stevens. The Indians had an eye-for-an-eye and tooth-for-a-tooth philosophy. In western Washington the classic example was the beheading of Isaac Ebey. Ebey was not even remotely involved in the incident which resulted in his death. Bolon's murder could have been the result of the incident in which the Indian maiden had been ravished by the gold miners.

It could have been even more direct.

Maybe Bolon was caught cheating at cards.

Whatever it was, the time had come for blood-letting.

And the whites chose to make Bolon the *cause celebre*, the Archduke Ferdinand of the Indian War.

When war is declared, truth is the first casualty

Granville O. Haller was dispatched from Fort Vancouver to chastise the Indians . . . and he got his pants licked off. Lieutenant William Slaughter was dispatched from Fort Steilacoom and got to the summit of Naches Pass where he realized the place was swarming with hostile Indians infiltrating western Washington. Wisely he fell back.

The whites used Indian hostility to get help from the federal government, saying they were under siege by a savage horde. The Indians also used it to try and get western Washington Indians into the affray.

It should be pointed out here that a state of war existed between the whites and the Indians from the time that Haller and Slaughter marched. Well aware that the 7,000 to 8,000 Indians in western Washington were a potential source of allies, fifth columnists sneaked across the mountains with an interesting and—to the local Indians—believable set of arguments.

Kamiakim announced he had enough war material to fight for five years . . . that "all tribes were invited to join him, and that all who refused would be held as foes who would be treated in the same manner as Americans—the adults killed and the children enslaved."

He pointed out with a certain amount of logic that, regardless of what they said, the whites were primarily interested in getting rid of the Indians. Either they would be exterminated or returned to the land of darkness from whence their ancestors had come.

The picture painted by the fifth columnists was one which caught the imagination of our local redskins. They would be crammed into steamships and hauled away. Except that they didn't call them steamships. They called them fire ships . . .

And not without reason.

Those early steamships on Puget Sound had a tendency to blow up, scattering the arms and legs and heads and torsos of the occupants all over the place. The local Indians were as afraid of the fire ships as they were of the white man's cannons.

Once packed like sardines in the fire ships, they would be hauled off to a place called "Polakly Ilahe," where no ray from the sun ever penetrated; where there was torture and death for all the races of Indians; where the sting of an insect killed like the stroke of a spear and where the streams and water were foul and muddy and unfit to drink."

In other words, Siberia.

The whites had been speculating for some years about the origins of the Indians and the general consensus was there once had been a land bridge across the Bering Straits. Western Washington Indians had landed in eastern Washington and had been driven to the coast by the tough Indians living in that part of the country. And enough of this had rubbed off on the Indians to make it believable.

The exterminators, of course, had no intention of doing that.

They were going to shoot 'em on the spot.

The Indians got plenty of demonstrations from the white men that whatever it was, their fate was not very good. Picnicking families of Indians were mowed down. Their ears, noses and hands were cut off, dried and shipped to friends elsewhere as trophies of the war . . . a little practice that had been initiated by the whites in Oregon a dozen years earlier.

The red brethren in eastern Washington had one clinching argument.

If the weak-kneed Siwashes in western Washington didn't join up . .

And if the whites didn't ship 'em off or kill them on the spot . . . then the war parties from eastern Washington would treat them the way they were going to treat the whites . . .

With torture and death.

Doc Maynard makes his move

Doc Maynard, the only man in western Washington who had prepared for the problem, moved swiftly to thwart the ambitions of the hostile Indians in eastern Washington and any of what he later referred to as "troublesome whites in Seattle" who might take it upon themselves to shoot some of the local Indians.

Having handed Mason what the latter knew would become a fortune in land, the doctor exercised plenty of clout in the councils of war in Olympia. And one of the first orders to emanate from the territorial capital was the evacuation of Indians on the east side of Puget Sound to Port Madison on the west side of Puget Sound. Mason ordered Mike Simmons to appoint the doctor as a sub-Indian agent in charge of the Indians at the internment camp which was named Fort Kitsap.

Putting Chief Seattle on the same reservation with Patkanim added up to signing Chief Seattle's death warrant. Chief Seattle would have to fight or die. He would have to fight the whites or he would have to fight Patkanim if both chiefs were on the same reservation.

But Doc Maynard had got his land out of the treaty . . . his city was named, owned and operating. And he no longer needed Chief Seattle. All of a sudden, he was a liability. In some of the biggest corporations of the civilized world of today, what a man in Chief Seattle's spot would get would be what we call "dumped."

The doctor moved with characteristic vigor.

Within a month of the outbreak he had the bulk of his 2,000 Indians at the internment camp. Armed with the necessary carpentry tools and lumber from the nearby sawmill operated by George Meigs, they were constructing buildings for what the doctor believed would be a long stay . . .

At least for the Indians.

He wasn't about to see Chief Seattle located at the Tulalip reservation with Patkanim . . .

Ever.

Nobody knew how many eastern Washington Indians had penetrated western Washington. But as far as rumor had it, the woods east of Lake Washington were loaded with belligerents ready to shoot the head off of any white man they could get in the sights of their guns.

Demonstrating considerably more courage than anybody else in town, the doctor insisted on covering the territory east of his town to collect any stray Indian families that might be caught between opposing forces in the war zone.

Governor Mason furnished him with an armed guard.

Bagley writes: "On November 9, he (Dr. Maynard) went up the Duwamish and Black rivers, thence along the east shore of Lake Washington and notified all Indians to come to Seattle to be conveyed across Puget Sound."

The doctor combed those fearsome forests for a whole week . . .

Realizing that at any moment he could be shot in the back.

He returned with some seventy-five Indian men, women and children. By November 20, 1855, they were joined by another 175 who had come to Seattle in their canoes from elsewhere on the Sound and were accordingly shipped off to Fort Kitsap.

Before anybody knew what had happened, the doctor had swept the east side of Puget Sound clear of non-belligerent Indians.

And the squawks weren't long in coming.

Henry Yesler blows his whistle . . . his cork and his stack

At five o'clock in the morning of November 21, Henry Yesler blew the whistle of his steam sawmill to summon his cheap Indian help to work.

And nobody showed up.

By November 24, he had rounded up some of the other members of the local business community who also were suffering from a lack of cheap labor—and feared that this lack might continue for some time.

And they fired off a letter to Acting Governor Mason.

It's a letter that never before has made any of our local history books and it's too good to leave out any longer:

"Seattle, Nov. 24, 1855

"Hon. C. H. Mason

"Sir we would beg leave to state that a short time since Col. M. T. Simmons came here and requested a meeting of the citizens for the purpose of determining the most suitable place to locate the friendly Indians during the present hostilities; stating at the same time that he only wished to know the will of the majority and he would be governed by the same. Accordingly it was determined by said meeting (called at his request) that the Indians should be located in this place on a plot of ground designated by a committee appointed by said meeting, in all of which the Indians have acquiesed [sic] with as little complaint as could reasonably have been anticipated.

"But just at the time when they had got their houses built and fixed to live in, they were required to break up and move on to their reservation; which is causing great dissatisfaction, and we fear will tend to provoke hostility with well disposed, and friendly Indians. A clear and decided majority of the inhabitants of this place have decided (as Col. Simmons well knew before he left here) that it was not safe to remove the Indians of this vicinity to their reserve, in fact it was to all appearances tantamount to a declaration of war against them.

"We would also respectfully state our firm conviction that the department can never give satisfaction to either whites or Indians in this part of the territory through the agency of D. S. Maynard inasmuch as it is *utterly impossible* for the department to obtain reliable information from him, owing to the fact that he scarcely consults any other Indian than Seattle, when the large majority of the Indians here are not his people and do not acknowledge him as their chief. Hence discord and difficulty must ever exist here until a different course is pursued.

"We must say in conclusion that we do not wish you to understand us, as preferring a charge against the government. But simply as wishing to give such information as will prevent trouble in the future. Confidently believing that the department has not heretofore been well appraised of the circumstances surrounding us here. Our request (as democrats) in the present case is, that the Dwamish [sic] Indians be permitted to remain here. They having voluntarily given up their arms to Captain Hewitt, and declared their willingness to obay [sic] his orders, and submit to his authority in all things, if they can be permitted to remain here. Will you please answer immediately in order that we may know how to act in this emergency and if possible prevent unnecessary bloodshed.

"With high considerations of respect
we are sir
your obedient servants

"H. L. Yesler
David Phillips
C. C. Lewis
S. Lamson Grow
Thomas Mercer

"P. S. If this does not belong to your department please send it to the proper person.

"H. L. Yesler."

I got a particular charge out of Henry's reference to the fact that all of the signators of the letter were Democrats. Mason just happened to be a Democrat, too.

It was politics as usual.

On November 27th, Mason replied to Yesler's complaint with:

"I have the honor to acknowledge the receipt of your favor of the 24 inst. and in reply to state that this office still places great confidence in ability and discretion of Mike Simmons, Esq. in Indian matters. Whether he agreed or not to be governed by a decision of a majority of the people as to the disposition of the Indians in your neighborhood, I know not; but have simply to state that the expression of the opinion of a majority can have no controlling influence upon the actions of the Indian agent—In addition to this, complaint already has been made by Col. Simmons that an unwarranted influence has been exercised by some of the citizens of Seattle with his efforts to provide for the Indians.

"As to the charge of 'unfitness' made against D. S. Maynard, Esq., 'it being impossible to obtain reliable information from him because he scarcely consults any other Indian than Seattle,' I have to state that 'Seattle' is recognized by the Indians as the head Chief of the Duwamish Indians, and it is part of the policy worked out to make the chiefs as influential as possible in order that they may have more responsibility. In conclusion I must say that I decline to interfere with any steps taken by Col. Simmons."

A war in the town of Seattle had begun.

Not between the whites and the Indians . . .

But between the whites and the whites.

Meanwhile back at the ranch

Until the incident of Indian Agent Bolon, the killing of Indians around Puget Sound was kind of a sometimes thing. For instance, Luther Collins might decorate his fence with Indian scalps, but he didn't go out *hunting* them. And when Masachie Jim got obnoxious, the entire population of Seattle had a hand on the rope that strung him up. The folks were horrified when they learned that Territorial Supreme Court Justice Edward E. Lander, newly-arrived in town, was serious when he said the parties who had participated in the hanging would, themselves, be hung if found guilty. So, the jury found everybody not guilty.

For their part, the Indians would cheerfully shoot somebody in the back, but a nose-to-nose confrontation wasn't anybody's idea of how to handle the situation.

Bolon's murder changed all that.

Well, not so much Bolon's murder . . .

People could understand that.

But killing his horse, too?

That *did* change everything!

Those eastern Washington Indians were really serious about this. We got the next horrible example of their seriousness on October 28, 1855, when nine people in the White River valley were massacred by Indians. Leschi became the goat and got hung for this, but post mortem testimony revealed he couldn't have been there at the time . . . and he said he wasn't there, even when they were putting the rope around his neck. And there's little doubt in my mind that it was those tough eastern Washington Indians who sneaked over the mountains and perpetrated the deed. But the massacre made one thing quite clear. This was no casual incident. It was deadly serious . . . so serious that a week later, Doctor Maynard had himself sworn in as a sub-Indian agent and started moving nonbelligerents to Port Madison, which he named Fort Kitsap.

And where was Stevens, the guy who had stirred all this up?

Clear off on the east side of the Rocky Mountains, treating with the Blackfoot Indians . . . a couple thousand miles away.

Under the initial enthusiasm of the murder of Bolon's horse, Acting Governor Mason was able to get together a troop of men who volunteered to make their way through the war zone east of the Cascades and bring home our chief executive . . . obviously the right man to direct the extermination of the redskins.

There was one problem.

The troops had no guns.

So, in a forced march, they descended upon Fort Vancouver, but by that time, General Wool had reached the conclusion that Stevens'

objective was the extermination of the Indians. So when the volunteers arrived at Fort Vancouver and asked for guns, they were told by
the regular army people something like, "that's a pretty dangerous
mission. Somebody could get hurt. One of you guys might shoot
himself in the foot . . . and besides, General Wool has declared
eastern Washington off limits to white people."

So they didn't get any guns . . .

And gratefully abandoned the mission.

Somebody had to make the trip, though, and it devolved on W. H.
(Bill) Pearson, who had been the governor's expressman on the
railroad survey and still was in the employ of the federal government.

On October 29, the day after the White River massacre, he leapt from
his exhausted horse and stumbled into the light of the campfire where
Governor Stevens was relaxing, a day's journey west of Fort Benton.

Pearson dropped his bombshell.

One historian was able to give us the direct quote: "A thousand blood-
crazy warriors are massed in the Walla Walla valley. They lurk behind
every hill, in every swale, to kill the Governor and wipe out his train.
Kam-i-ah-kan, Pu-pu-mox-mox, Young Chief, Five Crows, are in
command. They are spurred to savagery by the waving of fresh and
gory scalps torn from unarmed settlers and careless prospectors. The
Yakima passes are closed by thousands of warriors; the Walla Walla
country fairly crawls with them; the Columbia River trails, both lower
and middle, are blocked. The only open trail leads down the Missouri
River. Which way do we head from here?"

Presumably, after that, Pearson took a breath.

One of the dispatches in Pearson's pouch was from General Wool.

It explained in no uncertain terms that he (Wool) had declared all land
east of the Cascades off limits to white people. Six or seven thousand
Indians—nobody knew how many at that point—were ranging the
country on fast horses looking for an expeditious method of bloodying
their tomahawks . . .

Preferably with Stevens' scalp.

Wool was not about to give a bunch of hot-headed but naive villagers the opportunity of exposing themselves to death and burning. So there wasn't going to be any rescue party. And he had a suggestion or two. Inasmuch as Stevens was the firebrand who had lit the torch with his precipitous treaty-making, the best interests of all concerned would best be served if Stevens absented himself from the scenery for the next six months or so while the regular army brought things under control again.

Wool would have preferred having Stevens return by way of New York and Cape Horn, with possibly a long visit to Washington D. C. enroute. What he suggested was that Stevens try going down the Missouri and Mississippi Rivers, to New Orleans, the Isthmus of Panama, San Francisco . . . and then take a leisurely cruise back to Olympia.

Stevens was not amused.

The man and the muscle

Doc Maynard was not as much pro-Indian as he was anti-annihilation. In the development of his city he had from time to time ridden rough-shod over a number of people, but he usually did it in a way that you couldn't pin it on him. What usually happened was something like Denny's deprivation of the postmastership. One day he was post-master, and the next, this little plum had been snatched from his grasp just as he was about to take a nice bite. But, when Doc placed himself on the side of the Indians, he became a clear-cut pariah to his peers.

The most powerful of these peers, of course, was Governor Stevens. Stevens was a friend of the President of the United States. His was the power of the office of Governor . . . the superintendency of Indian Affairs.

And more than either of these, the power of public opinion which was ninety-nine and forty-four one hundredths percent with him.

Yet, above and beyond all of this was the personality of the individual involved. And, in order to gain further understanding of the doctor, it is essential to appreciate that of his principal opponent during the Indian Rebellion.

To begin with, Stevens was a born over-achiever, with a father who compounded this particular form of delinquency. Stevens' biographer makes note of the fact that Stevens tried harder than anybody else in school and was driven to even greater lengths by his father . . . to the point that the man who would become our first governor begged for relief from his schooling for a time.

Isaac's notion of relaxation was a job in a woolen mill, working ten or twelve hours a day, six days a week.

He was ten years old.

The biography continues with: "So Isaac went to work in the factory . . . rising long before daylight that he might eat a hurried breakfast, walk a mile to the factory, and begin the day's work at five o'clock in the morning, and toiling ten to twelve hours a day. The best weavers were women, it seems, and able to run two spindles apiece. Isaac determined to excel the most capable; and before he left the factory, succeeded in reaching the goal of his ambition, and managed four spindles unassisted."

Enroute home after a year at the factory, Stevens saw some hot gingerbread that cost a penny. But he didn't buy it. His puritannical upbringing required that he give his father all the money he had earned during the year. And what did his father say when Isaac asked for one penny out of that year's earnings?

"No!"

Father did one more small favor for Stevens. This one was physical rather than psychical. He drove the boy so hard in the haying fields that the lad got the rupture that plagued him for the rest of his life.

Stevens was constitutionally incapable of slowing down to a walk. There are regular references in his biography like, "in his zeal, he overworked himself, and was prostrate with severe illness in consequence." Another goes: "Mr. Stevens was never a sportsman or fisherman; indeed, he kept himself in work as never to have time for field sports." A schoolmate noted that Stevens was a small, insignificant boy . . . "But the impression of insignificance vanished as soon as one regarded his large head, earnest face, and firm, searching and fearless dark hazel eye."

He was a whiz at mathematics . . . A hell of an engineer . . . And the victim of continuing pain from an inguinal hernia.

The principal exterminator

When Governor Stevens returned to Olympia on January 19, 1856, there was an urgent message on his desk from Captain E. D. Keyes, commanding officer of the army headquarters for the Puget Sound District.

Keyes wrote: "I have heard directly and indirectly from Leschi, and the temporizing course I am pursuing, I feel certain, is the reason why he and the hostiles have ceased their depredations . . . *I deem it necessary to record my opinion that a forward movement at this time would not hasten the termination of the war, but might and probably would, induce the hostiles to recommence their depredations . . .* " (Italics mine.)

A day or so after Stevens arrived, the *Olympia Pioneer and Democrat* reported, "All was joy and gladness. The cannon was charged to the muzzle and our citizens seemed to look upon him as their deliverer—their hope."

I'll say the cannon was charged to the muzzle.

They gave him a thirty-eight gun salute.

Seventeen over what the President gets!

On January 19, the governor spoke to a joint session of the legislature in which the fellas were hanging from the rafters.

He said: "The war will be prosecuted until the last hostile Indian is exterminated . . . I am opposed to treaties; I shall oppose any treaty with these hostile bands. I will protest against any and all treaties made with them.

"Nothing but death is mete punishment for their perfidy!

"Their lives shall pay the forfeit!"

I don't know whether they fired off another thirty-eight gun salute, but

Stevens was able to gather from the thunderous applause that he had hit the nail of public opinion on the head.

Doc Maynard would quote Chief Seattle in writing to the governor later as saying that the whites were unable to determine through the sights of their guns in the woods which Indians were hostile and which ones were friendly. At that point, the number of friendly Indians killed had equalled the number of hostiles who had met their demise.

Governor Stevens carried his great message of extermination to the residents of Seattle on January 25, adding, "The town of Seattle is in as much danger of an Indian attack as are the cities of San Francisco or New York."

The next day, Seattle was under attack.

The Battle of Seattle—Part I

The "Battle of Seattle," which occurred on January 26, 1856, always has been billed in our history books as the turning point in the so called Indian War in western Washington. And the most-often quoted authority on the battle has been an account written by then Rear Admiral Thomas S. Phelps in 1881.

According to Phelps, 2,000 Indians attacked the town.

Opposing the hostile horde were ninety-six U. S. sailors plus eighteen marines and five officers . . . 119 men from the sloop-of-war *Decatur*. They subsequently were joined by seven civilians, four of them from G. A. Meigs' mill at Port Madison . . .

North of the blockhouse was a deep and difficult ravine at about Columbia Street. The main access to town was a well-beaten trail that ran up Yesler Way and continued on out to Lake Washington, which was where most of the hostile Indians from eastern Washington were supposed to be coming from.

After the attack, a breastworks consisting of timbers five feet high and eighteen inches apart—filled in between with dirt, and a blockhouse at Occidental Avenue and South Main Street would be built. But neither the breastworks nor the south blockhouse—presently occupied by the

Pioneer Square Branch of the Seattle First National Bank—was there at the time of the attack.

Oh, yes, I forgot.

According to Phelps, there were fifty "volunteers" from among the residents of Seattle and a few other places . . .

Unfortunately there were two doors in the blockhouse . . .

A front door . . . and a back door.

And only one sergeant-at-arms.

With his loaded carbine, he could drive the volunteers out one door to join the battle, but they just circled the fort and came in the other . . . and he finally gave up. At least, that's the way Phelps tells it. Our history books say: that was a "damned lie!"

After the smoke of battle cleared at the end of the day, there were two casualties. One was a young boy who poked his head out of the door of the blockhouse when he should have kept it in and the other was a soldier who got up to get a drink of water at the south end of town.

No, there were three casualties.

Before the attack of the Indians a sailor from the *Decatur* got drunk and tried to rape a young lady. Her thirteen-year-old brother shot the intruder in the head with a small fowling piece and killed him.

Maybe, you would have to say four casualties.

Years later Dexter Horton, Seattle's first banker, was warming his behind at a stump being burned for clearing land when one of the old shells from the *Decatur* went off . . . with the result that for some time thereafter Mr. Horton worked the front counter of the bank standing up and ate his meals on the mantle-piece at home.

This absence of casualties with 2,000 savage Indians attacking 126 stout hearted men was clear evidence that The Lord was watching over us. He was especially helpful at noon on the day of the attack. Phelps could see that about a thousand Indians were about to descend on him and "strike for the annihilation of my division."

His "division" consisted of himself and fourteen men.

Phelps continues with: "Quickly arranging my command to meet the tremendous odds to be launched against it, I had only time to impress in their minds with the certainty of our scalps ornamenting an Indian wigwam in the event of any weakness on our part in the assaults to be made . . ."

And it was here in the heart of the battle that Phelps recorded the great quote of the war.

The fourteen men said in unison: "Never fear for us, sir; we will stand by you or die in our tracks."

In the midst of battle . . .

Fourteen men, as one, came up with the greatest quote in Seattle military history.

At least, Phelps put quotation marks around it.

Now picture this. A thousand armed and angry Indians came within ten feet of Phelps and his fourteen men . . . The Indians were firing as rapidly as they could load their guns.

Phelps writes: "At this moment the fate of Seattle hung by a thread. With two bounds, three at the most, the third division of fourteen men would have gone down like grass before a mower's scythe, and in a few moments the battle would have been won, the people given up to indiscriminate slaughter, and the village in flames; but failing to make those bounds, the town remained in our possession, and the Indian cause was forever lost."

Man, talk about God being on our side . . .

None of the men was even scratched!

Well, that did it for the Indians. When they saw that God had stuck out his invisible shield like that and was on our side they slunk off into the underbrush and never came back.

Battle of Seattle—Part II

A good many of the more naive residents of Seattle slept in the blockhouse for most of 1856, but Seattle merchant, J. R. Williamson was not among them. Williamson was the guy with the spy in the Indian camp who had alerted the military officials on the night before the attack that this time the thing was for real—Governor Stevens to the contrary and notwithstanding.

Williamson also was privy to the fact that this was the first and would be the last attack on the town by the Indians. He had his own peculiar intelligence system and one which he had found to be entirely reliable. And while it hasn't as yet made any of our history books, it is to be found in a letter which Dr. Maynard wrote to Governor Stevens, contributing to Stevens' education on the subject.

Maynard may have been at Port Madison, but he was completely apprized of anything and everything that happened in his town. And what he wrote to the governor was that Captain Lander had been tipped off that the few remaining hostile Indians were leaving town to join with the hostile Indians on the east side of the mountains. Inasmuch as it was Williamson who had tipped off the folks about the original attack, it probably was Williamson who tipped them off that the last detachment of hostiles was headed east.

The doctor writes: "The Duwamish Indians being suspected of visiting the enemy rather often, and not altogether to our advantage, a company of the volunteers under Capt. Lander went up to an advantageous point enroute and watched their movements. Sometime towards morning three canoes with upwards of thirty Indians in them arrived, many with guns. On their drawing near, the volunteers fired upon them, killing two and supposed to have killed more . . . They took one canoe from them which had on board a quantity of provisions . . . which it is supposed they were carrying to the enemy, all of which, together with the canoe, was destroyed . . ."

It was not without irony the doctor wrote: "The history of this case will convey somewhat of the feelings and disposition of these Duwamish Indians. I believe they will bear close watching and careful management for a while, especially their leaders, Tecumseh, William and Curley."

Some of Governor Stevens' best friends were Indians . . .

Chiefs like Tecumseh, William and Curley.

The fun part of all of this is the role played by Williamson.

The day before, he had sold to the Indians the arms and supplies which Lander confiscated the next day. In other words, he cheerfully had been trading with the enemy.

No wonder Seattle became the major city.

No wonder Williamson ended up owning Ballard.

Battle of Seattle—Part III

The question of how many Indians participated in the attack on Seattle has steadily been revised downward with the passage of the years. In 1881, Phelps' estimate of 2,000 sounded pretty good to the people of Seattle because—nearly thirty years after the fact—we had been unable to collect all of our war reparations from Congress. A dozen or more years later, when the money either was collected or given up as hopeless by the second generation of the creditors, Phelps, himself, dropped the figure to 1,000.

In the 1920's, it had dropped to 300.

The most recent estimate I've seen was thirty.

Now, if there's one thing you can be sure of, it's that the merchants of Seattle—not the Christers who were marching around and pointing their guns at things—had a pretty good yardstick of what was going on. The local Indians were not what you could call a very belligerent bunch. Charging them with participating in the attack was like suggesting that the family dog had joined a union and was marching against its family. Everybody, with the possible exception of Stevens, knew which Indians he could trust or not trust.

On the other side was Commander Gansevoort of the sloop-of-war *Decatur*.

After the attack, Gansevoort insisted that guards be posted all night. On the first night, volunteers were assigned the duty. Phelps writes: "At 9 P.M. these volunteers were sent to their stations, and at ten o'clock, when the officer went on his rounds, every soul of them had gone home to bed, leaving their guns behind to represent them."

Gansevoort played the military game by the book.

Years before when he was the executive officer of a Navy training ship, he had played the game by the book with a bunch of midshipmen who had been charged with mutiny. What he did was string two of them from the yardarm.

One of the two was the son of the Secretary of War. Gansevoort was able to beat the court martial. But he wasn't able to beat the "system."

His future advancement had passed . . . and he was handed the rock-bottom assignment of the whole Navy—a little mudhole called Seattle.

But he still played the game by the book.

He couldn't control the volunteers, but he could control the men in his command. So, in addition to working all day at hard labor, like clearing away stumps in front of Madam Damnable's, they had to stand guard duty at night.

Phelps, who also belongs in the eager beaver class, suspected that the men from the Decatur were not attending to that night duty as seriously as they should be. The real casualties of the Battle of Seattle were beginning to come in.

Not from enemy bullets . . .

But from head colds.

Head colds which they caught when they decided during the night to take a nap in the frost-bitten ditches on either side of the road. Phelps' spies suggested that these were not called "naps" in Navy parlance, but "passing out."

Phelps, got out of his warm hammock to check on what was happening on January 28, 1856—two days after the attack on Seattle.

He provides another significant word picture.

"The occasional barking of a dog alone disturbed the stillness of the night, which was passing quietly away, when, at two o'clock in the morning, the most unearthly yells that ever greeted mortal ears, accompanied by oaths in the highest order of blasphemy, arise from the hen-coop (Plummer's), which instantly brought me to the scene, feeling sure the savages had succeeded in eluding the sentries, and were at their deadly work of slaughtering my men, when, pushing open the door, spectacle presented beggars all attempts at description.

A whirligig of arms, legs, heads and bodies met my view. Ten out of the twelve occupants were 'roaring drunk,' and mingled in a promiscuous mass of revolving humanity, fighting, biting, kicking, shrieking, and cursing, rendering futile all unaided efforts on my part to untangle this human ball of raving maniacs . . ."

The military authorities squawked to the merchants for selling liquor to the sailors.

The merchants protested indignantly that what with the war and all these men were the only customers they had.

Two weeks later, though, more men reported to sick bay with severe head colds.

It was the bloody end for Captain Guert Gansevoort.

He declared the town his men were supposed to be guarding "off limits to military personnel."

The scarlet letter

Along about the time that Doc Maynard was moving a whole bunch of Indians to his personally-financed reservation at Fort Kitsap, Lieutenant William A. Slaughter reported from the field that Chief Patkanim and a bunch of his tough warriors "are dogging my foot-steps." Slaughter, who had been around for a while and knew Patkanim well, feared that this bunch of Indians was up to no good and asked Mason to haul in some of the Chief's relatives as hostages. The idea was to help Patkanim "keep the faith" and not get off on a killing spree.

Arthur Denny offered to lay his life on the line by going after Patkanim and bringing him in, but the authorities wouldn't hold still for it. Denny's argument was that Patkanim was the best Indian friend the whites had and why should we antagonize him. People who knew Patkanim from another picture were, at the very least, suspicious. History generally has concluded that Denny was right, that Slaughter had made an unaccountable mistake. On the other hand, Patkanim and his men were loose in an area that had been declared as a "war zone." Any Indians in that zone were supposed to be presumed hostiles.

And unknown Indians killed Slaughter.

At the same time, Doc Maynard, who was moving nonbelligerents to Fort Kitsap, wanted Patkanim and his wild bunch on the reservation about as much as he wanted a couple cases of cholera. But what are you going to do when all nonbelligerents were supposed to be on the west side of Puget Sound and out of harm's way?

The doctor was equal to the occasion.

Patkanim was a son of the profits . . .

And the thing to do was put him on the payroll.

So out of it all came one of the more remarkable documents in the military history of the Indian Rebellion . . . a letter to Acting Governor Mason attested to by Mike Simmons, Lieutenant A. D. Drake and the doctor. Dated November 4, this interesting missive has heretofore eluded historians:

"I learn slanderous reports are in circulation regarding my actions and tumtums. I therefore improve this opportunity to state facts as actually exist.

"First I will furnish 100 Good men Subject to Your order at the Inst. of Your Call, to fight, anywhere this side of the Cascade range, But I cannot at this time consent to go onto the other Side of the Mountain.

"Second, I will arrest any and all Such as I can find within my Jurisdiction who May appear as Enemies to the Bostons, and forthwith Bring the Same before you.

"In consideration of the above I require that You furnish adequate means to carry the Same into Effect—& Compensate us as the other Bostons are paid.

"I will see you in answer to your order without delay.

"To the Above I subscribe myself
"Respectfully yours to serve

"Patrick "X" (his mark) Canam"

That first proviso was pure Patkanim for you. He didn't want to get stuck waging war against those tough eastern Washington Indians.

(This may be where Arthur Denny got the notion of giving Patkanim two names. Actually, the copy of the letter in the state archives is not in Doc Maynard's handwriting. It's in that of a young navy lieutenant named A. D. Drake. Patkanim couldn't read anything in the letter but his own "X," and wouldn't have cared, anyway. Subsequent scholars have concluded that it was all one word. Otherwise we'd be referring to some of the other chiefs like "Leschi" as Les Chi, and "Kitsap" as Kit Sap . . .

"Sap" County, Washington.

I'm sure the people living in Kitsap County wouldn't sail for it.)

In those days, friendly Indians frequently were used as hunters, scouts and expressmen in the communications network. Patkanim would go for whichever side could pay him and his men more money.

So, he was wandering around loose in the war zone when Slaughter was killed. The Denny family figured he was maligned and helped erect a monument to him in the 1920's. The local newspaper obituary at the time he died sixty years earlier opined that it was just as well that he had gone to his great reward because "we never trusted him anyway."

But Doc Maynard was reasonably assured of knowing where he *wasn't* . . .

At Fort Kitsap.

Charge!

Governor Stevens launched his plan of annihilation with his accustomed zeal, vigor and energy by addressing the legislature and announcing that "I am ready to take the responsibility of raising them (an armed force independent of them (the U.S. Army) . . . Let not our hearts be discouraged, I have an abiding confidence in the future destiny of our Territory. Gloom must give way to sunlight. Let us never lose sight of the resources, capacities, and natural advantages of the Territory of Washington. Gather hearts. Do not now talk of leaving us in our hour of adversity, but stay till the shade of gloom is lifted, and await that destiny to be fulfilled. Let us all put hands together and rescue the Territory from its present difficulties, so we may all feel that we have done our whole duty in the present exigency."

The governor's son reported that "to this manly and clear-sighted appeal the legislature made haste to respond with alacrity and heartfelt sense of relief, and renewal of hope and courage, with which men in the extremity of danger ever turn to a natural leader, and, so far as lay in its power, gave him unlimited authority to take measures necessary to save the settlements from extinction."

Then came the Battle of Seattle.

Man, alive!

Those damn Indians shot back.

Two of our guys got *killed*.

We had cannons . . . and we had rifles . . . and we had pistols . . . and we peppered the hillside behind the town with enough cannon balls and bullets to "salt" a lead mine. There wasn't a leaf left in a tree and enough stuff was expended to keep explosions going during the land-clearing operations for a decade and nearly blow the behind off of the town's leading banker . . .

And we didn't hit a single Indian.

Our Leader had assured us the night before the attack that Seattle was as safe from an Indian attack as were the cities of New York and San Francisco. That night, the governor assured the assembled townfolk that with "ten good men, I can kill off every hostile Indian between nere and Snoqualmie pass."

Stevens was in the approximate position of a coach giving a pep talk to a team that trailed its opponents by ninety-one points at the half. If The Lord was trying to promote the extinction of the Red Race, he sure was exhibiting some mighty mysterious methods. Those guys were shooting *back*.

Then, General Wool sent in a bunch more federal troops under Lieutenant Colonel Silas Casey who, on January 31, informed the governor that he now had a sufficient number of troops to replace the volunteers and "occupy all those points now held by your men, (the volunteers) and which I consider in any way necessary for the protection of the country within the region of recent hostilities." Casey, who had mustered two volunteer companies into the service of the United States army, announced that he did not need any more of the governor's volunteers.

The fact is that after the Battle of Seattle, the Indians on the west side of the mountains were in a retreat that amounted almost to a rout. They were able to stage one final battle on March 10 at a place called Connell's Prairie, near Puyallup. But that was the end of it for the Indians in western Washington.

But, it wasn't the end for Stevens.

Acting under the authority granted him by the legislature, he issued a call to arms for eighteen companies, twenty captains, twenty First Lieutenants, eighteen Second Lieutenants, and 1,002 non-commissioned officers and privates for the territorial militia . . . a total force of 1,060 men. The response around Puget Sound was lukewarm to say the least. Ultimately, he was forced to recruit down as far south as northern California to fill his quotas. He finally was able to submit a bill to the federal government for a payroll of 133,259 man days . . . with a price tag of $1,019,090.20.

But that was a year or so later.

Before he negotiated his first Indian treaty, the governor wrote a letter to the Bureau of Indian Affairs in Washington, D. C., saying: "The great end to be looked to is the gradual civilization of the Indians, and their ultimate incorporation with the people of the territory. It is ob-viously necessary that a few reservations of good lands should be large enough to give each Indian a homestead and land sufficient to pasture their animals, of which land they should have exclusive occupation.

The location and extent of the reservations should be the peculiar wants and habits of the different tribes . . ."

"In conclusion, I would express the hope that the administration of Indian affairs in this new and interesting field may illustrate not so much the power as the beneficence and paternal care of the Government."

But now the governor had forgotten about the "great and good end" was the civilization of the Indians . . .

What he wanted was blood . . .

Redskins' blood.

And that's the frame of mind he was in when Chief Patkanim's letter floated to the top of the pile on his desk in Olympia. Here was a fighting man after his own heart! And, as his son was wont to say, he "threw himself into his work with even more than his accustomed zeal."

If the whites wouldn't kill the Indians, then he would have the Indians kill Indians.

There were 4,000 to 5,000 Indians lolling around on reservations like the one at Fort Kitsap. They weren't even being shot at. The least they could do was provide him with a bunch of Indian battalions. So he broached the subject to Chief Patkanim . . .

And Chief Patkanim said, "I'll tell you what. I'll make you a deal . . ."

The comical side of the Indian war

I suppose every war has its comical side and the way our history books have handled it, it was Chief Patkanim who did it for the one with which we presently are concerned. Lieutenant Phelps started it, but it's been generally quoted since. Phelps tells about Patkanim's appearance on one occasion upon his return to Seattle from Olympia "after being paid off." "He was arrayed in citizen's garb, including congress gaiters, white kid gloves and a white shirt with standing collar reaching halfway up his ears, and the whole was finished off with a flaming red necktie."

Paid off?

For what?

Patkanim was hired by the governor to kill hostile Indians. The deal was that the chief and his men would get eighty dollars a head for every chief he killed and twenty dollars a head for the average run-of-the-mill Indian. James Swan makes note of the fact that he accompanied Patkanim on the first expedition. "The chief brought the heads of his slain as trophies to Colonel Simmons, who did not participate personally in the fight, except by being *constructively* present, that is, in a tent nearby."

(Mike served as sort of a federal government meat inspector. It wasn't as good as being the Territorial Delegate to Congress which Mike had tried for and missed, but it was a living.)

The heads were taken to Seattle in a big bag and placed on board the sloop-of-war *Decatur* which then, with its crew of 156, sailed off into the sunset, depositing the heads on the governor's lawn where they were counted and payment made.

Patkanim soon objected to Mike Simmons' presence on the grounds that the chief was an artist and couldn't do his best work with a government inspector looking over his shoulder. Furthermore, there was no need to use a whole U. S. battleship to haul the heads. For a few extra bucks, he would take them to Olympia for the count, himself.

And that's the way it worked.

There are those of today who are somewhat skeptical that this kind of thing was done, but, preserved in our state's archives, is a sample receipt issued by the Washington Territorial Government to this Indian chief. And inasmuch as it is an integral part of our history and the character of Doctor Maynard, it needs to be bound between the pages of a book instead of moldering away in the archival vaults.

This is what Patkanim got for his work:

30 Printed Handkerchiefs
60 Yards Muslin
30 Yards Muslin Delaise
6 Covered Pans
6 Covered Pans
50 Yards Green Baize
50½ Yards Scarlet Baize
30 2½ Point Blankets
44¾ Yards Bed Ticking
2 Pounds Thread
36 Thimbles
4 Pairs Fine Cloth Pants
2 Pairs Fine Cloth Pants
12 Pairs Fine Cloth Pants
1 Pair Fine Cloth Pants
20 Pounds Crop Wire
89 Cotton Shirts
24 2½ Point Blankets
2 Pairs Large Hose

The aftermath of this is that on June 29, 1924, a beautiful monument to Patkanim was unveiled at the Tulalip Indian Reservation. One of our Eagle Scouts blew "Assembly, out of respect to the military character of the Chief," according to Edmond S. Meany in *Washington Historical Quarterly*. "Skookum George, Chairman of the day, then called on Father O'Donnell, of Marysville, who opened the program with a prayer. The American flag was then raised." This was followed by addresses by a number of Indians and by Arthur Denny's granddaughter, "Mrs. Florence Heliker, (who) gave a brief address referring to the fine old friendship between her grandfather and the great Chief in whose honor the meeting was assembled."

Without Mike Simmons on hand, Chief Patkanim reverted to his normal system of profiteering. What he did was cut off the heads of some of his slaves—worth only twenty bucks—and sent the heads in as those of chiefs—worth eighty bucks.

Which in time came under the scrutiny of the Territorial Auditor, who apparently brought the entire operation to a standstill with the charge that the territory was paying for too many chiefs . . . not enough Indians.

Target numero uno

Bancroft notes in his chapter, "Extermination of the Indians," that, "It was the unpopular side to defend the Indians during this war. There were (however) many among the officers and servants of the United States brave and manly enough to do this."

(They were the ones who made the difference in the Pacific Northwest as opposed to the exterminators of Nazi Germany eighty years later.)

In the Washington Territory, there were two of record, Doctor Maynard and John Swan, of Olympia. And neither man was under any illusions about the precariousness of his position. Except for some relatively casual comments about the fact that attempts were being made to murder him, the doctor passed the whole thing off in his letters to his commander-in-chief as a normal, run-of-the-mill business.

Doc Maynard had about 2,300 Indians in his charge. To give you an approximation of what he was up against, it is noted that the number of Indians he was caring for constituted a population twenty times that of any white settlement on the Sound. Indians were encamped all around him in a dense forest. His camp consistently was infiltrated by the enemy fifth columnists. And there was no way he could tell how many hostiles from eastern Washington surrounded the camp. At the time of the attack on Seattle, he and his wife were the only white people in this crowd . . .

Two in two thousand.

If the hostiles could have persuaded even a hundred to join with them on the attack on our town, it would have fallen.

He was target numero uno.

Here's how he handled it in his correspondence after the attack: "We have some hostiles in our camps—how many, I do not know. On

Tuesday the Fifth at about half past seven in the evening one of them was discovered crawling about my camp and trying to look in at the apertures . . . last night they were discovered again and an attack was expected."

His final commentary is illustrative: "These symptoms of trouble and danger I must acknowledge rather absorb all other matters. But with the apparent determination of the Indians to fight when they do come, I am in for one frolick at all events unless I learn their numbers are too small."

The doctor and the head-hunter

Immediately following the attack on Seattle, Governor Stevens launched a program of enlarging in the scope of Patkanim's activities by enlisting head-hunters from the tribes on Squaxon Island, Fox Island, and the Chehalis and Cowlitz Rivers. His theory was one of deadly simplicity. If he could get Indians killing other Indians—and getting killed themselves in the process—the total number of aborigines would be reduced.

The doctor's objective was the prevention of just that.

How he did it is as reflective of his character as anything in this book.

The correspondence on this one is a little bit one-sided because only the doctor's letters are on file. What the governor was up to has to be pieced together from other sources. But you must keep in mind that Stevens was lethal in direct confrontations. When he was in the army, he went up against his own Chief of Staff during the presidential campaign in which Franklin Pierce was elected. He came within an ace of getting James Douglas fired as Governor of British Columbia, and only a miracle avoided his precipitation of the United States and Great Britain in a shooting war over the controversy about which country owned San Juan Island. He took on the Secretary of War without getting himself fired on the question of the Northern Pacific Railroad. And, before he was through, General Wool was recalled. He gave Company "A" in Seattle a dishonorable discharge . . . and threw the Chief Justice of the Territorial Supreme Court in jail and got away with it.

Doc Maynard, on the other hand, was a different matter.

He never let Stevens get a clear shot at him.

It started when Stevens ordered the doctor to produce a troop of Chief Seattle's braves to join with Patkanim and Captain Lander in an attack on the hostiles at the confluence of the Snohomish and Snoqualmie Rivers.

Here's how the doctor handled that one. He wrote that he had recruited 103 braves who were ready, willing and able to march immediately, adding, however, "I believe the enemy are aware of the movement in sending out the Snoqualmies (Patkanim's men) but have no evidence of it to lay before you. I have the names of 103 men under my charge which list I will send you in by next express. Please advise."

"Please advise," that's the way the doctor whipped him. By the time of the next express, of course, Captain Lander had marched on the enemy at the confluence of the two rivers and had learned, as the doctor had predicted, that the enemy was not there.

The governor then apparently told the doctor he needed some volunteers to beat the underbrush east of Seattle to search out hostiles. And Maynard replied with an inquiry. "Chief Seattle and his band," he wrote, "have heard that volunteers in the militia are being paid to stand guard in the settlement of Seattle and they wonder if they, too, shouldn't be paid for standing guard at Fort Kitsap. Please advise."

The governor then apparently pointed out that Patkanim and his men were making a small fortune killing hostile Indians at eighty dollars a head for chiefs and twenty dollars a head for other hostiles. Doc Maynard immediately upped the ante. He wrote the governor, "I have posted a bounty of $100 for the scalps of the Indians around the camp who have been trying to murder me," adding, "Am I justifiable in offering a bounty for the scalps of the enemy under these circumstances. Please advise."

Meanwhile, the list of the 103 willing warriors never appeared to be produced. The governor sent Captain Lander to Fort Kitsap demanding it. This time, a list was forthcoming. In it were the names of the Indians, but the bottom line of the resolution read: "We will fight whenever we have the consent of our Indian agent, the aforesaid D. S. Maynard."

Stevens blew his cork.

He demanded that the doctor produce the warriors. Doc blandly replied, "Some of my Indians have expressed impatience and are anxious to engage themselves in scouring the woods east of Seattle, but I do not feel safe in guaranteeing their fidelity. I do not wish to be understood as trusting these volunteers, yet I would be glad of further evidence of a fixed determination to render themselves profitable on such an undertaking. As soon as I am able to determine the number of volunteers at this point—I will report same to Captain Lander."

At this point, Stevens ordered the doctor to come to Olympia and laid down the law. The doctor carefully responded in writing after his return to Fort Kitsap.

"On my return from Olympia, I found them unwilling to risk themselves in the field exposed to the threat of the whites about Seattle. I conferred with Captain Lander about the subject and he expressed doubt about their safety at present. Please advise."

The problem was that all Indians looked the same in the sights of the settlers' guns . . . and everybody concerned—including Stevens— knew that the settlers would welcome the opportunity of shooting an Indian, any Indian, in the back. The doctor was not about to expose Chief Seattle and his men to such a risk.

And that's when the governor played his ace.

I wonder why it never has appeared in a Seattle history book.

What he did was call upon the talents of his wife's sewing circle in Olympia. The story appears in Stevens' biography: "The ladies of Olympia, under the head of Mrs. Stevens, made blue caps with red facings, with which these red allies were equipped to distinguish them from their hostile kindred."

Doc Maynard trumped the governor's ace.

He wrote that Chief Seattle and his men were hot to trot under the

captainship of Lander, but added: "I submit to the governor their expressions and await instructions what course to pursue. I find, however, they are destitute of guns. They say they have been unfortunate in gambling (with the enemy infiltrators in camp) for some time back and have lost all their weapons . . .

"Please instruct me by return express."

Mrs. Stevens' sewing circle made baseball caps for eighty-two of Chief Patkanim's men . . . fifteen for Squaxon Island Indians . . . seventeen for Chehalis Indians . . . nine for Cowlitz Indians . . .

And none for Doc Maynard's Indians.

At that point, the governor threw in the sponge.

VII

"Having accomplished my purpose . . ."

Somewhere in the neighborhood of ninety-nine per cent of the Indian Rebellion in western Washington took place in King County. What with the county running from the summit of the Cascades to the Pacific Ocean, however, it wasn't hard for the folks to get in the fighting without stepping out of the boundary. At any rate, the last battle was fought on Connell's Prairie on the White River on March 10, and the doctor submitted his resignation as "Special Indian Agent" on March 28.

By that time, he had successfully thwarted Governor Stevens' enthusiastic efforts to exterminate the Indians. He had arranged for Secretary of State James Mason to go back to Washington, D. C. and obtain $300,000 to take care of those same Indians.

Our history books say that the doctor remained at Fort Kitsap for a year, when it actually was only four months. I guess the history books rely on the memory of Catherine Maynard to whom it *seemed* like a year. But it only was four months, and the doctor was a busy man indeed during those additional eight months . . .

Preparing for the peace.

At any rate, and for whatever reasons, the doctor's letter of resignation has lain moldering in the State Archives for 118 years now. And since it provides us with such a splendid example of how he behaved in that period of his life, it must be incorporated in our history if we are to know who we are.

The letter, written in Olympia, probably because the governor had refused to even talk to him, reads:

"Dear Sir: Not having had an opportunity and failing to make report (as I designed), to Lieut. Col. Crosby at Seattle, I therefore report to your honor at this place. There has been no material change among the Indians under my charge since my last report. Col. Crosby is evidently deeply engaged in so regulating the troops at Seattle as to render them useful that he has found little time to assaying matters of our Indians, or rather the troublesome whites. I understand he has called at my camp since I left. Of which he will undoubtedly report. I am requested by Chiefs Seattle and Now-Ohisy to report to you the conduct and disposition of, Stuttering George, Enoc-O-Lin and One-Eyed Tom, which I do in their own words, to wit:

"They are bad men and evil disposed toward the whites, have threatened to kill me (Ed. note, Maynard) and twice drawn their knives to do it but were stopped by Chill-Whale-Ton, are spending a part of their time with the Duwamish Indians who are urging them on to evil acts, are dangerous *Tamahnous workers* and are about to cause all them to sicken and die.

"They earnestly pray that these three be taken from among them and either closely confined or put to death. I believe this matter should be noticed and suggest that it may be attended to as soon as may be after the report of Col. Crosby upon the subject.

"To further acquaint yourself with the matters, I refer you to Col. Simmons and L. M. Collins.

"My Asst. at Fort Kitsap having ingraciated [sic] himself meritoriously among those under my charge together with the assurance of having effected the object of my appointment *(at all events the object I had in accepting it)* [Italics mine] together with the impairment of the health of my wife appear in justification while I ask at this time to be discharged from further duties and responsibilities under my appointment as Spl. Ind. Agt. [sic] and ask that Mr. Haley, my Asst. be appointed in my place.

"I await your decision upon this matter and most cheerfully I continue to submit myself.

Respectfully yours to serve
D. S. Maynard, Spl. Ind. Agt.
Seattle Division, W. T."

In matter of Chief Curley

The doctor's reference to the hostile Duwamish Indians needs some background information to be understood. There was almost as much antagonism between the members of the Duwamish tribe and Chief Seattle as between Chief Seattle and Chief Patkanim . . . even though Chief Seattle gets listed as the principal chief of the Duwamishes. It dates back to pre-Maynard days when Chief Seattle was chief of the Suquamish Indians. the fishing wasn't much over at Port Madison. And the Suquamish Indians liked to come to Elliott Bay and fish the mouth of the Duwamish. It was for this purpose the Suquamish Indians had a fishing camp at Maynard's Point.

The Duwamish Indians, under their chief, Curley, had their main camp at about where Renton is located today. Under the cover of darkness, it was their wont to swoop down on the Suquamishes, kill the men and take the women and children as slaves.

One night Chief Seattle, who owed most of his success to the grapevine he maintained, heard there was going to be a raid and had his men fell a tree across a bend in the Black River, which fed into the Duwamish. The first canoes of the raiding party hit the log and dumped their occupants into the water. Chief Seattle and his men, who were lying in ambush, jumped into the river and killed the raiders. The following canoeists beat a strategic retreat and were forced to submit to the rule of Seattle as their new chief.

Chief Curley wasn't even invited to be a speaker at the Point Elliott Treaty. His resentment, already smoldering, grew as he watched Doc Maynard unobtrusively appropriate what once had been his domain for the city of Seattle. The resentment flared into active resistance when the doctor tried to force him to live with Chief Seattle at Port Madison. The doctor, who was sensitive to the situation, provided the

Duwamish Indians with an eight-acre tract on Bainbridge Island, across the port from the main band of reservation Indians.

Most of the Duwamishes went peaceably to the new location.

But not Chief Curley.

In those days, Indian chiefs attached themselves to the white man they figured could do them the most good. Chief Seattle lucked out in making himself Doc Maynard's "dog robber." Patkanim attached himself to Arthur Denny. And Chief Curley performed the same service for Henry Yesler.

In other words, politics worked the same in those days as it does today.

Being under the aegis of Yesler, Curley was not required to place himself at Fort Kitsap. So he was loose in Seattle at the time the hostiles arrived from eastern Washington. He counselled them on the attack of the town, specifying that Henry Yesler's life was to be spared when the other townsfolk were killed. Curley made himself useful to the hostiles by supplying them with guns and ammunition and information about what strategy the whites had in mind.

When he placed the Indians at Fort Kitsap, the doctor had in mind protecting them from extermination. But when it came to Curley, the doctor sought to protect the whites. He wanted no part of Curley anywhere in the neighborhood.

The doctor, who didn't want Indians to get a foothold anywhere near his town, intervened and forced Curley and the remaining members of his tribe to move to Bainbridge Island.

In the summer of 1856, the whole thing came out in the open when Commander Samuel Swarthout of the *U. S. S. Massachusetts* and newly assigned to duty on Puget Sound, listened to Henry's side of the story and dispatched a letter to Governor Stevens. It's a letter which provides us with an insight into the rebellion on the part of some of the whites to the doctor's arbitrary rule.

It dates back, of course, to the fact that Henry always was in financial trouble . . . and was in even worse trouble after the doctor had removed the cheap help from the mill at the end of 1855.

Swarthout's letter, written on August 31, 1856, reads like this:

"A short time ago "Curley" and his tribe of Indians, were removed (agreeably to their wishes and with your approbation) from the "Seattle" reservation to a Reservation contiguous to "Alki Point" and nearly opposite this town, where they are living happy and contented, molesting no one and interfering with nobody; perfect harmony prevails among themselves and between them and the white inhabitants of this vicinity, and yet, I am informed, there are some evil disposed persons exerting all their influence to disturb the tranquil state of affairs by having these "Indians" removed again; the most prominent actor among these mischief makers is an individual named "Maynard" for whose character the most respectable people of this town entertain no respect. I am constrained to place reliance upon the report alluded to because I know that Captain Hewitt, who was appointed a Sub-Agent over "Curley's" tribe, by Col. Page, with your acquience [sic], has been lately removed by Col. Simmons, through the interference of this man "Maynard." I will submit to you, Sir, that if an effort is made to remove these "Indians" against their wishes, they will resist and it can be accomplished only by coersion [sic], in which case I will decline rendering any assistance toward so unjust a proceeding. I have, however, an abiding confidence in your sense of equity which, I flatter myself, will prevail over the influence of these designing men."

The Swarthout letter, instigated by Henry Yesler, was an attempt at rebellion on the part of the folks who chaffed some at Doc Maynard's arbitrary rule of the town.

At this stage of the game, the governor was a little leery about the unexpected things that happened to him when he crossed the mild-mannered doctor . . . and he let the order stand.

Doc Maynard retained control of his town.

The "education" of Arthur Denny

The most venerable building on the University of Washington campus is called "Denny Hall" in tribute to the fact that Arthur Denny donated the piece of prime land so Seattle could get the first university in the territory—and the thirty thousand bucks it cost to build it.

This generally is accepted as the most important single contribution that Arthur made to the town. In understanding it, you also must understand that he was the world's most notorious tightwad. That's what shocked the folks out of their socks. Further consideration must be given to the fact that his principal asset was keeping his ass set on downtown property.

What Denny gave was eight-and-a third acres of land where the Metropolitan Tract containing the Olympic Hotel, IBM Building, Stimson, Cobb and Rainier Tower are located today. How he happened to give it generally has been attributed in the Denny-dominated history books to his deep spirit of altruism.

But how it came about is quite another story.

Providing the town with an institution of higher learning was part of the doctor's grand plan for the city . . . and it was with this in mind that he set aside a thirty-acre tract of land at the top of a hill overlooking Elliott Bay for that purpose. This was a big deal for the Reverend Mr. Benjamin A. Close who, as you will recall, performed the ceremony uniting the doctor and Catherine in marriage. Close was new to the Methodist-Episcopal Conference, and it was a great feather in his cap to report at his first conference—as a new minister—that this generous gift had been made.

The Methodists were hot for this kind of thing at the time. They had a university at Salem . . . sold lots around it . . .

And made lots of money.

Normally, the doctor required that some kind of a building be constructed within three months on any land he sold or gave away. But because of his friendship with Mr. Close, he gave the church three years to do something—anything—with the property that would indicate it would be used for purposes of higher education.

Denny, being the leading layman of the church in Seattle, was made chairman of the board of trustees and instructed to see that the conditions of the conditional sale were fulfilled. Others on the board were Edmund Carr, Nelson Barnes, Philip Northeraft, R. H. Lansdale, George Hughbanks and William Morse.

Of course Denny was so busy trying to bring about Prohibition that he neglected to do anything about legally acquiring the property.

Now, under ordinary circumstances, the doctor would have let things go along until the church got around to taking advantage of his offer. But he was in big disrepute among his peers for thwarting their ambition to dispose of the Indian "problem" with bullets. But every time they went after the doctor, things boomeranged and somehow they found themselves kicking their own posterior extremities.

Catherine was different.

She didn't stay home and raise a brood of kids. She helped the doctor in his medical practice—which included treating paupers, Indians and even Negroes if they happened to be sick. She sank to a low ebb by accompanying the doctor to Fort Kitsap and helping him take care of the members of what officially had been determined as that "wretched race." (To understand the spirit of the times you have to keep in mind that the first session of the legislature had passed a law providing a fine of up to $500 against any minister who made so bold as to perform a marriage between any one hundred per cent white person and anybody who was more than twenty-five per cent any other color.)

But most significant of all was the matter of Catherine's premarital relationship with the doctor on the Oregon Trail. During the Indian rebellion, the Christers concocted the bright idea of entering into our history books that Catherine had planted the first dandelion in the Pacific Northwest. The other women planted sweetbriar, or roses, or pansies, or sweet William, or clover . . . but Catherine planted the dandelion.

The barbs they sank in her emotional hide were invisible, but they hurt just as much as any you could put in a blow gun.

And so it was that when the Maynards returned from Fort Kitsap Catherine was located by public opinion on the "other side of the railroad tracks" . . . twenty years before we even got a railroad.

Doc Maynard blew his cork.

And when he got mad, somebody got hurt.

His very first act upon his return was to notify the church that the terms of the conditional sale of the thirty acres had not been met and that he was cancelling the deal. No amount of pleading on the part of anybody would change his mind.

The deal was cancelled on April Fool's Day, 1856.

And the elders of the church would never let Denny live it down.

So it was that the Reverend Mr. Daniel H. Bagley came to Seattle five years later at the behest of Mr. Denny. Mr. Bagley had this great ambition to create a new university in the territory, but he had to have a bunch of land on which to put it. Knowing the background of the situation, Bagley leaned on "brother" Denny for the land. And it was with that in mind that the two men prowled Denny's donation claim for a suitable hunk of real estate. Denny tried to pawn off the side hill below the present site of the Pike Place Market.

But Bagley knew he had his parishioner on the spot and would sail for nothing but the best piece of view property on Arthur's donation claim. On April 16, 1861, Denny signed a quit claim deed to eight and one-third acres . . . land that was rounded out to 10 acres by Charlie Terry and Edward Lander—both of whom have halls named in their honor on the campus today.

Doc had his sweet revenge.

Today the University derives between four and five million dollars a year in leases on the property.

The post war real estate boom

While the eager beavers of the governor's extermination corps were out giving the Pacific Northwest a bad name by killing off berry-picking Indians and sending dried Indian scalps, ears, noses, and hands to friends who weren't able to be here and enjoy the fun, Doc Maynard set about the business of reconstruction.

On April 15, 1856, he sold Plummer and Chase seventeen town lots for an average of $130 apiece . . . a total of over $2,200. This was the highest price he had obtained for a single lot and nearly as much land as he had disposed of during the entire previous year. And later the same day, he nearly doubled that amount by selling Franklin Matthias, the housing contractor, two lots for $500.

The fifteenth was a big day for the doctor. By that time, it was becoming evident that it was unnecessary to dedicate the finest piece of property in town to a whorehouse. The men bent on whoring would happily take their business where this occupation was practiced—without regard to the view. And it was then that the doctor sold to Seymour Wetmore a piece of property next to the garbage dump that would in time become the basis of the town's red light district . . . which would arrive here along about the time we got the University.

On the seventeenth he sold W. D. Van Asselt and Jacob Maple a pair of lots real cheap, like for $100 and later an adjoining lot for another $100. These men already owned land in the Duwamish Valley, but they subsequently would bring to town the first furniture factory. On the eighteenth, he liberated $1,000 from J. R. Williamson. Williamson previously had made a small down payment on a couple of lots in the block where the Grand Central Arcade is today. Williamson had made a lot of money supplying both sides in the Indian Rebellion and paid the doctor $1,000 to get a warranty deed. David Maurer, who wasn't all that bright anyway but owed the doctor for keeping his head out of a noose after hanging an Indian, punked up $500 for the restaurant in the same block as Williamson . . . where Maurer already was operating the best restaurant in town.

On the twenty-ninth, the doctor collected $100 from Lewis Wyckoff, around whom has been based one of the favorite legends in our history.

The legend, of course, has been used to beat Doc Maynard's reputation to death on a post-mortem basis. The idea is to show how stupid the doctor was. He was trying to get a blacksmith shop going—just for no reason at all. There wasn't a horse within fifty miles of town. Along came Wyckoff, who was a blacksmith . . .

And the doctor gave him the land and the shop . . .

The whole works for twenty bucks.

What doesn't come into the legend was that the doctor had been advertising for a blacksmith for a year before he made the deal with Wyckoff . . . that he had to have a blacksmith shop if he wanted the town to grow. Henry Yesler's mill, for instance, was shut down as often as it was operating. He had to have parts made in Portland or San Francisco and remain closed down until the order could go south, the part made and returned . . . or send to Port Madison where G. A. Meigs had a blacksmith shop. In which instance Henry had to pay triple the going rate for the part.

In those days Seattle had four major rival towns—Olympia, Steilacoom, Port Madison and Alki. Port Madison had the blacksmith shop and because of it was outdistancing its rivals.

Wyckoff's foundry was to be the other metal industry that would start to make up Seattle's industrial district on Doc Maynard's claim. This, in turn, would make Seattle competitive with Port Madison as the Sound's other ship-building town.

So, he *needed* a Wyckoff.

At a time when the going rate for lots in any town on Puget Sound was between twenty-five and a hundred bucks, Wyckoff's first twenty bucks was the down payment. He made the next payment of $100 for the property on April 29.

That was the same day that Dan K. Howard, a Seabeck lumberman, was eased into a lot in the doctor's claim for a measly thirty dollars.

"Typical of the doctor giving away land!" the history books have said.

The truth is that Doc Maynard never disposed of his land just for the fun of making a sale. If he sold it cheap, he had a reason for selling it. And he had a good reason for selling a lot for thirty bucks to Daniel K. Howard of Seabeck. It isn't apparent on the warranty dead. And, unless it's linked up to the reason for the sale, it doesn't make sense.

Doc's reason for selling to Daniel K. Howard will shortly be made apparent.

In the meantime, in the month following his retirement as Special Indian Agent, the doctor sold $4,500 worth of real estate. If you discount the more or less forced sale to the Olympia consortium the previous year to finance Fort Kitsap, the sales in the month of April, 1856, constitute about half of all the income he had derived from real estate sales during the previous three years.

Postwar inflation had set into Seattle real estate six months before any of the other towns on Puget Sound had come to the realization that the war was over.

And, on May 1, he made one of the most significant sales in Seattle's financial history.

Dollars from Dexter Horton

Doc Maynard always was on the lookout for bright, hard-working young men in his embryo town.

One of the bright young men who impressed the doctor was Dexter Horton, who had an engaging personality and a capacity for work that had employers in Port Townsend and Port Gamble bidding for his services. In the spring of 1853, the twenty-eight-year-old Horton did a little work for William Bell at $2.50 a day. He was lured to Port Townsend with wages of ten dollars a day for a short-term job.

Then in September he fell into a bonanza.

Cyrus Walker, the big boss of Puget Mill, which was the local operation of the Pope & Talbot people, made Horton and his wife an offer that no sane couple could refuse. In those days Walker could hire a man to work an eleven-and-a-half-hour day for thirty dollars a month. He worked from six o'clock in the morning until six at night, with a half-hour off for lunch, six days a week. He could be sure of a roof over his head and good food.

The cook, on the other hand, arose at four o'clock in the morning to prepare breakfast for the mill hands and worked until eight o'clock at night.

What Walker did was hire Horton and the latter's wife, Hannah, as a team for the 60 men in the mill . . . with room and board thrown in.

Not for thirty bucks a month . . . or sixty bucks a month . . . or even a hundred and twenty bucks a month.

They got $130 a month!

When Dexter Horton went to work for Cyrus Walker, he was fifty dollars in debt to Thomas Mercer for financing his trip here. His clothing consisted of a pair of overalls, a hat and a pair of somebody else's cast-off boots. In the nine months they worked at Port Gamble, the pair paid off their debt, acquired suitable wardrobes and saved $1,100.

He was just the kind of a man we needed in Seattle. Henry Yesler offered the couple more money cooking for his crew of fourteen men along with shorter hours. The job required their services from one o'clock in the afternoon until midnight. So they went to work for Henry in June, 1855, and worked there until the Indian Rebellion shut down the mill five months later.

Then Horton went to work hunting Indians for Governor Stevens.

Five months later Doc Maynard talked Dexter Horton into going to work for himself. The doctor persuaded him there was need for another general store in town and sold him two lots on the northwest corner of First Avenue South and Washington Street. Horton acquired as a partner one David Phillips.

And on May 1, 1856, the doctor issued the two men a deed to the two lots for $100.

There was a small detail that had to be taken care of here. Three years earlier, on September 1, 1853, the doctor had sold the same land to one Miles Fowler. But Fowler hadn't constructed a building on the premises and the doctor repossessed the land.

The rest of the story is one you can find in any history book on Seattle. Horton & Phillips became an important general store. The two men warranted the trust of the people in town . . . started holding gold dust, etc., in the bottom of a coffee barrel in individual sacks.

Fourteen years later Horton opened the first private bank in Washington Territory at this location. In time his establishment acquired the name that it has today . . .

The Seattle First National Bank . . .

And the site?

It presently is occupied by a branch of the Seattle Trust & Savings Bank, which has become one of the most imaginative loan institutions in betting its bucks on the rebirth of Seattle's birthplace in Pioneer Square.

(In fairness to Seattle First, I am compelled to note that it has a colorful Pioneer Square branch at the site of the old South Blockhouse at Occidental Avenue South and South Main Street.)

The passing of the bar

Doc Maynard quit his job as sub-Indian agent on March 31, 1856 . . . just three weeks after the last battle with the Indians on the west side of the Cascades. On May 1, he made that significant sale of real estate to Horton & Phillips.

Then he disappeared from public view for the next six months.

Meanwhile, the volunteer army marched around killing stray Indians wherever they could find them. These included a Hudson's Bay Company employee plowing a field for the company . . . and a party of thirty-one Indian women, children and old men picking berries on the banks of the White River.

During this period Governor Stevens threw a Territorial Supreme Court justice in jail twice and handed dishonorable discharges to the members of Company "A" in Seattle for insubordination.

Then, on October 30, Adjutant General James Tilton disbanded the Volunteers of Washington Territory, noting in the process that "the most cordial thanks of the commander-in-chief are given for the signal gallantry, resolute endurance and excellent discipline they have maintained during the six months' arduous, faithful and efficient service. The people of Washington Territory will know how to honor for all time the devoted and fearless men who have maintained the foothold of civilization upon the remote frontier."

They knew what to do all right.

They elected Stevens to Congress.

Why?

That six months had cost the federal government nearly a million dollars in scrip to pay for the wages, supplies and ammunition of the volunteer army. A century later, historians Charles M. Gates and Dorothy O. Johansen would comment that the army expenditures and circulation of scrip with which the volunteers were paid was "advantageous to farmers and merchants alike . . . This was not an insignificant sum in a frontier economy."

The doctor was among those who derived the greatest benefit. Downtown Seattle had been cleared of stumps, at a cost of $175 an acre. At federal expense the blocks had been surveyed, the streets laid out, and ditched . . . a leveling process that had enhanced his real estate sales in April and May. Of the fifty buildings in town, forty-five were located on his town plat.

But the doctor was off on another tangent at the time.

The doctor could look with pride on his accomplishments to that date. In the first place, Alki had gone out of business at the time and young Charlie Terry was evidencing great interest in becoming a part of Seattle, an interest which the doctor looked upon with great favor. Charlie was the liveliest young man on Elliott Bay. He already had bought a sizeable chunk of land from Carson Boren and saw eye to eye with the doctor on what was needed for the construction of a city.

Doc Maynard was nearing retirement age and, as the biggest land-owner on Elliott Bay, looked to the future for a comfortable living in real estate sales. However, there was a missing ingredient in town. His own lawyer, George McConaha, had drowned in a canoeing accident off Vashon Island two years earlier and the town was without a member of the legal profession.

So, while the rest of the male population was marching around the territory and quarreling among themselves, the doctor applied himself to the studies necessary for admission to the bar in Washington Territory. And, at the October session of the District Circuit Court in Madam Damnable's establishment, his efforts bore fruit. The court record reads:

"Elwood Evans, Henry R. Crosbie, and William H. Wallace testified that having examined the qualifications of David S. Maynard for his qualifications for admission to the bar as an attorney and counsellor, and having reported favorably, Maynard was, by order of the court (Judge Chenoweth) admitted to practice as an attorney-at-law and solicitor in chancery in all courts of the Territory."

Elwood Evans, who originally had served as secretary to the governor, got a choice lot in the heart of the central business district in Seattle for a mere fifty bucks out of the deal.

Doc believed in making his land work for him.

Half a loaf is better than one

I have mentioned on more than one occasion that Arthur Denny's principal objective in life—aside from making money—was the creation of a "dry" town. He introduced Prohibitory laws in the legislature in 1854 and 1855. On the second occasion, the rest of the territory voted "Wet," but King County voted "Dry," primarily because the big mill towns on the west side of the Sound were operated by New England prohibitionists like Walker and G. A. Meigs. (You will recall that at that time, King County extended from the summit of the Cascades to the Pacific Ocean.)

Doc Maynard had no intention of permitting his county to be dry, but the Indian Rebellion intervened in 1856 and he was too busy to do anything about it. And so it was that after he had passed the bar examination, he could turn his attention to the little matter of thwarting Denny again.

While the latter was killing Indians, Doc got busy.

He had to get rid of that dumb ban on the sale of alcoholic beverages which had been imposed in the county by the big Denny Prohibition Project.

The Doctor selected as his vehicle one Timothy D. Hinckley.

Mr. Hinckley arrived in the area in 1853 and took up a donation claim on Lake Washington. He was one of Doc Maynard's fellow

Democrats and the two men became friends at the regular meetings of St. John's Lodge of the Masons, which the doctor created. Hinckley found that farming wasn't that hot and after the Indian War got a job as engineer for George A. Meigs at Port Madison. The record doesn't show whether Hinckley was for or against booze . . . just that he wanted a good hefty license of $500 a year on the people who sold the stuff. He also bought a lot of property and subsequently would develop the Hinckley Block at Third and Columbia, where the Seattle Chamber of Commerce is today.

Having persuaded Hinckley that his investment in town lots would pay bigger dividends if Seattle was a wet rather than a dry town, and when the legislature convened in December, 1856, they went to work.

With the following results:

On January 9, 1857, Hinckley presented a petition as resident of King County, praying that the west half of King County be set off in a new county to be named "Madison." The county boundary was to commence in the main channel of Colvo's passage and go along the old boundary of King County to Case's inlet, thence westerly to the head of Hood's canal and then following the main channel of the canal to Admiralty Inlet; thence following the main ship channel of said inlet to its junction with Colvo's passage; thence following the main channel of said passage to the point of beginning.

The bill became law on January 16, 1857.

King County was cut in half.

It had taken exactly one week.

King County was "wet" again.

A face that only a father could love

You read the average description of the town of Seattle at the end of the Indian Rebellion and you get a pretty unprepossessing picture. For one thing, there were no streets north of Yesler Way, which was the northern boundary of Doc Maynard's claim. There were, however, seven ravines, one of them as deep as a seven-story building, lying

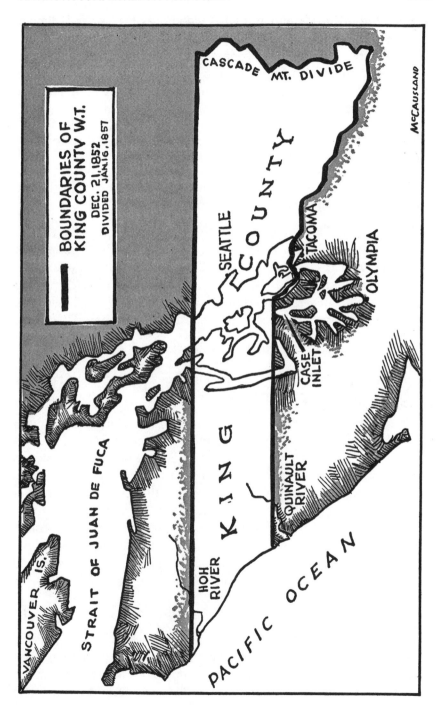

between the doctor's claim and what we know of today as Belltown, about a mile north . . . all along what we know of today as the downtown business district. Today, First through Fourth Avenues provide us with a gradual upward slope of some twelve blocks. But, if you looked under the streets, you'd find either fill or trestles. You also would find a labyrinth of drainage pipes.

If they ever got clogged up, downtown Seattle would slide into Elliott Bay.

It was twenty years before the city council took the bit in its teeth and ran streets through rather than around stumps.

In Doc Maynard's time, there were two ways of getting from Maynardtown to Belltown. You took a boat from the level land of Maynardtown across a crescent-shaped bay to Belltown, or you drove along what was called the "Beach Road." The Beach Road failed to function at high tide. Maynardtown was at sea level. Belltown was about 175 feet above the beach. So, you had to be prepared to climb.

What there was of Seattle was Maynardtown.

An eight-acre pimple at the northeast end of 1,500 acres of tideflats, but the doctor saw beyond the mud.

His vision encompassed trade with China . . . with Seattle as the major U. S. port for that trade . . . and in this connection it is of interest to note some comments by William Bunge who was employed by the State of Washington to do an economic study of the Puget Sound Region a century later. Bunge noted that shipping costs over oceans are one-tenth those of land, adding: "In terms of economic distance, Seattle is closer to Tokyo than it is to Chicago . . . within a few years these Oriental economies can mean to the West Coast what the European economies mean to the East Coast . . . China's annual economic growth is an astronomical twenty -three percent."

But Bunge has an even more interesting commentary to make on the population movement within the Puget Sound Region.

He points out that for about a century, the trend of migration has been from the rural to the metropolis. The general store which once served the hamlet now has moved to the middle sized communities. "The driving force is the change of transportation which shrinks the cost and time to cover the longer distances . . . The rural hamlet depended for life on the inconvenience of travel. Now the farmer's wife can reach downtown Seattle department stores easier than she could formerly hitch up the team and is obviously going to frequent the Seattle stores with their wider variety and special services. In a study of Marysville Washington (1960 before the advent of Interstate 5) it was found that the improvement of U. S. Highway 99 caused a loss of 83 percent of the higher functions . . . doctors, dentists, entertainment, etc . . ."

Bunge's study clarifies the cutting edge of the town that Doc Maynard invented when it is placed in juxtaposition with a similar analysis resulting from observations made by Bagley a century earlier.

Bagley points out that at the end of the conflict with the Indians there were thirty-nine ships of one kind or another functioning on Puget Sound. Seattle was located at the geographic center of the Sound. It had the best harbor, the best port facilities. It became the principal port of call for every vessel.

Writing in 1916, Bagley sums it up like this: "Port Blakely, Port Orchard and Port Madison all built large vessels in the early days. These points across the Sound were like suburbs of Seattle, for all of them did their shopping and marketing here. Like the street cars of today, which bundle the suburbanites off to the city markets every Saturday evening and return them to their homes in the outlying districts, loaded down with provisions for the week, the water craft of the pioneer days were the public service vehicles, which brought the shoppers to the Seattle market."

Bagley went on to say that in "1857 King was the banner county of Puget Sound."

He continued with: "Large mills were in operation at Seabeck, Port Gamble, Appletree Cove, Port Madison, Port Orchard, Alki and Seattle. In 1857, when Kitsap County was taken away from King, all but the latter two were taken away but their trade and friendly intercourse remained as before. This was particularly true of Port Madison and Port Orchard and later of Port Blakeley.

"The company store in each milling town supplied the standard foodstuffs and the clothing for the men but the women came to the

DOC MAYNARD, THE MAN WHO INVENTED SEATTLE

little town in King County for the finer articles of women's and children's apparel.

"Gradually men and families came to Seattle for better school facilities, social opportunities and business investments.

"From Seabeck came Capt. J. R. Williamson who put up a large mill across the bay at West Seattle, and Marshall and Blinn who made a large fortune at Seabeck invested largely in Seattle town lots and King County timber lands. Also, from there came Daniel K. Howard to make considerable investments.

"From Port Gamble came John Collins, John S. Condon, Stephen Hovey, Hiram Burnett, M. S. Drew and Cyrus Walker. All these made large investments in Seattle and King County, but small in comparison with those of Pope and Talbot, who were the Port Gamble Milling Company. Their holdings were large and today (1929) are almost beyond estimate in value, including many buildings scattered about Seattle. (In 1857 when all of this began, Cyrus Walker, for all practical purposes, *was* the Pope and Talbot company on Puget Sound.)

"From Port Madison came John Webster, Capt. J. W. Edwards, Capt. John Cosgrove, Andrew B. Young, P. J. Primorose, William A. Jennings and others although A. J. Meigs, the founder of Port Madison contributed little toward the early growth of Seattle and King County, nearly all the wages of its employees were spent here. Meigs brought with him down-east views regarding temperance and morality and made of Port Madison a 'closed town.' He established a large community hall and reading rooms, but the rough element of the logging camps and mills and deserting sailors preferred to come to Seattle to spend Saturday evenings and Sundays and holidays, of course."

Where they spent their time, of course, was at Madam Damnable's, Charlie Plummer's pool hall and what Bagley dismisses as the "usual assortment of saloons."

During the day, however, they found the widest variety of goods at Horton & Phillips, Plummer & Hinds, J. R. Williamson or Bettman Brothers, nee Charlie Terry's. There usually was one general store in the little hamlets on the Sound.

There were four sets of aggressive merchants in Seattle. The circuit court still functioned at Madam Damnable's . . . And real estate . . . Doc Maynard was the *only* real estate man in town. He also was the only doctor . . . the only lawyer.

The nucleus for the major city in the Pacific Northwest had been established. All it had to do was divide and grow.

The heir apparent

Doc Maynard lifted his nose from his lawbooks during the summer of 1856 to make the arrangements for Seattle's first spectacular wedding. What he did was set it up for Charlie Terry to be married by Chief Justice Lander in Patkanim's canoe . . . with Chief Seattle along in the canoe as Charlie's "best man." The event occurred in Fort Kitsap's front yard in the middle of Port Madison, with a couple thousand delighted Indians watching the show from shore.

It was the Doctor's way of telling the world at large and the Indians in particular that he had selected Charlie as his heir apparent in the construction of his town.

The event took place on July 13, 1856.

Charlie was married to Mary Jane Russell, daughter of King County's first sheriff, and those of you who have read *Sons of the Profits* will know that he was the only man in town besides Doc Maynard who had a sense of humor. It was at his house at Alki Point that David E. Blaine, Seattle's first minister-in-residence, gave his first sermon— even before taking up his residency here. Charlie took up a collection afterwards with the famous quote, "I don't know much about Methodism, but I sure know about this." Later, when Mary Jane heckled him for some chamber pots, he sent a wagon around to every store in town and had a whole wagon load dumped on the family front porch.

Charlie, who gets even more of a kiss-off than the doctor in Seattle's early history books, disenchanted the Dennys by stealing Alki Point from under their noses before the doctor arrived on the scene. He committed the further heresy of selling liquor in his store.

Charlie was an admirer and emulator of Doc Maynard—the sincerest form of flattery. Twenty-two years the doctor's junior, he didn't have the slightest idea of how to put a town together. When he first established his town, he named it New York after his native state. But when he saw the doctor's success in naming his town, Seattle, Charlie changed the name of his town to Alki.

When the doctor platted a town, Charlie platted a town. When the doctor got Henry Yesler to establish a sawmill in town, Charlie got William Renton to build a sawmill at Alki. When the doctor advertised his town in the *Olympia Columbian,* Charlie advertised in the *Olympia Columbian.*

The only basic difference between the two men was that while Doc Maynard couldn't care less about making a buck, Charlie had a deep interest in the pursuit of the dollar. The doctor, of course, had no way of knowing that he would outlive his pupil, who died at the age of thirty-seven in 1867 . . . but not before he had acquired a huge amount of land in town and served as the chairman of the first board of town trustees.

Doc Maynard had been on hand to watch Cleveland and Ohio City behave like the Gingham Dog and the Calico Cat, eating one another up . . . with the exception that in Ohio, real human blood was shed. Maynard did not believe there was room for two towns on Elliott Bay, but Charlie was stubborn, which the doctor had to admire. But it wasn't Maynard who persuaded Charlie to come to Seattle. It was the lack of protection from the north wind, which caused Renton to move his mill to Port Orchard a few months after he got it started. And it was a lack of a sufficient supply of running water.

But the doctor wooed Charlie from the beginning.

On June 6, 1855, for instance, he sold Charlie four lots in Block Eleven for $150. This was Charlie's first tentative investment in Seattle. The site later was occupied by Lou Graham's fancy whorehouse. Today, one of the lots is occupied by the unique park which United Parcel Service, which got its start at the spot, has given to the city of Seattle.

The following year, Charlie bought out Bettman, and then on July 11, 1857, the doctor and Charlie effected the big exchange which has made all of the history books . . . in a way that has been designed to make Doc Maynard look like the village idiot. What the doctor did was swap Charlie 260 acres in the vicinity of downtown Seattle for Charlie's donation claim of 320 acres at Alki Point.

Some cogent details have, naturally, been left out.

The property which the doctor swapped with Charlie was outside the platted part of town. It ran from Dearborn Street south to Holgate Street, and from the waterfront to Thirteenth Avenue South. If you take the time to look at a map, you quickly will learn that half of this property was under water at high tide . . . and the other half of it was on the side of Beacon Hill.

What Charlie bought the property for was a nice piece of fertile land along the Duwamish where he could establish an onion farm. And he had good reason. Onions were selling for $4.58 a pound at the time . . . three times what Charlie and Judge Lander paid per acre for their purchase of their acreage from Carson Boren.

So that was the swap between the two men.

One other detail has been left out.

The doctor sold Charlie 55 lots in the platted part of his claim for $3,300 . . .

Which surpassed the sale to the Olympia consortium by $800 . . . and became the biggest real estate transaction in any town on Puget Sound to that date.

Doc Maynard acquired a $5,000 mansion at Alki Point in the bargain. To that date, including the sale of the huge acreage in the unplatted part of town to Charlie, the doctor had disposed of 320 acres of land. Because he and Catherine had arrived earlier than anyone else, they had started with 640 acres. So they still owned 320 acres . . .

Which was what all of the other couples had started with in the first place.

There always has been a big hooran about the real estate exchanged between the doctor and Charlie Terry. The way it goes is that the doctor exchanged downtown property that was "worth millions" for worthless property at Alki Point. The doctor got $3,300 for his property—seven months after the Indian Rebellion was history and real estate values on the Sound were as close to zero as they ever got.

So what about the millions that Charlie realized on the deal?

Millions?

Not quite.

Charlie's estate was probated on July 29, 1875—when Seattle already had become the major town on the Sound.

Charlie's executors had sold the land for $18,736.

Shell-a-bration

There must have been other occasions, but Chief Seattle's ineptitude only appears on the record three times. The first, of course, was on Whidbey Island in the presence of every Indian on Puget Sound when he opened his big mouth and got himself in a pickle with Chief Patkanim. The second big one came when he made the "Great Speech" with his left hand on Stevens' head. Finally, there was the matter of the big social gathering on Puget Sound.

It was the fore-runner of the Seattle Seafair Celebration . . .

Only this one was to be the world's biggest clambake.

Chief Seattle and the members of his tribe undertook the responsibility of providing the clams.

Charlie, who was deep in the mosquito fleet business himself as captain of the steamer *Fairy*, which was engaged, among other things, in hauling coal barges down the Black and Duwamish Rivers and in delivering his crops of onions to market, worked out a transportation deal with Captain John Scranton.

This was a big splash.

Scranton was captain of the *Julia*, originally named *Julia Barclay* by one of her California owners. But she was the first steamer built on Puget Sound, and the pride of every person on the Sound. She was a sleek, fast, 145 foot sternwheeler and everybody on the Sound wanted a chance to ride her. Obtaining her services for the first big celebration on Puget Sound was the first of many similar coups that has made Seattle the major city.

Charlie Terry's brand new mansion on the onion farm near the present site of Georgetown, was the headquarters for the visiting dignitaries. There was to be a big ball in the Snoqualmie Hall that night and it was here that the ladies were to change their clothes . . .

And see Charlie's fancy new home.

What Charlie needed if he was to be sure that the ladies could be hauled up the Duwamish without getting stuck on a sandbar someplace was a high tide . . . and he was just the kind of a guy to think of that kind of thing. Chief Seattle, on the other hand, was the kind of a guy who would say to Doc Maynard, "yessir, boss. Anything you say, boss!" whether he intended to or could do what he promised or not. And in this instance the hopes of the chief were incompatible with the needs of Charlie Terry.

"In order to give zest to the entertainment," the advertisements read, "Dr. Maynard, hyas tyee of the Seattle tribe of Indians, will superintend the grand clambake. The clams and other shellfish will be cooked on heated stones in the ancient style of the aborigines of our territory."

The town put its best foot forward. Madam Damnable's normal operation may even have been suspended for the occasion. It, along with Charles Plummer's and Charlie Terry's mansions would be the first opportunity for most of the folks on the Sound to see real lath-and-plaster buildings . . . together with the new-fangled green blinds that you pulled right down in case the sun was shining, or if you didn't want any Indians peeking in the windows at night. Other novelties for a number of the folks were the glass-paned windows, polished floors . . . and a magnificent fireplace in every room.

Seattle had cornered the mansions on Puget Sound.

Two hundred people—everybody on Puget Sound who could borrow, beg or steal three bucks for the tickets and could get himself loaded on board the *Julia* came.

And Seattle set out to show them that this was the biggest, finest and most important town on the Sound.

To begin with, we had the biggest population. There were 123 grown men . . . twenty-five women . . . thirty-four children.

One-hundred-and-eighty-two white people.

Wow!

And every one of them with his best foot forward. There was Yesler & Denny's sawmill, kind of dinky alongside of some of the big mills on the Sound, but shined up fit to kill.

Outside of the huge mansions, center attractions were Horton & Phillips, Williamson & Greenfield, Plummer & Hinds and Charlie Terry's stores. The stores contained a myriad of household supplies, outfits for logging camps, carpenters' tools, agricultural instruments, ships' stores, flour and feed, coal, coal oil and tobacco . . .

And booze.

You couldn't buy booze at Steilacoom or Port Madison, or Port Orchard or Port Gamble or Port Ludlow—the other big towns on the Sound. But in Seattle you could get every potable beverage in the books.

L. C. Harmon had the hotel you could write home to mother about. David Maurer, Manuel Lopez and S. B. Simon had the restaurants. A whole bunch of people had saloons, but those didn't get mentioned in lists of enterprises in Seattle at the time. The only one which slid through the automatic censorship was Plummer's and that only made it because he was the first man in King County to punk up the $500 necessary for a liquor license.

Doc Maynard had gone out of the grocery business, but the shingle on his door informed the folks that they could get either legal or medical services. And he was immediately adjacent to the mail dock operated by postmaster Plummer.

At that point Doc Maynard had a corner on both the medical and legal services in town. Dr. Smith, lived way out at Salmon Bay. There was another man, Josiah Settle who advertised himself as a doctor, but the local historians commented that he was "more of a nurse than a doctor." In listing the other lawyer in town, Jasper W. Johnson, the commentary was, "he had little professional employment excepting conveyances and notarial work."

Thomas Mercer, L. V. Wyckoff and Hillory Butler were the teamsters who handled the merchandize from the docks, "the cordwood down the hill and the lumber about the village. Mercer and Wyckoff also had good farms that occupied their spare time." Wyckoff, of course, also had the blacksmith shop.

Mercer also had another sideline. He had invented a patent medicine that was liberally-laced with opium and advertised as curing everything from falling of the womb to cancer.

Charles H. Gorton and Harvey L. Pike were the housepainters . . . and Pike was an adept sign-painter. Henry Atkins, William H. Surber and William Cheney dominated the pile-driving business on the Sound and had their headquarters in Seattle. Besides Charlie Terry, there were Samuel D. Libby, H. H. Hyde, John S. Hill and his brother, David, in the steamboating business.

Having served his purpose in creating the new county, T. D. Hinckley had moved back to town. George Frye was Yesler's other partner and head sawyer in the mill. And then there was Nils Jacob Ohm, mentioned so prominently in *Sons of the Profits* as the chief sawdust dumper of the Yesler-Denny mill.

John Pike, Franklin Matthias, Thomas S. Russell, Harry Hitchcock and Solon B. Abbott were the carpenters and housebuilders . . . with Matthias in his cabinet shop next door to Plummer's store by far the biggest. M. D. Woodin and his son did all of the tannery business on the Sound. Jacob Wibbens ran Charlie Terry's bakery and cracker factory.

Others in the act were: L. B. Andrews, gunsmith; Hugh McAleer, plumber and tinsmith; William W. White, blacksmith; John Welch, tailor.

Plummer had a brick factory and commercial carriage house in addition to his other activities . . . and most of the 664 barrels of salmon that were shipped out of Puget Sound were processed in barrels that had been made in Seattle. Coal from Renton, while not big, produced several hundred tons a year. It was a good quality and came down the Duwamish in scows along with the prolific supply of gorgeous fruits and vegetables which were on display in the stores to impress the visiting folk.

All of the businesses were in the Central Business District, which was on Doc Maynard's claim in an area that had come to be known as "Maynardtown." Only half of Yesler's mill was on Doc Maynard's original claim. The other half was on Carson Boren's.

The Doctor was so busy with his other preparations he didn't pay attention to Chief Seattle's promise to produce the necessary shellfish. A computer analysis providently provided to me by Ron Westley of the State Department of Fisheries and Eugene Collias of the University of Washington's School of Oceanography reveals what the chief's problem was. Chief Seattle, who had been digging clams around Puget Sound for the previous fifty years should have known what the computer of today revealed. He was faced with what today are termed "climbing tides" beginning on July 18. On July 17, there was a .1-foot tide. The next day there was a 1.1-foot tide. And that was really his last chance to dig enough clams for 200 people.

Doc Maynard got madder at Chief Seattle over those damned clams than he had for any of the dumb things his whipping boy had done in the previous seven years . . .

They had this big clambake . . . And there were no clams.

Mine the miners

Two months and ten days after the doctor informally turned the reins of his town over to Charlie Terry, Dr. William F. Tolmie of the Hudson's Bay Company inserted the first of a series of small classified advertising notices in the *Olympia Pioneer and Democrat*. The ad warned all miners and prospectors to keep out of the Fraser River district unless they were prepared to "pay a fee of twenty-two shillings a month to the British Crown."

Considering the amount and quality of the "Come to Canada" advertising that British Columbia inserts in the local news media today, it was quite a modest approach. And the average tourist must be prepared to spend considerably more than twenty-two shillings a month to the British Crown . . . or is it the the B. C. Government?

And eighty percent of the American tourists who venture into the big Canadian Province north of Seattle do so through the Seattle Gateway.

It all started on December 28, 1858, through that small notice in the *Olympia Pioneer and Democrat . . .*

And we've collected our fair share of the cumshaw since . . .

Which proves it pays to advertise.

Dr. Tolmie was operating on instructions from James Douglas, on behalf of the British Crown. In December of 1857 Douglas wrote the British Foreign Office saying, "The auriferous character of the country is becoming more extensively developed, through the exertions of the native Indian tribes, who have tasted the sweets of goldfinding, and are devoting much of their time and attention to that pursuit. The reported wealth of the mines is causing much excitement among the population of the United States territories of Washington and Oregon, and I have no doubt that a great number of people from those territories will be attracted thither, with the return of fine weather this spring."

And a good thing the Bay Company had been making out of the goldfinding of the Indians. With the aborigines the company pegged the price of gold at the price of lead.

Governor Douglas had a neat plan for enriching the monopoly which he had served so long and so well. He would franchise the Pacific Mail Steamship Company to haul prospectors up the river and collect two bucks a head for Hudson's Bay in the process. But the Foreign Office, aware that Douglas was attempting to expand the operation of his company, informed him that he only had a license to deal with Indians . . . and on Vancouver Island. The British Government itself, would take care of collecting money from the prospectors. So the new province of British Columbia was created. Great Britain liked his approach to things so much that it offered him governorship of the new province . . . and he liked the idea so well that he accepted it.

In the meantime, the weekly ads continued.

In March, 1858, Charles Prosch, who had established the *Puget Sound Herald* in Steilacoom, informed his readers that miners on the Fraser were reaping twenty-five to fifty dollars a day in gold . . . and that squaws were hauling in ten to twelve dollars a day. The implication was that if squaws could do it, anybody could. Copies of the Herald were sent to San Francisco where at first they sold for a buck apiece . . . and then five bucks apiece . . . and then galley proofs sold for five bucks apiece.

On April 25, 1858, the *San Francisco Herald* picked up the cry, stating that the "Fraser River excitement" in the Atlantic states equalled that which had stimulated the "rush" to California nearly a decade earlier.

And the Fraser River goldrush was on.

By mid-May, steamers from California were landing hundreds of passengers in the Pacific Northwest. On May 20, the steamer *Panama* landed 500 prospectors in Bellingham Bay. A month later, 1,800 were landed at the same place within three days, and during the same period 1,000 were landed in Victoria. By July 1, Bellingham Bay was a town with eleven general stores, two butcher shops, three bakeries and two restaurants.

The population was considerably larger than Seattle's 182.

Bellingham Bay had 10,000 people.

Among them was Ezra Meeker of the Puyallup valley who had figured out a way of hauling cows there on a scow and selling milk at a dollar a quart. In his memoirs on the subject, Meeker leaves us with a priceless piece of Seattle's heritage. There were, of course, the usual camp followers attendant to a gold rush. Referring to the many boats in the bay, Meeker writes: "There were but a few women in this crowd, but ashore, quite too many, a large majority of whom (those on the ground will remember), were too much like their arch representative, 'Old Mother Damnable,' well and truly named. But I draw the veil."

Within the next six months, 100,000 prospectors "rushed" the Fraser . . . through Victoria . . . through Bellingham Bay . . . up the Columbia . . . over Naches Pass and over Snoqualmie Pass.

A lot of them starved to death.

The mills on Puget Sound closed as their crews joined the rush. Ships in the bays were abandoned by their crews. Soldiers at Fort Steilacoom deserted. The population of Seattle emptied out like water in an overturned bucket.

"Let's go!" Charlie Terry said.

Doc Maynard had been through a gold rush before and had failed to be stampeded. He pointed to a small notice that had been issued by a beleaguered Canadian government. Thousands of the prospectors were starving to death. The government listed the supplies that were needed for ten men for six months. The bill came to $1,800.

"Mine the miners, not the mines," Doc Maynard counselled.

The potential take for outfitting miners was $18,000,000.

All we had do was get our fair share.

The following year, Seattle businessmen lobbied through the

legislature a bill calling for the construction of a road from our town to Bellingham Bay. Charlie Terry, Dexter Horton, Charles Plummer and Joseph Williamson outfitted pack trains that went over Snoqualmie Pass to the diggings.

Within six months, the population on Bellingham Bay would drop from 10,000 to ten. But during the next ten years, 250,000 miners would produce about $50,000,000 in gold from what came to be known as the "Golden Caribou."

Thomas Prosch would write later that: "Seattle shared in the excitements, and her people received their full share of the financial benefits resulting therefrom, the place being locally prominent as an outfitting point."

The Fraser River was the first of Seattle's important gold rushes.

The second came in 1864, when the miners rushed to Boise, Idaho.

The following year there were reports of gold strikes on the upper Columbia and in the Coeur d'Alene mountains. In 1878, there was a minor rush to diggings on the Sultan River. A year later came news that gold had been found on the Skagit. By that time, Seattle merchants had developed a keen sense of the importance of gold rushes to our economy and subscribed a sum to finance the construction of a trail to Ruby Creek.

Part of that trail was so awful we gave the name Diablo Canyon to that section . . . and years later we would build Diablo Dam at that location. It may have been the "Devil" to travel or later build a dam on. But in 1880, four hundred miners outfitted themselves in our town. We thoughtfully kept track of how much they spent.

It came to $50,000.

Our merchants were impressed.

We were even more impressed when returning miners initiated one of Seattle's early real estate booms.

The final and most important gold rush came in 1898.

Writing about this one, J. Willis Sayre says: "It is virtually impossible to overestimate the value, to Seattle, of the sixth and last gold rush . . . Seattle, in common with the rest of the United States, had suffered severely from the hard times which began in 1893 and continued for several years.

"There was a saying, in 1895, that the location of every twenty-dollar gold piece in Seattle was known. Leading merchants carried their lunches with them to their stores to save money.

"Then the gold rush suddenly and literally began pouring millions of dollars into this city. Outfitting stores, specializing in the needs of gold seekers, centered the trade here. Working night and day, they struggled to keep up with their orders; the sidewalks were piled with goods awaiting shipment north. The town was jammed with incoming hosts and money was spent upon a scale never known here."

Wise old Doc Maynard said, "Mine the miners."

Now, let's see . . .

What was that about an Alaska pipeline?

The tale of Asemath Ann

There have been various versions of the tale of Asemath Ann in Seattle history, and finally an enterprising reporter for the *Chehalis Bee Nugget* tried a drastic new approach to the legend and published it on August 28, 1931.

What he did was get it from the mouth of the lady, herself.

The story is prefaced by the fact that on December 15, 1863, Dr. Maynard and Catherine opened Seattle's first hospital on First Avenue South between South Main and South Jackson Street. There is some disagreement among authorities on where the doctor and Catherine were living at the time. Some say that they were living in the hospital. Asemath Ann's story reveals they were living in a far more pretentious place. Knowing the doctor, I'm inclined to agree. When he was at Alki Point, which he was for a time, he lived in what would be the equivalent of a $50,000 mansion constructed at current pre-inflation prices. The doctor always succeeded in living high on the hog.

One of the employees in the doctor's hospital was eighteen-year-old Christopher Columbus Simmons, the Simmons' fifth child. Prior to his arrival in Seattle, Chris wooed and won the heart of Asemath Ann Kennedy, daughter of Franklin Kennedy, the first probate judge in Mason County.

What Chris and Asemath Ann wanted to do was get married, but both families frowned on the idea. Chris was banished to Seattle and Asemath Ann was trundled off to school in Steilacoom. Chris pined for his loved one and one night in the summer of 1864, Chris "borrowed" a rowboat from the doctor and headed for Steilacoom. Asemath Ann takes up the story from there:

"Chris stole me. Just think! I was only thirteen. He just carried me off, but I didn't make much fuss about going. And he got my brother-in-law and a brother of mine to go along to Seattle. They did most of the rowing. Chris and I were in the stern of the canoe. We rowed all night and all day to Seattle. Uncle and Aunt Maynard took us into their big new home. And gave us the wedding. Here's a picture of the house and the corner room upstairs there was Auntie's. That's the room we were married in. Rev. Daniel Bagley married us. It was the 23rd of August, 1864—almost 67 years ago. Quickly uncle took a slip of paper, wrote the number '18' on it. He made me take off my shoe and put the number in the heel of it. He says to me, 'you look so young he will likely ask you how old you are and you must say right off, 'I'm over 18.' "

Well, it worked.

They were married.

Asemath Ann continued with: "Father and mother were mad as a wet hen and so were Chris' folks, but they got over it."

So they were married in the upstairs corner room of the Maynard Mansion. One of two mansions in town at the time. The other belonged to Charles Plummer.

The money machine

Ten years ago, with information collected to that point, I wrote in *Sons of the Profits* that it was the story of how the fellas who built

Seattle made their money. Adding, "If they could have made more money by *not* building a city, then that is what they would have done."

Further research has revealed that Doc Maynard invented a money-making machine.

All they had to do was crank it.

Research on this book began with the Pioneer National Title Company records dating back to the time when the land was owned by the United States Government. I then found who got what donation claims . . . to whom they sold it . . . and what the people who bought it did with it. Subsequent research took me back even further than the U. S. Government ownership to when the land belonged to the Indians . . . and how Doc Maynard got the land, on which Seattle was built, into his hands. It was a relatively simple matter to look through the archives and find out how he used it to invent the city.

The whole thing was a game with Doc. He was like a kid with a new toy. According to actuarial statistics, he should have been long gone, and here he was with eighteen years of experience in city building in Cleveland and a shot at the greatest project of his life. He was Pygmalion to our Galatea. He was solely responsible for putting her together and breathing life into her.

His was the creative genius that made our city. He ran her, as Arthur Denny complained in his book as though he thought he "not only was monarch of all he surveyed, but what Boren and I surveyed as well."

Oh, what a Freudian slip that was!

Except for one major detail, when Denny screwed up our street system on his land and in defiance of the doctor, Maynard ruled the destiny of his town for the first seven years of her existence . . . and any competent behavioral psychologist will tell you that's long enough to bend the twig the way the tree will grow.

Denny fails to mention, for instance, that he didn't sell a single piece of property of any kind to anybody until after all of the events that have occurred so far in this book had taken place. Yet, thirty years later, when the people who could refute him were dead, he took credit for being father of Seattle.

And frankly, that kind of stuff ticks me off.

Twenty-five years after the doctor got here, the *Seattle Intelligencer*, (now the *Post Intelligencer*) put together Seattle's first directory of businesses. There were 208 of them—not counting somewhere between eighteen and fifty houses of prostitution which were thoughtfully omitted from the directory and had to be compiled from other sources.

Of the 208 businesses, *196* were in Maynardtown.

(Maynardtown's what today we call the Pioneer Square Historic District.)

These included every architect, attorney, bank, baker and confectioner, billiard parlor, blacksmith, boot and shoemaker, brewer, candy and nut store, chop house, drugstore, cigar manufacturer, Chinese laundry, butcher, commission merchant, civil engineer, dentist, restaurant, florist, whorehouse, fruit and vegetable market, gristmill, gunsmith, hotel, department store, jeweler, beer tavern, saloon, ladies wear store, marine architect and wholesale house.

Wholesale house.

That's the one that made Seattle important.

There were sixteen of them . . . five times as many as any other town on Puget Sound . . . even more wholesale houses than saloons . . . of which there were only thirteen.

But all of them were in Maynardtown.

Maynardtown was the heart of this city for the next fifty years.

The last hurrah

Doc Maynard died on March 13, 1873. Two days later, all of the shops in town were closed, and anybody who was anybody at all attended his funeral.

Presumably, that was the last hurrah for the man who invented Seattle. Fifteen years later, Arthur Denny wrote the first history of

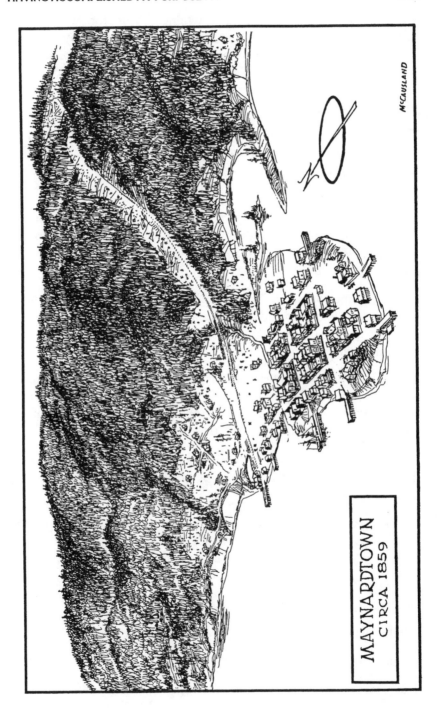

MAYNARDTOWN
CIRCA 1859

McCAUSLAND

Seattle. He began the process of writing the doctor out of Seattle history. Following Denny's book there was a larger volume edited by Frederick James Grant, who frankly conceded in the preface that he had relied almost entirely on Denny for his information about the city's beginnings. Ninety-nine percent of the city's history has stemmed from Grant's volume.

Then, in 1906, Thomas Prosch wrote a slim monograph on David and Catherine Maynard in which he generally followed the "Party Line," but with one or two significant observations like the following:

"He was a home buyer, a protectionist, a friend to his nearest neighbors. Stepping into a shop one day he told the keeper, whom he had been patronizing for years, that he would not see him there anymore. 'Why doctor, what's the matter?' inquired his astonished friend.

"We are going to have a shop in Maynardtown, and I always stand by my own side and help my own people,' the doctor replied. The shop he was giving up was on Yesler's land, about sixty feet from Maynardtown.

"It was always this way with him. He favored the United States above all other nations; Washington Territory above all other American commonwealths; Seattle above all other towns or cities; and his own nearest neighbors above all other peoples."

When Harborview Medical Center was dedicated in 1931, a bust of the doctor was placed in the lobby. (It subsequently has been moldering away in the library.)

In 1951, when Murray Morgan's *Skidroad* appeared, his research revealed a quote from the floor at the doctor's funeral, "Without him, Seattle will never be the same. Without him, Seattle might not have been."

Now nearly thirty years later, this volume.

Is it the last hurrah?

I doubt it.

The Doctor, of course, couldn't have cared less what posterity

thought of him. As far as he could tell at the time, there was nothing posterity ever had done for him. And he sure left the folks with plenty to think about—like "up your nose with a rubber hose" in his last public appearance. The doctor never minded astonishing the people of the town.

Let's face it, he enjoyed it.

Shortly before his death, an early-day shyster who made a practice of finding flaws in donation claims, discovered one in the doctor's. A question was raised over which of his wives was legally entitled to half of his donation claim. It obviously belonged to Catherine. She'd helped him develop it. And as long as the question remained with authorities in the territory, there was no problem. But when it got into the bureaucratic red tape in Washington, it became very serious indeed.

For $500 the shyster bought from Lydia whatever might be her rights to half of the Maynard donation claim. And, shortly before Maynard's death, she appeared on the scene . . .

Broke, naturally.

On the day of her arrival, Doc Maynard entered his favorite barber shop. (They were known as "shaving saloons" in those days.) "Dixon," he said, "I want you to fix me up in your best style." "What's up, doctor," the barber asked. "What are you going to do?" "I'm going to give the people here a sight they never had before and may never have again. I'm going to show them a man walking down the street with a wife on each arm." So Lydia lived with the doctor and Catherine while she was giving her depositions designed to deprive them of half their donation claim.

I can understand Lydia doing it . . .

But how in God's name did he talk Catherine into it?

And what a curve to pitch at the Sons of the Profits.

From the doctor's standpoint, he had accomplished his objective. Seattle was a vibrant, functioning city. But the Sons of the Profits had bought and paid for half of his donation claim. Would they have to pay for it again . . . At ten, maybe a hundred times the original price? As far as Doc Maynard was concerned, that was *their* problem. And, oh, yes. There was one final irony.

Madam Damnable was long gone . . . and the doctor and both wives were living in her mansion . . . on Maynard's Point . . . with a fabulous view of Mt. Rainier.

POSTSCRIPT

The Story Behind the Story

The first bound volume of any kind that deals with the history of Seattle was published by Arthur A. Denny in 1888. Entitled "Pioneer Days on Puget Sound," it came out fifteen years after David S. Maynard's death and was eighty-three pages long. It was obviously Denny's version of what happened.

Thanks entirely to Arthur Denny, who believed that anybody who took a drink was a "drunk," Doc Maynard's role in our history has been billed as that of the "town drunk." Whether or not he became the victim of what we now recognize as a disease called alcoholism in his later life is moot. He certainly was functioning with all of his faculties a month or so before his death. And it is completely evident that during the "Maynard Years," when the character of this city was formed, that disease was not at issue.

ACKNOWLEDGEMENTS, SOURCES, BIBLIOGRAPHY

The essence of this book lies in a labyrinth of hitherto untapped archival information. And particular thanks goes to the guides who provided me with conducted tours of the records.

The book is based on information provided by LEO BOYAJIAN of the Pioneer National Title Company. We traced ownership of the land from the original Donation Claims, found out who it was sold to and then determined what contribution these people made to the invention of Seattle. Most of the people who participated in the invention were left out of the early books, the first of which were not written until thirty-six years after the original stakes were driven . . . fifteen years after David S. Maynard's death.

The most astonishing piece of information revealed in this phase of research was that Arthur Denny, who always has been billed as the father of our city, didn't sell a single piece of land to anybody for the first six years . . . in other words, the period covered in this book.

I am totally indebted to NANCY PRYOR, TOM MAYER and KATHRYN HAMILTON of the Washington Room of the Washington State Library, who cheerfully unearthed archival information which I would not have believed possible. Tom uncovered the great gem of the book, which was the amount of money Doc Maynard got for the woodpile which financed the invention of Seattle. The question I put to Tom was, "How much did a cord of firewood sell for in San Francisco in 1851?" He went after the information with such aplomb that later somebody queried, "Did he ask, 'Let's see . . . was that alder, fir or cedar?' " Tom didn't ask that, but he did find out that firewood sold for forty dollars a cord in San Francisco at that time.

RUBY EL HULT provided me with in depth research in her unpublished manuscript, *Seattle: A Different Sort of Pioneering.*

I am particularly indebted to JACK and BARBARA HOLLOPETRE and my nephew, JACKIE HOLLOPETRE, who painstakingly unearthed the history of Cleveland, Ohio, for the period during which Doc Maynard functioned as physician and businessman there.

Further kudoes go to JIM McALPIN, Washington State Archivist, and to JIM MOORE who is in charge of the vast supply of archives stored at Western Washington University in Bellingham . . . to the MUSEUM OF HISTORY AND INDUSTRY of Seattle, which has some of Doc Maynard's actual surgical instruments . . . to DR. MARC SCHUCKIT of the Alcohol and Drug Abuse Program at the University of Washington whose advice has led to the conclusion that, historic legend to the contrary and notwithstanding, the disease of alcoholism played no role in the invention of Seattle.

I also wish to extend a vote of appreciation to LETA EDWARDS, director of community relations for Harborview Medical Center, for finding the bust of Doc Maynard where it had been kept from public view for fear that one of the Sons of the Profits might appropriate it for his own use.

To PAT ROBERTS, for work over and above the call of duty in keeping the proofs straight, and to BOB CRAM for the cartoons and jacket design, BOB McCAUSLAND, for the scenic illustrations and maps.

For seventy-two years the only extant picture of Doc Maynard has been a less-than-satisfactory rendition of him which appeared in Thomas Prosch's biography of the doctor in 1906. The sketches of the doctor which appear here and on the book jacket capture the spirit of the man at a glance. They were done by TED RAND, one of the Pacific Northwest's most talented artists. The Rand sketch was taken from a tintype of the doctor which Jim Hermanson of Port Townsend discovered in the files of the old Seaman's Hospital in Port Townsend, where the doctor practiced medicine occasionally in his later years.

I finally am indebted to MURRAY MORGAN who in 1951 captured the essence of Doc Maynard in his chapter in his book *Skidroad* entitled "Doc Maynard and the Indians, 1852-1873."

I am also indebted to BRUCE and RILEY GETTYS of Beaufort, South Carolina, for the interior description of Madam Damnable's handsome establishment. We visited the Gettys in the spring of 1978 and found their lovely home bore a striking resemblance to Seattle's first mansion. Through their kind permission, we took pictures of the interior and thus were able to provide the description which has been missing in all of our histories.

JIM HERMANSON of Port Townsend came up with a real find in the tintype of Dr. Maynard, from which the Ted Rand sketch on the cover of the jacket and the frontispiece were made.

Special thanks also go to newspaperman JACK LELAND, of Charleston, South Carolina, for the quote concerning the character of the people in that town and for directing us to the "Big Brick," Charleston's most famous House of Ill Repute, which functioned from 1819 to 1946 and proves that Seattle's was not the only fine establishment of its kind in the United States at the time.

Although I have not made as much use of their facilities in this book as I have in previous volumes, the Main Branch of the SEATTLE PUBLIC LIBRARY provided a comparison of the value of the dollar between 1852 and 1978 . . . and the UNIVERSITY OF WASHINGTON LIBRARY provided a copy of the letter about Dr. Maynard sent by Commander Swarthout to Governor Stevens.

Additional thanks to go MARY FLINTON of the Washington State Library who came across the story in the Lummi Indian magazine on the Point Elliott Treaty . . . and to ANNIE SWENSSON, who uncovered material on filling in of the tidelands.

SELECTED BIBLIOGRAPHY
BOOKS

(In this bibliography the presumption is made that people wishing to pursue the subjects further will have access to the normal published histories of Seattle, King County and the state of Washington. So they are not listed except in instances where direct quotes have been used.)

BAGLEY, CLARENCE B., *History of King County, History of Seattle;* BANCROFT, HUBERT HOWE, *History of Washington, Idaho and Montana, History of Oregon;* BEATON, WELFORD, *The City That Made Itself;* CANTWELL, ROBERT, *The Hidden Northwest;* COMAN, EDWIN T. Jr., and GIBBS, HELEN M., *Time, Tide and Timber;* CORNING, HOWARD M., *Dictionary of Oregon History;* COX, THOMAS R., *Mills and Markets, A History of the Pacific Coast Lumber Industry to 1900;* DENNY, ARTHUR A., *Pioneer Days on Puget Sound;* DENNY, EMILY INEZ, *Blazing the Way;* EVANS, ELWOOD, *History of the Pacific Northwest;* FEDERAL WRITERS' PROJECT, *Washington, Oregon;* GATES, CHARLES M., *The First Century of the University of Washington, Readings in Pacific Northwest History;* with DOROTHY O. JOHANSEN, *Empire of the Columbia;* GRANT, FREDERIC JAMES, *History of Seattle;* HENDRICKSON, JAMES E., *Joe Lane of Oregon;* HAZARD, JOSEPH T., *Companion of Adventure;* JOHNSON, EDWIN F., *Railroad to the Pacific, Northern Route;* KENNEDY, JAMES H., *The History of Cleveland;* LONGSWORTH, BASIL, *The Oregon Trail;* LYONS, CICELY, *Salmon, Our Heritage;* McCARTHY, RAYMOND G. and DOUGLASS, EDGAR M., *Alcohol and Social Responsibility;* MEANY, EDMOND S., *History of the State of Washington;* MEEKER, EZRA, *The Busy Life of Eighty-Five Years, Pioneer Reminiscences of Puget Sound;* MORGAN, MURRAY, *Skid Road;* MORRIS, RICHARD B., *Encyclopedia of American History;* NEWELL, GORDON, *Rogues, Buffoons & Statesmen;* PARKMAN, FRANCIS JR., *The Oregon Trail;* PROSCH, THOMAS W., *David S. Maynard and Catherine T. Maynard* and *A Chronological History of Seattle From 1850 to 1897;* ROSE, WILLIAM GANSON, *Cleveland: The Making of a City;* ROSENBERG, CHARLES E., *The Cholera Years;* SAYRE, J. WILLIS, *This City of Ours;* SNOWDEN, CLINTON A., *History of Washington;* STEVENS, HAZARD, *Life of General Isaac I. Stevens;* SWAN, JAMES G., *The Northwest Coast.*

GENERAL

BEGINNINGS, PROGRESS AND ACHIEVEMENTS IN THE MEDICAL WORK OF KING COUNTY; C. B. BUSSELL, *Tidelands, Their Story;* HERRICK, RUTH E., *Cherry Grove;* ILLINOIS GUIDE & GAZETTEER, *Abingdon Through Zion;* AKIN, JAMES JR., *(Oregon Trail) Journal;* BEARDSLEY, ARTHUR S., *The Bench and Bar in Washington, First Fifty Years,* (unpublished manuscript No. 35, Washington State Library photocopy of restricted manuscript); BODEMER, CHARLES W., *Glory, God and Gold: Medicine Comes to the Pacific Northwest;* BUNDY, GEORGE, *Maynard Point and Its Upstart Neighbor, the Community of Seattle;* CARVER, MARGARET R. AND FRED E., *The Ancestors and Descendants of Jonathan Simmons and Mary Troutman and of Their Children;* CHEHALIS BEE

NUGGET, August 28, 1931, A Review of Three Pioneer Lives of the Southwest; COLLIAS, EUGENE E. and WESTLEY, RON, Tide Heights for July 1859 at Seattle; CONOVER, C. T., (Seattle Times, October 11, 1959), Charles Plummer had Many Business Activities; COWLITZ COUNTY HISTORICAL QUARTERLY, February, 1967, The Blanchet Family; DIMOCK, ARTHUR H., Transactions of the American Society of Civil Engineers, 1926, Preparing the Groundwork for a City; The Regrading of Seattle, Washington; DORRIS, JONATHAN TRUMAN, (Ye Galleon Press, Fairfield, Wash.), The Oregon Trail; EL HULT, RUBY, (unpublished manuscript), Seattle: A Different Sort of Pioneering; FARRAR, VICTOR J., Diary of Colonel and Mrs. I. N. Ebey; FINGER, JOHN R., Seattle's First Sawmill, 1853-1869; GENINI, RONALD, (Journal of the West, Vol. 11, No. 3, July, 1972), The Fraser and Cariboo Gold Rushes and Contrasts with California; GRIFFIN, RICHARD T., (Penthouse Magazine), Grandma Was a Junkie; HINES, GEORGE, (manuscript, Washington State Library), Biography of George A. Barnes; HOWARD-JONES, NORMAN, (Journal of the History of Medicine and Allied Sciences, Oct., 1972), Cholera Therapy in the Nineteenth Century; THE INTELLIGENCER, (Monday, March 17, 1873), Death of Old Pioneer—Dr. David S. Maynard; LENOX, EDWARD HENRY, Overland to Oregon; LOCKLEY, FREDERICK (Ye Galleon Press), Recollections of Benjamin Franklin Bonney, Reminiscences of Col. Henry Ernst Dosch, Captain Sol Tethero, Wagon Train Master, and, To Oregon by Ox-Team in 1847; LONGSWORTH, BASIL NELSON, Memorandum of Thoughts, Reflections & Transactions as Transcribed on His Journey from Washington Township, Guernsey County, Ohio, to Oregon in the Summer of 1853; KRENMAYR, JANICE, (Seattle Times, January 5, 1975), "The Earth Is Our Mother," Who Really Said That?; LOVETTE, LELAND P., (United States Naval Institute, 1939), An Attempt at Mutiny; McBRIDE, DELBERT J., (curator, State Capitol Museum), Governor Isaac Ingalls Stevens and the Treaties with the Nisqually Indians, An Examination of the Promises Made to the Indians in December, 1854, and the Manner in Which They Were Kept; McDONALD, LUCILLE (Seattle Times, March 28, 1954), Washington's First Territorial Secretary; (Seattle Times, May 25, 1958), James Tilton, Territorial Surveyor; MAHLBERG, BLANCHE BILLINGS (Pacific Northwest Quarterly, October, 1953), Edward J. Allen, Pioneer and Roadbuilder; MEANY, EDMOND S. (Washington Historical Quarterly, July, 1924), Chief Patkanim, (Washington Historical Quarterly, January, 1922), The Cowlitz Convention; Inception of Washington Territory; OREGON STATESMAN, November 8, 1853, (Story about George N. McConaha); OREGON SPECTATOR, December 4, 1850 (Prices obtained for the sale of firewood in San Francisco); PHELPS, THOMAS (Ye Galleon Press), Reminiscences of Seattle, Washington Territory, and of the U.S. Sloop-of-War Decatur During the Indian War of 1855-1856; RICH, JOHN M., Chief Seattle's Unanswered Challenge; PRATT, FLETCHER, The Navy, A History; SEATTLE GAZETTE, January 9, 1864, p. 3, ads for Doc Maynard's Hospital, Plummer's and Dexter Horton's stores and A. B. Rabbeson's saloon; SEATTLE TIMES, July 4, 1896, Aged Mrs. Maynard; She Talks About Seattle; SQUOL QUOL, Vol. 1, No. 1, 1973 (Lummi Indian magazine), Point Elliott, 1855; STRACHAN, MARGARET PITCAIRN (Seattle Times, Dec. 3, 1954), Early-Day Mansions, No. 14—Plummer; SYME, LEONARD, Personality Characteristics and the Alcoholic; TARBILL, V. V.,

(Harvard Business Review, July, 1930), *Mountain-Moving in Seattle;* WALKER, ANNA SLOAN, (Washington Historical Quarterly, April, 1914), *History of the Liquor Laws of the State of Washington, and, WARD, D.B., Across the Plains in 1853.*

GOVERNMENT SOURCES

BUREAU OF INDIAN AFFAIRS, U.S. DEPARTMENT OF INTERIOR, DOCKET 109, *The Duwamish Tribe of Indians, petitioner, vs The United States of America, defendant, July 6, 1959;* CONGRESSIONAL GLOBE, pp 540-542, Feb. 8, 1853; HOUSE JOURNAL, WASHINGTON TERRITORY, March 25, April 12, April 14, 1854, Prohibition legislation; JUDICIAL RECORDS, Division of Archives, State of Washington, Third Territorial District Court, 1852-1859, King County Probate Court, 1852-1891; SISLER, H. H., *Fifth Annual Report of the King County Road Engineer, 1939;* MICROCOPY OF RECORDS IN THE NATIONAL ARCHIVES, WASHINGTON SUPERINTENDENCY OF INDIAN AFFAIRS, 1853-1874, Microfilm Number 5. *Letters from Sub-Indian Agent, David S. Maynard, Fort Kitsap, to Governor Isaac Ingalls Stevens; Letter from Henry L. Yesler to Acting Governor Charles H. Mason, and Mason's Reply to Yesler;* WASHINGTON (TERRITORY) VOLUNTEER RECORDS, 1854-1858, Manuscript Number 28 at Washington State Library, *Receipt to Chief Patkanim for Indian heads and amount paid him and his tribe* and *Letter from Bishop A.M.A. Blanchet to Governor Stevens;* OREGON HISTORICAL SOCIETY, Papers of the Provisional Territorial Government of Oregon, 1841-1859.

INDEX

Doc Maynard's preliminary page portrait is by Ted Rand. Text illustrations by Bob Cram. Terrain maps and sketches by Bob McCausland. Composition by Vashon Graphics, Vashon, Washington. Design and production by William C. Speidel.